THE SCOTTISH HOME

THE
SCOTTISH
HOME

EDITED BY

ANNETTE CARRUTHERS

NATIONAL MUSEUMS OF SCOTLAND

We are grateful for assistance from the National Museums of
Scotland Charitable Trust towards the publication of this book.

Published by
National Museums of Scotland Publishing
Chambers Street
Edinburgh EH1 1JF

Produced for National Museums of Scotland Publishing by
White Cockade Publishing
71 Lonsdale Road
Oxford OX2 7ES

British Library Cataloguing in Publication Data
A catalogue record of this book is available from the British Library

ISBN 0 948636 72 6 hardback
ISBN 0 948636 85 8 paperback

Editing and design by Perilla Kinchin
Cover design by Gerald Cinamon
Printed in Great Britain by Ebenezer Baylis & Son Ltd, Worcester

Title page: A life of leisure photographed by Victor Albert
Prout at Corriemulzie Cottage, Deeside, in 1863. Antlers were
not usual in a fashionable drawing room but this was a holiday
house in a shooting area.

The contributors

Annette Carruthers is a lecturer in the School of Art History
at the University of St Andrews. Her publications include
Edward Barnsley and his Workshop, 1992, and *Good Citizen's
Furniture: the Arts and Crafts Collections at Cheltenham*, 1995.

Helen Clark, Keeper of Social History at Edinburgh City
Museums and Art Galleries, was responsible for setting up
The People's Story Museum in Edinburgh, which opened in
1989, and a new museum in Newhaven in 1994. She writes
frequently on museum and social history topics.

Ian Gow is Curator of the Architectural Collections of the
National Monuments Record at the Royal Commission on the
Ancient and Historical Monuments of Scotland. He is the
author of *The Scottish Interior*, 1992, and joint editor of *Scottish
Country Houses, 1600–1914*, 1995.

David Jones is a lecturer in the School of Art History at the
University of St Andrews. A furniture historian, he is Editor of
Regional Furniture, and contributes many articles to this and
other journals.

Juliet Kinchin is a lecturer in the Department of Historical and
Critical Studies at Glasgow School of Art. She is co-author of
Glasgow's Great Exhibitions, 1988, and has written extensively
on furniture and interiors, including recent contributions to the
Encyclopaedia of Interior Design and *The Gendered Object*, 1996.

Miles Oglethorpe is Head of the Industrial Survey at the
Royal Commission on the Ancient and Historical Monuments
of Scotland. He is joint author of *Brick, Tile and Fireclay
Industries in Scotland*, 1993.

Naomi Tarrant is Curator of Costume and Textiles at the
National Museums of Scotland, and has written numerous
books and articles, of which the most recent is *The Development
of Costume*, 1994.

Contents

Acknowledgements

First thanks must go to the Leverhulme Trust, which from 1991 to 1994 funded a fellowship to study 'Form and Function in the Scottish Home, 1600-1950', and to the National Museums of Scotland Charitable Trust, which gave a grant to support the production of this book.

The project was initiated by John Frew of the School of Art History at the University of St Andrews and John Shaw of the Department of Science, Technology and Working Life at the National Museums of Scotland. Both have provided ideas and encouragement throughout and the success of the project has been in large part due to them.

Staff in the School of Art History at St Andrews have been a great help and I would particularly thank David Jones, Martin Kemp, and Dawn Waddell. At the National Museums of Scotland, the former and current directors, Robert Anderson and Mark Jones, have taken an active interest in the project and many others on the staff have given information and expertise. Special thanks are due to David Bryden, Hugh Cheape, George Dalgleish, May Goodall, Ann Grant, Morvern Hardie, Helen Kemp, Irene Mackay, Andrew Martin, Angus Neale, Veronica Thomson, and Elizabeth Wright.

The Editor wishes to thank all the museum curators in Scotland who have opened up their stores and records and contributed information, especially Carol Anderson, Margaret Blackburn, Anne Brundle, Gavin Grant, Rosalind Marshall, Janice Murray, Ross Noble, and Ian Tait.

Special thanks are due to Veronica Steele at the RCAHMS and Dorothy Kidd at the SEA for help beyond the call of duty, and to Iain Gordon Brown, Ron Caird, Rachel Hart, and Janet McBain for information or images from their archives and libraries.

This research has been helped considerably by the contribution of speakers at two series of study days held in the Royal Museum of Scotland. Their lectures demonstrated the variety encompassed by the subject, helping to open up discussion. Thanks are due also to Alexander Fenton, John Hume, Katherine Mercer, Stana Nenadic, Sebastian Pryke, Mrs M Jarvis, David Walker, Gavin Watt, Priscilla Williamson, Ian Wolfenden, Sydney Wood and Kenneth Wright.

We are grateful to Sir John Clerk of Penicuik Bt for permission to quote from letters in his collection at the SRO and to Ralph Glasser for passages from *Growing up in the Gorbals*.

Annette Carruthers would like to thank Alan Saville and all the authors of the chapters of this book. She particularly thanks Perilla Kinchin, its producer, whose editorial skills and management of the complex arrangement of text and pictures have made an enormous difference to the quality of the work.

Helen Clark thanks Alison Done for her time and patience in typing her chapter.

Ian Gow wishes to thank Simon Thurley of the Historic Royal Palaces, and all the participants at a 1995 symposium on royal dining for their help and ideas. He also thanks Annette Carruthers, Mary Cosh, Perilla Kinchin, Veronica Steele, Elizabeth Strong, and the photographers at the RCAHMS.

David Jones is grateful to June Baxter, Annette Carruthers, Fay Ireland, John Lowrey, Martin Pursloe, and Geoffrey Stell.

Juliet Kinchin is most grateful to Annette Carruthers, Jolyon Hudson, and Francis McKee for drawing additional material to her attention; also to Ian Gow, the staff of the Strathclyde Regional and Glasgow University Archives, the Hunterian Art Gallery, Glasgow Museums, and above all, to Perilla Kinchin and to Paul Stirton for their constant help and encouragement.

Miles Oglethorpe thanks James T Robertson for his notes and advice on the history of the water industry in Scotland, and Robert Burgon of the Scottish and Northern Ireland Plumbing Employers' Federation. He would also like to acknowledge Armitage Shanks, whose recent gift of catalogues to the National Monuments Record of Scotland greatly assisted his research.

Naomi Tarrant wishes to thank Annette Carruthers, Ian Gow, Stana Nenadic, Margaret Swain, and Elizabeth Wright.

Illustrations

1. RCAHMS/Scottish National Portrait Gallery
2. Shetland Museum
3. NMS/SEA/C11197
4. Shetland Museum
5. RCAHMS/Richard Hewlings
6. NMS/SEA/C12678
7–8. RCAHMS
9. Paisley Museum
10. Patricia & Angus Macdonald
11. RCAHMS
12. Orkney Photographic Archive
13. NMS/SEA/50/43
14. NMS Library
15. National Gallery of Scotland
16. The Royal Collection© Her Majesty The Queen
17. National Gallery of Scotland
18. NMS/SEA/37/8/11
19. The Duke of Buccleuch & Queensberry KT/Joe Rock
20. NMS/SEA/C19504 & Göteborgs Historiska Museum, Sweden
21. NMS/SEA/56/44/18
22. NMS/SEA/C8787 & Tain & District Museum
23. John Murray Publishers
24. Paisley Museum
25. RCAHMS
26. NMS/SEA/C699
27. Private Collection
28–9. RCAHMS
30. NMS/SEA/Scotch Myths Archive/P2672
31. NMS Library
32. NMS/SEA/51/56/5a
33. NMS/SEA/51/54/7
34. NMS/SEA/C9197
35. Peter Adamson
36. Orkney Photographic Archive
37. NMS/SEA/Scotland's Magazine Collection/57/12/15/A C Cowper
38. National Trust for Scotland
39. Historic Scotland
40. NMS/SEA/C8339
41. Shetland Museum
42–3. Peter Adamson
44. Scottish National Portrait Gallery Archive
45. St Andrews Preservation Trust Museum
46. Alexander Neish
47. St Andrews University Library
48–9. National Gallery of Scotland
50. David Jones
51. Fife Folk Museum, Ceres/Peter Adamson
52. Shetland Museum
53. Temple Newsam House, Leeds/Pratt Collection
54. John Frew
55. Edinburgh Old Town Library
56. Edinburgh Museums
57. Paisley Museum
58–60. Edinburgh Museums
61. Richard Rodger
62. Strathclyde Regional Archives
63–4. Glasgow Museums/Alf Daniels
65–6. Paisley Museum
67. Dundee District Archives
68–71. Edinburgh Museums
72. Dundee Museums/the late Joseph Paterson
73. Hulton Deutsch Collection
74. Springburn Museum
75. David Livingstone Centre, Blantyre
76. Springburn Museum/Andrew C Lillie
77. Paisley Museum
78. Edinburgh Museums
79. Dundee Museums/the late Joseph Paterson
80. Dundee District Archives
81. Perth Museum
82. Shetland Museum
83. Orkney Photographic Archive
84. Dr Iain Gordon Brown
85. NMS
86. National Library of Scotland
87. SRO
88. National Gallery of Scotland
89. The Duke of Buccleuch & Queensberry KT
90. SRO
91. Falkirk Museums
92–3. RCAHMS
94. Paisley Museum
95–6. Shetland Museum
97. RCAHMS
98. Country Life Picture Library
99. Glasgow Museums/Alf Daniels
100. D C Thomson & Co Ltd, Dundee/The Sunday Post
101. RCAHMS/James Hardie
102. David Jones/Thomas Justice Archive
103–4. RCAHMS/Inglis Collection
105. The Earl of South Esk
106. RCAHMS
107–9. Peter Adamson
110. Private Collection
111. Peter Adamson
112. Peter Adamson/The Wardens of Trinity House
113. David Jones
114. Peter Adamson
115. David Jones
116–17. Peter Adamson
118. SRO
119. RCAHMS/Private Collection
120. St Andrews University Library
121. Peter Adamson
122–3. RCAHMS
124. NMS/SEA/C24664/Mrs John Raven
125. Edinburgh University Library, Special Collections/Scott Morton Collection
126. RCAHMS
127. Peter Adamson
128. Orkney Photographic Archive
129. Peter Adamson
130. RCAHMS
131. Country Life Picture Library
132–3. RCAHMS
134. RCAHMS/Newhall Estate Trustees
135. The Paxton Trust
136. RCAHMS/The Paxton Trust
137. National Trust for Scotland
138. RCAHMS
139. Hunterian Art Gallery
140. RCAHMS
141. The Royal Collection© Her Majesty The Queen
142. Perth Museum/Magnus Jackson Collection
143. RCAHMS
144. Private Collection
145. Scottish National Portrait Gallery
146–7. RCAHMS
148. RCAHMS/Mrs D Stogdon
149–50. RCAHMS
151. Private Collection
152–3. RCAHMS
154. RCAHMS/Bedford Lemere
155. Edinburgh Museums
156–7. RCAHMS
158. RCAHMS/Hopetoun House Preservation Trust
159. National Library of Scotland
160. Aberdeen University Library/George Washington Wilson Collection/C2383
161. Private Collection
162. Glasgow Museums
163. Lucy Parr & Graeme Shearer/Chris Gascoigne
164. Juliet Kinchin
165. RCAHMS
166. Glasgow Museums
167. Kirkcaldy Museum & Art Gallery
168. Edinburgh Museums
169. Private Collection
170. Falkirk Museums
171. Shetland Museum
172. Paisley Museum
173. Orkney Photographic Archive
174. Juliet Kinchin
175. Tankerness House Museum, Kirkwall
176. Juliet Kinchin
177. Glasgow Museums
178. Hunterian Art Gallery
179. David Jones/Thomas Justice Archive
180. National Trust for Scotland
181. Trustees of the Tate Gallery
182. Board of Trustees of the Victoria & Albert Museum
183. The Minneapolis Institute of Arts
184–5. NMS
186. Board of Trustees of the Victoria & Albert Museum
187. RCAHMS
188–9. The Paxton Trust
190. RCAHMS/Inglis Collection
191. The Paxton Trust
192–6. NMS
197. RCAHMS
198–9. NMS Library
200. Edinburgh Museums
201. RCAHMS
202. NMS Library
203. National Trust for Scotland
204. Perth Museum
205. Springburn Museum
206–8. RCAHMS
209. Edinburgh Museums/The Interior Archive Ltd/Fritz von der Schulenburg
210. Annette Carruthers
211-30. RCAHMS

Preface

From the beginning this project on the home in Scotland has involved the co-operation of many individuals and institutions and the book has been written by seven contributors. They have brought to it an immense depth and range of expertise, demonstrating the value of approaching a subject from different angles. Architectural and design history are represented here alongside the study of furniture, textiles, and the decorative arts, social history and women's studies, oral history, and industrial archaeology. The authors' interpretations are sometimes surprising, they often challenge assumptions, and they will undoubtedly raise further questions.

It was always clear that an attempt to describe the homes of people throughout Scottish society from 1600 to 1950 would have to leave out a great deal, but it seemed worthwhile to outline a big story rather than to cover a small part in detail. The date range chosen reflects the fact that evidence for domestic life in Scotland before 1600 is very scanty and after 1950 is overwhelmingly abundant. In several places we have strayed outside the allotted period, but it remains the main focus of study.

As the research developed – investigating the variety and contrast seen in the houses of country and town dwellers, of rich and poor, of fishers, farmers, and merchants – some common themes recurred. Looking through the illustrations in this book you will notice, for instance, the important place of the hearth, not simply for warmth (though this is clearly a concern in a northern country) but as the symbolic centre of the home. Or you may be struck by how many Scots have shared their homes with animals – several breeds of dog can be found here, along with numerous cats and a few birds and cattle (not to mention the dead creatures spread on floors and displayed on walls as trophies). Short captions cannot do justice to the immense amount of information contained within the illustrations but observant viewers will notice contrasts and similarities echoing between images.

One of the pleasures of the research has been discovering the variety of regional elements within Scotland, helped by the extraordinary resource of the local museums and their curators. It was to be expected that there would be major differences in the way people live in the Highlands and Lowlands (the conventional divide), or in the Central Belt and in the Western and Northern Isles; but the distinctions between, for instance, Orkney and Shetland, or Aberdeenshire and Morayshire, were more of a surprise.

This diversity is reflected in the vocabulary of the home, a rich subject in itself: the word for the 'best' room in a small house, for example, can be 'ben' as in 'but and ben', 'room' as in 'room and kitchen', 'parlour', or 'spence' – this last used mainly in the south west. A passage can be a 'lobby', a 'trance', or a 'hallan'. Use of language also differs in ways that can be misleading to people from other English-speaking areas: 'house' is often used in Scotland to describe what English people call a 'flat' and Americans an 'apartment'. 'Flat' in Scotland usually refers to one floor of a building, while 'apartment' is a room.

In gathering information and images for the book we have tried to give adequate representation to the collections of museums around Scotland, though there is an inevitable emphasis on two major resources in Edinburgh, the Scottish Ethnological Archive of the National Museums of Scotland and the National Monuments Record of the Royal Commission on the Ancient and Historical Monuments of Scotland. Official record material has been used extensively, but some of the most enticing evidence is that provided by individuals recording memories of their childhood homes. Anyone who has

2. 'Reestit' mutton, a Shetland speciality, is a surprising addition to the classical decoration of this living room in Lerwick. Jack and Jessie Rattar, with their cat Tony (named after the politician, Anthony Eden), were photographed in December 1939.

lived in Scotland can contribute in some way to the study of the Scottish home and most curators in local museums and in the relevant national institutions would be pleased to hear from people with photographs, sketches, or vivid memories.

The Scottish home has proved to be a subject of continuing fascination. This book is not a comprehensive survey, but I hope that it will inspire readers to look again at familiar surroundings and to answer some of the unanswered questions.

Annette Carruthers

1 Studying the Scottish Home

ANNETTE CARRUTHERS

'… she had no taste for poking into pantries, and chimneys, and cellars, or of hearing any of the inelegant minutiae of life detailed.'

Susan Ferrier, 1824[1]

3 & 4. The fireplace, the focus of the home, is a recurring image throughout this book, bridging differences of class and place. *Above:* Katherine Menzies, the wife of a lawyer, in what was probably the morning room or parlour at Larchgrove House, Balerno, near Edinburgh, in about 1897–8. *Below:* William, Margaret, and David Sinclair in a crofthouse in Whalsay and Skerries parish, Shetland, about 1910. The shelf of books may support the view that the much-travelled Shetlanders were a well-educated people.

Today the home is familiar territory to most of us, our personal experience enlarged vicariously through television and film. We probably know more about how our neighbours live than people in the past, and certainly more than they saw of the houses of those in different social classes from themselves. This superficial familiarity has led to misconceptions about historical change within the home and has perhaps blunted the curiosity which might lead to understanding.

There have been enormous changes, however, not just in the style of buildings or the range of goods we own, but in the ways the home is used and perceived by its inhabitants. Some of the evidence may have vanished beyond recapture, but enough can be retrieved from varied sources to provide new insights.

The home has a wide popular appeal – as witness the numerous magazines and television programmes devoted to DIY, style, and decoration – and it provides an accessible key to the study of history. Our homes reflect our working lives, the state of our national economy, our social relations and aspirations, our status in the community. The appearance of our houses and the nature of our household goods indicate very directly the values of our society.

Writers on 'the British home' tend to assume that Scotland follows patterns similar to those of England and Wales, or that it is so different it can be dismissed in a section on 'primitive survivals' or omitted altogether. With a few honourable exceptions, the Scottish home has not been given the attention lavished on the English or American dwelling in recent years.[2]

Among the few histories of the home, its decoration and its use in Scotland are John Warrack's *Domestic Life in Scotland, 1488–1688*, published in 1920, and several social history works on a similar theme, based mainly on written sources, though Jean Faley's *Up Oor Close* provides numerous vivid oral accounts of tenement interiors.[3] Ian Gow's recent *The Scottish Interior* analyses Scottish decorative schemes through visual sources, but is largely limited to the upper and middle classes because of the nature of the illustrations available. Most works dealing with this subject are 'lifestyle' oriented, focusing on the sumptuous furnishings or faded grandeur of the architect-designed houses of a minority, as inspiration for interior decorators.[4]

Much has been published on Scotland's rich tradition of building and diverse house types. The earliest literature focused on polite architecture and those most dramatic and evocative of Scottish buildings: castles, country houses, and palaces. This remains a fruitful area of study, though attention usually concentrates on building history and style rather than on how these monuments were used – on Great Hall and Withdrawing Room more than kitchen and corridor.

What more do we wish to know, and what sources of information are available to us? The challenge is to discover what the Scottish home was really like for its inhabitants, how their mode of living influenced the appearance and working of the house, and how the form of the dwelling constrained or liberated behaviour. Which historical trends affected Scottish society at large? Which were specific to the homes of certain social groups? This book aims to provide both an outline history of the Scottish home over the past four hundred years and some deeper studies of particular aspects which indicate the wealth of information available.

Many of the finest houses are displayed to the public with their successive overlays and accumulations of furnishings. Visitors familiar with, for instance, the custom in the seventeenth and eighteenth centuries of arranging furniture formally against the walls, can visualize by an effort of imagination how a cluttered Edwardian-style room would have looked two hundred years earlier; those less familiar might assume it to be just as it always has been. Information

5. Late Victorian clutter fills the drawing room of Stevenson House, East Lothian, photographed in about 1900. The house itself dates from about 1700 and the bow window from around 1820. Originally this room would have been sparsely furnished, with furniture ranged formally against the walls and few textiles.

COTTAGES AT BARRA.

6. Thick walls and curving forms kept blackhouses relatively warm and quiet in spite of the driving winds of the Western Isles. They had small windows and no chimney, so the interiors were dark and smoky. A photograph from about 1909.

is rarely provided to help the casual visitor disentangle the strands of history. How difficult it is to recognize the difference between the arms and armour decoratively arranged in the Victorian hall and the practical fighting equipment kept ready in an earlier age, especially when items in the Victorian display may have been in the house for generations. And how hard to imagine, in immaculate rooms peopled by wandering tourists, what the atmosphere would have been with purposeful everyday activities going on. It is hoped that this book will help visitors in such houses to read and understand the interiors.

Small buildings in the countryside have also, more recently, received attention, but little survives of structures built before the mid eighteenth century. This is largely because land was held on short leases and there was scant incentive for tenants to invest labour and money in sound construction. Houses were built of materials which came to hand in the locality, and those who study rural dwellings almost inevitably concentrate their detective work on identifying techniques and classifying regional features. Most attention has been given to northern and western areas, where house types appeared primitive to housing reformers earlier this century and have been officially discouraged. The 'blackhouses' of the Western Isles and Highlands, for instance, look as if they might have survived from prehistory, with their thick double walls, rounded corners, and curved roofs of heather thatch weighted by large stones: but some were built at the same time as the Forth railway bridge only one hundred years ago. Such houses do not conform to the modern idea of a home, but they represent the evolution over centuries of forms built to cope with a particular climate and terrain, especially to provide protection from the cold and noise of high winds. They evolved to suit the life of labour dictated by these conditions, and their interiors reflect this.

Less is recorded of rural dwellings in the Lowlands. Analysis of the design of the symmetrical stone houses found all over the country has shown surprising diversity in the proportions of houses in different areas, and other regional variations, in materials or the shapes of gable ends and windows.[5] Interiors have usually been destroyed by modernization, but the founding of the Regional Furniture Society in 1986 has provided a focus for work on the furnishings made and used away from fashionable urban centres. A great deal more is known now than ten years ago.

Houses in small towns developed in much the same way as in the countryside, but city dwellers needed different forms to accommodate a new way of life. Purpose-built, multi-storey tenements had appeared in Edinburgh by the late seventeenth century, partly because the land available within the city walls was limited: the only possible place to build was up.[6] Structures of ten storeys or more were feasible only because of a conjunction of circumstances. Abundant building stones provided a solid basis for construction, not easily destroyed by fire. Coal for fuel was found within easy reach of Edinburgh and Glasgow and was transported by sea to other major cities, replacing peat, which gave off less heat and would have been too bulky to store in cities. Perhaps also trading links with mainland European countries confirmed the Scots' liking for this kind of dwelling, which developed also in other great cities like Paris and Prague.

Histories of the tenement have generally concentrated on architectural features and the economics of building, though the reminiscences of former inhabitants have filled out the picture (tending however to focus on working-class experience). The Scottish tenement has been rehabilitated, both metaphorically and in its fabric, and the word 'tenement' no longer carries the

SHOPS AND FLATS ERECTED FOR THE GLASGOW CORPORATION TO IMPROVE HOPE STREET. THEY ARE BUILT OF RED SANDSTONE FROM LOCHARBRIGG'S QUARRY. THERE IS A FLAT ROOF COVERED WITH ASPHALT. THE OUTSIDE WOODWORK OF THE SHOPS IS OF TEAK, WHILE THE INSIDE FINISHINGS ARE OF YELLOW PINE STAINED AND DULL-VARNISHED. THE BUILDING IS FIREPROOF THROUGHOUT. SEE PAGE 70

John Keppie, F.R.I.B.A., Architect
Honeyman, Keppie and Mackintosh

7. Even tenements designed to be inexpensive and built for Glasgow Corporation made a significant architectural contribution to the city and provided thoroughly respectable housing – a reminder that 'tenement' is not synonymous with 'slum'. This development of shops and flats is as illustrated in Walter Shaw Sparrow's *Flats, Urban Houses and Cottage Homes* of about 1906. For a plan of the layout, see pl 227.

automatic connotation of 'slum'; but it is perhaps still not widely realized why this reputation arose. Some tenement blocks provided accommodation on a grand scale, with lavishly fitted interiors which attracted middle-class residents until the 'servant problem' after the First World War made them increasingly difficult to manage, and improved urban transport made the suburbs more attractive. This type sometimes became run down in the mid twentieth century, but has regained popularity for a variety of reasons. City-centre locations make them convenient, and cheap power for heating dispenses with the need for servants to carry coals and clean up after open fires.

Other tenements were built to lower standards or were dragged down by industrial development in their neighbourhood, and became slums because they were occupied by very large numbers of people existing in poverty. In 1901, nearly half the population of Scotland lived more than two people to a room and 57 per cent of dwellings consisted of only one or two rooms. Some homes were in the small houses which now usually accommodate single families but which ninety years ago often housed four or five separate households. The greatest overcrowding, however, was in tenement blocks in Glasgow, Paisley, and Edinburgh. One form of building thus catered for very different ways of living, within a shell which appears similar, though high-status tenement housing was usually differentiated architecturally through decoration, cupolas and turrets, or bay windows. Study of the building type tells us about the cityscape, but a different approach is needed to understand how these houses were used as homes.

Clearly other housing types could be mentioned. Grand terraced rows of houses grace the major cities; conveniently placed villas sit in the suburbs; and co-operatively built workers' housing clusters in small scattered communities. Developments in the twentieth century, especially the provision of public housing, have changed the nature of the Scottish home, bringing new standards of space and comfort. It is also salutary to remember that only 2.8 per cent of the housing stock (evaluated in 1987) dates from before 1871, and only just over one quarter from before 1918.[7] The Scottish home as we see it today is almost entirely a twentieth-century creation, and there are obvious hazards in trying to understand its history from buildings alone.

One starting point for an alternative approach is the study of surviving household objects. As Kenneth Ames suggested in 1982, 'the commonplace artifacts of everyday life mirror a society's values as accurately as its great monuments'.[8] Information on household things provides essential background. Surviving objects cannot, however, give a full picture of life in the past because, like standing buildings, they represent only part of what has been. Things survive because they were precious in financial or sentimental terms, because they have become obsolete and unusual, because they are made of tough materials, or because their owners had room to keep them. Other things which were of equal importance have disappeared because they were taken for granted, because they had become obsolete and were discarded, because they were fragile or were used and adapted to destruction. Textiles are the most obvious example of commodities which played a vital part in making the home comfortable and pleasing, but which often simply wore out or faded away. In addition, many museums have failed to collect local material or to record where and how things were used. Evidence from objects has to be balanced with information from other sources.

For grand houses of the upper classes there is no shortage of documentation after about 1700: architects' designs, paintings, prints, drawings, and inventories of possessions, augment what we can gather from surviving buildings. People of this class often stayed in an area for generations, and paintings such as *John Francis Erskine, 7th Earl of Mar and his family* by David Allan symbolize their pride in family, house, and land.[9] Middle- and working-class people have generally been more mobile and any possessions considered worth keeping would be moved with their owners. Photographs of flittings or

8. High-rise flats at Kirkton Avenue in Glasgow, built by Wimpey in 1965. By the mid twentieth century, tower blocks were seen by many municipal authorities as the solution to problems of overcrowded tenements. However these proved to have their own social problems, and from the 1970s housing campaigners preferred the rehabilitation of tenements to such new schemes.

evictions, showing furniture in front of the house or precariously stacked, give information about the goods found in smaller homes but otherwise this mobility obscures the evidence.

Archaeology could offer valuable information about abandoned houses, but little has been carried out on post-medieval dwellings. There has been some excavation in the major cities, revealing, for instance, the extent to which timber was used in buildings before the seventeenth century.[10] In rural areas, archaeological investigation has occasionally been undertaken in conjunction with surveys but there is little incentive to spend money excavating late domestic sites which are not threatened by destruction, though the many abandoned dwellings in the Scottish countryside must conceal much vital material (pl 10).[11]

Surveys of standing or ruinous buildings offer more ample evidence. Fine drawings are available in the collections of the Royal Commission, though the proportion showing domestic buildings is quite small. A typical example, of weavers' cottages at Carlops in Peebleshire, is interesting for its depiction of the original kitchen fireplace and the placing of box beds, but gives no information about decoration and furnishing.[12] Members of the Scottish Vernacular Buildings Working Group also undertake surveys and this is an important contact for anyone interested in rural buildings.

Architectural records include designs for buildings and depictions of finished work. Apart from what they reveal about architecture, these sometimes give evidence of the arrangement and use of furniture. This subject has been widely studied in Europe and Scandinavia in the past thirty years, but little has been published in Scotland. A particularly revealing example is a scheme for the rearrangement of a flat in Edinburgh's High Street, showing the proposed

9. An elderly couple evicted from their cottage in Potterhill, Paisley, about 1900. Their meagre furniture and belongings have been piled up in the street, The house next door shows how such buildings could be transformed by the addition of dormer windows and slate roofs.

10. An aerial view of the village of Arnol in Lewis shows clearly how the place has changed during the twentieth century. The blackhouses were abandoned as the people built first the gable-ended houses and more recently, substantial bungalows, losing any identifiably Scottish character.

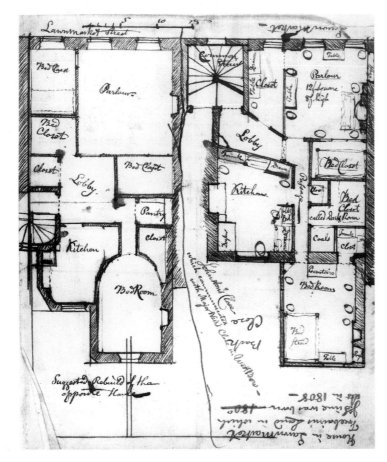

11. *Left:* John Sime's plan of his family's flat in the Lawnmarket, High Street, Edinburgh, is interesting for the naming of rooms and the arrangement of furniture.

Front Elevation.

Ground Plan

First Floor Plan.

Attic Plan.

change to a fashionable layout of 1808 and also the reality of how the family lived. When they are put together with painted images of the period and evidence from surviving furniture and textiles, much can be deduced from such plans (pl 11).

Even very basic architects' designs like the records of the Deans of Guild can provide information about general trends, such as when bathrooms became usual rather than a luxury, for example.[13] Dean of Guild plans also show the original layout of a building, the names for different rooms, and sometimes how alterations were made (pl 12). Those for 'ordinary' houses are usually more revealing about common practice than designs by top architects, who were trying to make a name for themselves by demonstrating individuality.

Other records, from banks, businesses, local councils, and government sources can illuminate a study of the home. Valuation rolls in conjunction with census returns are very revealing about properties and their occupiers; and government publications, such as the 1917 *Report of the Royal Commission on the Housing of the Industrial Population of Scotland, Rural and Urban*, provide graphic descriptions of the inadequacies of the dwellings of miners, farmworkers, and others.

Testaments and inventories are documents of especial value. These were usually made to record items to be shared out after a death or to settle debts after a bankruptcy, and for that reason they have limitations as evidence. They can be used, however, to identify known people and see what was in their possession at specific dates, or studied in groups to investigate the kind of goods owned by society in general. This last approach to inventories from the period 1660–1760 in different parts of Britain has produced valuable detail about which goods were common, which rare (and presumably luxuries), and how patterns of ownership varied in different areas. It is also possible to trace the

12. Details of a Dean of Guild plan for a villa at Brandiquoy, Kirkwall, Orkney.

13. Billhead of about 1910. At this date James Barrie may have been making furniture on the premises to suit his local clientele. By the middle of the twentieth century, few such small cabinetmaking firms were left and most people in centres of population bought from retailers.

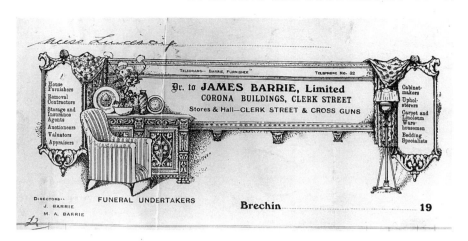

14. 'Inside of a poor weaver's cottage in ILAY', as published by Thomas Pennant in *A Tour in Scotland, and Voyage to the Hebrides; MDCCLXXII*, after a drawing by Joseph Banks. The weaver works at his loom on the left while the family clusters around the peat fire.

history of particular items, such as clocks or mirrors, over a long period to see how they came in or out of fashion.[14]

Business records also help in showing what goods were available at particular dates, but have to be approached with care since they do not always reflect what people really had. The billhead of a Brechin furnishing firm of about 1910 (pl 13), for instance, may depict furniture the proprietors considered fashionable rather than the kind they sold to customers in Brechin.

The feelings originally evoked by objects and their surroundings cannot be felt again, but some echo can perhaps be recaptured through literature, diaries, autobiography, and letters. Since writing requires leisure time, these sources are limited to certain social milieus. Elizabeth Grant of Rothiemurchus in the early nineteenth century is an excellent source, especially on the differences between Highland and city habits. One surprise in her account of fashionable life in Edinburgh is that when her father is declared bankrupt, the bailiffs cannot take the furniture because it is all on hire from Mr Trotter. How many people lived with housefuls of furniture owned by this cabinetmaking firm?

A few memoirs of working people also exist, such as Alexander Somerville's *The Autobiography of a Working Man* of 1848, which describes the wretched hovel in which his parents lived.[15] In the twentieth century, with wider educational opportunities, there are more first-hand memories such as Ralph Glasser's vivid accounts of his childhood in Glasgow's Gorbals.

Travellers' tales can be useful because the visitors came from outside and commented on the unusual, but they often ignored what they took for granted, sometimes exaggerated out of shock or chauvinism, and were occasionally inaccurate out of sheer laziness (they simply had not been to the places they described). Thomas Pennant published *A Tour in Scotland* after a journey made in 1772, and his portrayal of conditions in Islay is fairly typical of this kind of work, describing habitations which were

scenes of misery, made of loose stones; without chimnies, without doors, excepting the faggot opposed to the wind at one or other of the appertures, permitting the smoke to escape through the other, in order to prevent the pains of suffocation. The furniture perfectly corresponds: a pothook hangs from the middle of the roof, with a pot pendent over a grateless fire, filled with fare that may rather be called a permission to exist, than a support of vigorous life: the inmates, as may be expected, lean, withered, dusky and smoke-dried.[16]

Novels and poetry can give an insider's or outsider's view, and often reflect the way individuals felt about their homes. They also reveal the general attitudes of the period in which they were composed and indicate just how

15. *The Connoisseurs* by David Allan, about 1780. Although the furniture can be related to surviving pieces, the background here gives little sense of a real room. This seems to be usual in eighteenth-century Scottish paintings, where the focus is on people or land rather than on interiors.

important the home could be as a signifier of character. In *Crossriggs*, a popular novel of 1908 by Jane and Mary Findlater, the poor but plucky heroine, Alex, does wonders in creating a pleasant drawing room from worn and shabby furnishings, while her elderly neighbour, Miss Bessie Reid, 'was skilled in all the little arts that make home hideous. There was a specimen of her handiwork at every turn …'[17] Alex's good-natured but unimaginative sister marries a prosperous businessman and is delighted with his 'large, square, uninteresting' house and its plumply furnished dining room with its 'usual luncheon table, spread with the usual viands, and decorated with red geraniums arranged in accordance with Matilda's quite ordinary taste'.[18]

Similarly, in Catherine Carswell's *Open the Door!* of 1922 the Glaswegian Bannerman children are discomfited by the 'worldly grandeur' of the house of their Edinburgh aunt. Joanna, the heroine, visits the widowed mother of a suitor in her small flat in North Kelvinside, Glasgow, and instantly feels oppressed by the 'solid tastelessness', especially again in the dining room, where the tea looks 'like an exhibition of bakery' and 'the tall, forbidding tea-pot on its beaded mat, and the chairs of horse-hair and very ruddy mahogany which had been pushed up to the damask, did undoubtedly combine rather in the cold effort to defy criticism than in any spontaneous hospitality.'[19] In contrast, when Joanna arranges a room with her favourite family possessions, she looks upon it with pleasure because it is 'a room prepared for the beloved and therefore lovely'.[20] In part, such novels simply reflect their authors' attitudes to current fashions in interior design but they also demonstrate how much the characters, especially the women, are both shaped and revealed by their surroundings.

There are obvious limits on the period covered by novels, which only began to appear in the eighteenth century. We also have to beware of being seduced by, for example, Sir Walter Scott's prose into thinking that his historical information was accurate, just as we need to recognize the romanticism in his home at Abbotsford, Roxburghshire, where the impressive hall hung with armour is a deceptive mix of real oak panelling and painted plaster (pl 120).

16. Queen Victoria had watercolours painted at Balmoral both before and after it was 'tartanized' in the mid 1850s (see also pl 141). An earlier view of a bedroom depicts flowered wallpaper and a large print of the Crystal Palace. This one of 1857 by James Roberts shows Prince Albert's influence on the decoration.

Fiction by working-class authors did not appear until the late nineteenth century, when basic education for all was introduced: nevertheless, novels and poetry can provide insights into attitudes to homes and possessions, and enjoyable research material can be found in the work of Burns, John Galt, Robert Louis Stevenson, Willa Muir, Lewis Grassic Gibbon, and many others. The search for references to the home can also add interest to a few otherwise tedious stories.

In the early nineteenth century especially, painting in Scotland was often inspired by Scott or Burns and numerous depictions were made of *The Cottar's Saturday Night* and scenes from *Tam O'Shanter*. Despite romanticization, these usually contain elements which can be tied to other evidence, such as surviving furniture and household goods. A few rare artists, such as Walter Geikie, who drew numerous detailed cottage interiors, appear to have made closely-observed studies of everyday life, and many items in Geikie's views are recognizable types in museum collections (pls 17, 48, 49). History paintings, such as *Baptism in Scotland*, painted by John Phillip in 1850[21] but representing life in the previous century, are, like historical novels, of limited use as evidence.

Straightforward views of houses or rooms are not common in Scotland, although a few 'house portraits' exist from the early eighteenth century and glimpses of houses and interiors occur in paintings of other subjects. The so-called *The Connoisseurs* by David Allan, painted in the 1780s (pl 15), depicts a schematized room but the cabinet in the background is of a distinctive type by William Brodie, an Edinburgh maker, and can be related to a surviving piece

attributed to him .[22] *Sir Adam and Lady Ferguson* by David Cooke Gibson of about 1850,[23] is a more specific work, showing a fireplace with attached gas mantle, a selection of furniture, wall colour, carpet, and so on (pl 145). Recent research has identified the small portion of painting above Sir Adam's head as a portrait of his father, and the accuracy of this section suggests that the picture can be accepted with some confidence as a truthful depiction of the room.[24]

In the nineteenth century, the room as a subject appears more often, though it was never as popular in Scotland as elsewhere in Europe, perhaps because the picturesque landscape outside was regarded as the obvious choice for amateurs.[25] Queen Victoria commissioned meticulous watercolour views of Balmoral and Holyroodhouse, but of course these cannot be considered typical houses (pls 16, 141).[26]

Portraits came within the reach of almost everyone with the development of photography in the mid nineteenth century, but were at first usually taken in a studio, with studio furniture, so photographs of people rarely show their own possessions around them. The technical limitations of cameras made it difficult to photograph indoors, and there are fewer shots of interiors than exteriors.[27]

Early photographs reflect the lives of the middle and upper classes, though Hill and Adamson interested themselves in fishing communities near Edinburgh in the 1840s, and from the beginning photographs recorded the unusual and picturesque. They can be useful as evidence of buildings now demolished or altered, and of customs described but ephemeral, such as the decoration of the threshhold with patterns drawn in pipe clay (pl 18).

Some scepticism should be exercised regarding photographs taken for sale as postcards, because furniture was often moved or the people posed to suit the composition (see pl 83). This is probably easier to recognize in a recent

17. A typical drawing by Walter Geikie of a cottage interior around 1830. The panelled item on the right is probably a box bed and the classical pilaster in the right foreground is also part of a bed of the sophisticated kind made by wrights in the Lothians and Fife (see pl 43 and p 56).

18. Decorating the threshhold and entrance passage of the house with patterns drawn in pipeclay is a custom well documented in written sources. This 1880s photograph of a dairymaid, possibly from Lanarkshire, gives rare evidence of how these patterns looked.

photograph than an old one, since we know the difference between perfect images in advertisements or furnishing catalogues and the reality of our own homes. It is usually helpful to know why a photograph was taken, since this may reveal any hidden agenda. Sanitary Officers in several cities, for instance, had lecture slides made of unhealthy conditions for their campaign to improve housing in their area (pls 57, 65, 77). These provide an often shocking picture of the lives of the poorest inhabitants of common lodging houses and condemned buildings. The more widespread conditions of the comparatively crowded but decently maintained houses of the majority of the working people and middle classes feature less frequently in photographs, but we do find images which are apparently truthful records of a known house at a particular time. When matched with information from local trade directories and census returns, these can be extremely informative (for instance pls 3, 172).

Given the nature of cine film and the equipment required, the same limitations apply, but the medium can provide interesting evidence. Most films about houses and housing are either elegiac, made to celebrate a vanishing way of life; or campaigning, showing bad conditions to prick consciences. Educational films, usually aimed at young girls, also explain how furniture and equipment was used in the home, although they perhaps exaggerate.[28] The development of relatively cheap and easy-to-use video cameras means there will be more of this kind of evidence in future, though unless something is done to direct people's enthusiasm there will probably be many videos of similar things. Houses will be glimpsed as background to family celebrations and social events, and there will be little footage of everyday behaviour, such as people washing up or watching television. Few people film their bathrooms or cupboards under the stairs, or other areas of interest.

Oral history and reminiscence are other increasingly valuable sources, with obvious limitations of timespan, accuracy of memory, and tendency to nostalgia.[29] Like novels and diaries, these can provide insights into the uses and meanings of objects which cannot be discerned from their appearance alone.

Such rich resources of evidence present some difficulties of management. Perhaps a study of the functions of the home can provide a useful structure, identifying common patterns in places of very different appearance and relating appearance back to human needs? The investigation of the relationship between form and function has been an underlying theme of this project.

In looking at human needs it is necessary to begin with the people. Little is certain about the make-up of Scotland's population before the introduction of the Census in 1801, which counted just over 1.6 million people, about a third of today's total. Poll tax and hearth tax returns of the 1690s indicate that the greatest densities of population were in the firths of Forth, Clyde, and Tay, where good trade links enhanced the importance of productive agricultural

19. *The Arrival of the Country Relations* by Alexander Carse, 1812. The painter clearly realized that changes were taking place in society, altering the relationship of town and country and giving people in the middle ranks the opportunity to acquire fashionable new consumer goods.

20. Mrs Macmillan at Smerclate, South Uist, 1934. The Swedish anthropologist who took this photograph must have realized that this way of life was fast disappearing. On the rack the plates are displayed leaning forward to protect them from the haze from the peat fire on the central hearth.

land.[30] These tax returns also suggest that the household size (including servants) of the rich in Scotland was between seven and ten in the country and slightly less in towns, but this is uncertain.

There is some evidence of an increase in family size in the late eighteenth and early nineteenth centuries and of larger families in towns than in the country in the nineteenth century, with a particular contrast between the cities and the Highlands, where marriage took place at a later age.[31] The growth in population and the factors which led to people concentrating in the central belt have an obvious influence on the home in general, but conditions within individual households depend very much on the circumstances of the householder. A single labourer clearly has different requirements from a mother of ten, and a merchant needs housing which might not suit a farmer. In spite of such variation, human needs are fairly constant and the functions of the home relate closely to these.

The basic function is shelter for sleeping, epitomized by the tinker's bender of tree branches and fabric (pl 37). Along with shelter, warmth is essential for survival in a northern climate, and different fuels had a major influence on the changing form of the home and its equipment. Peat was once widespread and is still important in the Western Isles and elsewhere. It burns well on a low hearth and gives off a haze of peat reek which hovers about five feet from the ground if confined, as in the chimneyless houses of the Highlands and Islands. The use of peat had an obvious influence on the forms of fireplace and fire-irons, and a less expected effect on other items. Chairs were made low to sit under the smoke, and plate racks held dishes tilted forwards so the decorated surface could be seen from the low chairs and did not get covered in soot (pls 20, 39). Similarly, the increasing use of coal from the late seventeenth century necessitated new forms of fireplace to cope with the more intense heat and, in wealthy households, firescreens to protect those sitting near the fire.

Next after shelter as a function of the home comes security. This could be provided by the form of the building or fittings such as doors, bars, and locks, or it might depend on the constant presence of people or animals. It could be argued that the combination of security, physical or psychological, with shelter is the essence of 'home', and that the tinker's bender is home in a way that a common lodging house or a cardboard box in a doorway is not.

The main functions of the home, therefore, are to provide a sheltered and secure environment in which the essentials of human life can take place. Until this century the home was most often the scene of birth and death, and the removal of these events to hospitals and other institutions has affected how we think about them (pl 79). Attitudes to sex have also changed enormously over the past four hundred years, bringing new ideas about the use of rooms and furniture. The bed, in particular, has a very different place in the household today from that which it had three hundred years ago, when almost every room contained at least one. It was usual then to entertain guests in a room containing beds (pl 182), whereas now the bedroom is regarded as private space rarely seen by visitors.

Work is another essential of life which has changed dramatically in its relation to the home. Home-based work includes paid activity such as weaving,

21. Photographs of household servants were often taken by grateful employers but few show them at work. Here is Helen Mathieson, one of three maids in the home of a banker at Corrennie Gardens, Edinburgh, in 1903. The framed prints, papered wall and anaglypta dado, and Eastern-pattern carpet are typical of hall and staircase decoration at this time.

22. Dinner at Balnagown Castle, Ross-shire, in about 1900. Not unexpectedly, a social occasion is the focus of the photograph, but it also gives an indication of the rich decoration of the room.

shoemaking, painting, and similar tasks which need a certain amount of space and equipment. It also includes domestic service and unpaid household labour, such as washing, cleaning, and cooking. Until the beginning of the nineteenth century, a wide range of people worked at home or in workshops attached to the home, and their removal to factories and business offices changed attitudes. To the middle-class man, home became a haven from the dirty world of commerce and the 'sweet sanctities of domestic life' came to be seen as the woman's sphere. For some the leisured role of 'angel of the hearth' was entirely satisfactory, while for others the home now became a suffocating prison. In recent years, home-based working has become more common again, reflecting not simply the economic situation of the country, but changes in technology, and attitudes to work and domesticity.[32]

One hundred years ago, the home was a workplace for vast numbers of people, but the greater variety of jobs which became available to women early in the twentieth century gave them the chance to escape underpaid and over-controlled domestic service. The 'servant problem' inspired numerous books on 'the servantless house' and many *Punch* cartoons. It had a major effect on the form of household furnishings, the development of household equipment, and the use of rooms. Among these was the transformation of the middle-class kitchen from a bleak area fit only for servants to the 'cosy', country-style, family kitchen beloved of glossy magazines, and the changed role of the middle-class housewife from a manager of staff to an all-purpose domestic labourer.[33]

The storage and provision of food has an enormous effect on the form of household goods. Factors such as the availability of shops or the proximity of vegetable gardens influence the dwelling, and the provision of food as entertainment leads on to the next function of the home, as a place for leisure and celebration of the occasions of life (pl 22). In two-room dwellings all over Scotland there was usually a 'best room' reserved for visitors, and in larger houses there were dining rooms, billiard rooms, smoking rooms, and so on, all with their own distinctive features (pl 29).

These functions are fairly straightforward. More nebulous but undeniably important is the idea of the house as evidence of status — of the occupant's position in society. Sometimes this is manifested in the grandeur of the architecture, but often it shows in more subtle ways, such as the shiny brass letterbox which proclaims respectability or the display of prized possessions on a mantelpiece (see for instance pl 26). Inside the house, the furnishing reflects status considerations in ways which are so familiar we take them for granted – the best carpet in the living room, plainer mouldings and skirtings in the bedrooms. Even when a room is empty, it is usually possible to understand its role from its decoration or its position in the house. Conventions change, however, and for an understanding of the past it is necessary to know the rules. Dining-room fireplaces, for instance, were normally black in nineteenth-century Edinburgh town houses and elsewhere, while those in drawing rooms were generally of pale statuary marble. The dark dining room was considered a male preserve, while the drawing room with its light decoration and furnishings belonged to the women. Status considerations reflect not only class and money values, but also gender relations and power levels within families.

It is also evident that function can be defined by form (in spite of Louis Sullivan's dictum of 1896 'Form ever follows function')[34] and this too is related to status. Buildings often have an overawing effect on people, influencing their behaviour in a deliberate way. Architects can contrive such effects and home owners may use architects as a means of acquiring status.

A final category of function is the idea of the home as an expression of spiritual values. The building of a chapel as part of the house is an obvious example, but the creation of a beautiful room as a means of personal expression is another. This brings in the meanings implicit in certain colour combinations or decorative motifs: a cream-coloured room with flowered curtains, for instance, speaks of values different from those of a grey one with Venetian blinds. Victorian writers often associated the idea of art in the home with moral standards, and a pleasant, comfortable house was held up as both an example and an incentive by temperance campaigners.

The creation of a home is bound up with complex feelings about social and family life, and with wider affiliations, regional and national. It may not be possible to explain entirely, but why are there, for instance, distinct differences between Edinburgh and Glasgow tenements? Are some features there to demonstrate local affinities, as some homes clearly show a sense of Scottishness? Osbert Lancaster's view of Scottish Baronial in *Homes Sweet Homes* makes a joke of this, but the conscious adoption of a Scottish identity by Scots introduces questions about the development of interest in Scotland's history, of antiquarianism and antique collecting, and inevitably, such figures as Sir Walter Scott, whose passion for collecting from the past was combined with an enthusiasm for the most modern technology, such as gas lighting and pneumatic bell pushes. Scott's house, Abbotsford (pls 120, 138), is also an interesting example of the house preserved as shrine.

Looking at function thus provides a different slant, casting new light on familiar ground, especially in revealing parallels across social divisions which are often obscured by superficial but striking differences of style. If we want to concentrate on life as lived at home, however, another approach suggests itself. This is the way we see our own houses and those of our friends – looking round room by room. We have pursued this approach in the arrangement of the book, which investigates how rooms were used and how their use changed.

There are complications with this method. Changes in the furnishing and use of rooms can be rapid, and at any time there will be some who are considered modern in the way they live and others who are quite happy to keep things as they always have been. Customs survive in some places which have died out in others and generalizations have to be tempered with caution. It is often suggested that new ideas about architecture and the use of space originate

23. 'Scottish Baronial' by Osbert Lancaster from *Homes Sweet Homes*, 1939. Exaggerated as it is, all the distinctive elements in this drawing can be found in photographs of real Scottish rooms in this book (excepting the bear with lampshade).

with architects and their clients, 'filtering down' society over many years. Yet parallel cultures also appear within apparently similar groups, who yet have interests and traditions of their own. The conspicuous consumption of the middle classes of Victorian Glasgow contrasts with the more cautious taste of the capital's residents, while the fishing people of the East Neuk of Fife had a passion for pottery not shared by the fishers of the North East.

Further difficulties arise from the fact that people use various names for rooms which have essentially the same purpose. Three people in a terrace might each have a room similarly furnished which one calls the drawing room, one the sitting room, and the third, the lounge. Or members of a family might think of a single room in a different way. J M Barrie, setting the scene for his 1908 play *What Every Woman Knows,* describes a room belonging to a socially mobile family grown wealthy from granite quarrying, revealing also its place in relation to more formal apartments in the house:

> It is not the room you would be shown into if you were calling socially on Miss Wylie. The drawing-room for you, and Miss Wylie in a coloured merino to receive you; very likely she would exclaim, 'This is a pleasant surprise!' though she has seen you coming up the avenue and has just had time to whip the dustcloths off the chairs … Nor is this the room in which you would dine in solemn grandeur if invited to drop in and take pot-luck, which is how the Wylies invite, it being a family weakness to pretend that they sit down in the dining-room daily. It is the real living-room of the house, where Alick, who will never get used to fashionable ways, can take off his collar and sit happily in his stocking-soles …

In this 'living-room' the furniture is homely and mostly from the smaller house where the Wylies began. There is a 'large and shiny chair which can be turned into a bed if you look the other way for a minute', some horsehair-seated chairs, and a centre table. A bookcase of pitch pine gives Maggie the excuse to call this room the library, 'while David and James call it the west-room and Alick calls it 'the room', which is to him the natural name for any apartment without a bed in it'.[35]

There are also problems in tracing changes in the names of rooms over time, but it is possible to discern patterns and while the answers may not be

24. A comfortable living room (or parlour) at Townhead Terrace in Paisley, around 1900. The original photograph has written on the back that it was taken at 11.30pm by flash-light, but sadly gives no further details.

conclusive, the questions are worth further investigation. Almost all dwellings had a room specified as the kitchen, but in inventories from around 1700 other rooms usually appear as 'room' or 'chamber', often further described by their position: 'fore', 'mid', or 'back'; 'north' or 'south'. From listed items in inventories, these rooms often seem similar, but we can guess their function to some extent. In 1716, Robert Drysdale, a merchant burgess of Edinburgh, had similar items in his 'North roume' and 'mid roume', and both contained 'stouped' beds (p188). Several things in the mid room were described as 'old' or 'broken', however, and the value of the furnishings was less than half that in the north room, suggesting that this was the place in which he would entertain friends, if he entertained at all.[36]

A systematic survey of large numbers of inventories has been beyond the scope of this project but would be valuable. Other sources of evidence have been mentioned above, but those of special use for establishing the evolution of rooms are architects' plans, house agents' details, furniture makers' records, bellboards, and books.

Along with plans, comments by architects and their clients on the use of rooms are also of great interest. A letter of 1762 from Robert Clerk to his kinsman Sir James Clerk, who was designing his own house, is particularly revealing:

> In France where Men & Women live always together & their pleasures are never seperate, the Dining room & Drawing room must be both large & are better next one another … But in England & more so in Scotland, where Men's pleasures in Women consist chiefly in matters of fact, & those who are sincere & natural confess that they are more at their ease & enjoy society more when the Ladies are absent, it is proper that the Dining room should be a capital good room particularly in the Country & that it should not be next any room in which there is or can be any company. The Drinking & the conversation after dinner make this absolutely necessary. The Drawing room may be a room of less size. In the Country there ought to be another room upon the principal floor seperate quite from the Dining room & Drawing room which I call a loitering room & it ought to be a library & large. There people spend their time with pleasure who neither like to drink or to be with the Ladies …

Robert Clerk showed his letter to Robert Adam, who approved of his views, but Sir James replied that the library should be above the principal floor so that it would *not* turn into a loitering resort for the whole family.[37]

Details of houses for sale or rent appear in newspaper advertisements from the past few hundred years and give an outline of what rooms are called and how they change. In the *Glasgow Courier* of 28 January 1800, a notice of lodgings to let described:

> A large lodging, being the whole of the first floor … fronting George Street and High Street … consisting of a dining room 19 feet by 16 feet 4; drawing room 18 by 16, five good bed-rooms besides a light closet, kitchen, larder &c. and a spacious lobby. The tenant … may have two large rooms in a back house, having an entry from the stair head, well calculated for a laundry, servants' rooms, &c … Each lodging will have a Cellar, and the privilege of a Well in the back close.[38]

By 1860, 'Superior HOUSES of Three to Five Rooms and Kitchen' could be advertised as 'fitted up with Plunge and Shower Baths', though these were unusual at this time.[39] Present-day estate agents' particulars almost invariably include a bathroom and possibly a bathroom *en suite* with the 'Master bedroom' in a house of any size, while smaller properties often have a shower room squeezed into a closet space, indicating that bathing facilities are now considered essential.

Furniture makers' advertisements, estimates, and catalogues not only show the furniture considered suitable at different dates, but also suggest which rooms people had. In 1774 James Hamilton, an Edinburgh cabinetmaker, provided for Mr Thomas Mowat in Shetland 'a list of furniture made use of in the most fashionable houses', separated into Dining Room, Drawing Room, Bed Room, and Dressing Room.[40] Just over one hundred years later, advertisers in Worrall's *Directory for the Counties of Aberdeen, Banff, and Kincardine*[41], most commonly mention 'Dining Room, Drawing Room, Bedroom, Kitchen, and other furniture', while some include the parlour and others the hall and lobby.

Bell boards which hung in kitchens to summon the servant are a less obvious source of evidence, but can often be dated accurately and provide information specific to one house or family.

25. A bell board at Arniston House, Midlothian, provides evidence of the number and names of rooms in about 1900. Bell boards sometimes survive in houses of much more modest size, indicating that as late as the 1930s, even with only two bedrooms, a household could have a domestic servant.

Books of advice on decoration, which started as a trickle and became a deluge in the Victorian period, give a more general picture. Sometimes these focused on a single room, such as *The Drawing Room* by Lucy Orrinsmith. Other writers produced *Suggestions for House Decoration* or *A Plea for Art in the House* and dealt with the different rooms in passing, often chapter by chapter.[42] The kitchen is usually absent from such works before the twentieth century, presumably because it was considered only a work area and not suitable for artistic treatment.

In small houses the rooms were known simply as kitchen and chamber, spence, or room; or but and ben. The names seem to reflect regional differences in language rather than use, though the usage must also have varied with local occupations.

Until this century the majority of the Scottish people lived in small houses, mostly in overcrowded conditions: the 1901 census showed that 50.5 per cent occupied houses of only one or two rooms.[43] Because such a large proportion

26. By the 1930s when this photograph was taken at Ballachulish, Argyllshire, it was less usual for people in the country to be living in a house so small that the bed had to be in the living room. Much care has obviously been taken with the symmetrical arrangement of items on the mantelpiece.

historically coped with the exigencies (and some pleasures) of living in close proximity, the book begins by considering life in one or two rooms. For single people or couples without children, such small houses can be convenient. For large families, this kind of dwelling could satisfy only the most basic functions of a home, providing shelter and security but little more, though considerable effort and ingenuity often went into maintaining the status of respectability in the most difficult conditions.

In 1801 when the first census was taken, only about one-fifth of Scots lived in centres with 5000 or more inhabitants and until the 1880s, most people lived in the country or in small settlements. Chapter Two therefore deals with the small house in the country.

For the first time in 1891, census returns showed that over half the population lived in towns and cities, mainly concentrated in the Lowland belt between Edinburgh and Glasgow. Chapter Three investigates how these different circumstances prompted new ways of dealing with life in a small space.

Inevitably, the rest of the book is about the homes of a minority, but it was a minority which had the greatest range of house types and the widest choice of furnishings. In the present century it has become the majority. At the beginning of the long period under study few people had more than two rooms, but expectations and provision gradually changed. By 1861, over a quarter of Scottish houses had three or more rooms, increasing to nearly half in 1911.[44] With the building of three- and four-apartment council houses after the First World War, rooms for separate purposes became available to a much wider section of society and by 1951, over two-thirds of Scottish houses had three rooms or more.[45]

Almost all dwellings of more than two apartments had a room named the 'kitchen', but its place in people's lives varied considerably according to the size and nature of the household. Although much influenced by the practicalities of food preparation, the kitchen has also altered in response to social change over time.

One feature of the home entirely determined by practical needs is the location of the hall or lobby, but even here there have been changes in attitude affecting its furnishing and use. John Marshall's *Amateur House Decoration* of 1883 indicates one such change and is of interest because Marshall lived in

Edinburgh and illustrated his book with drawings of his home (pls 27, 151). Of particular significance is that Marshall felt constrained by the formality of rooms dedicated to specific purposes. At this period the wealthy middle classes lived in substantial villas and the very rich built sprawling country houses run by armies of servants, with a room dedicated to almost every possible activity. Addressing an Edinburgh audience with architectural interests, Marshall suggested a relaxation of the rules governing the arrangement of rooms, starting with the transformation of the hall into a casual lounging area, if necessary by knocking through into the seldom-used morning room. A similar change had already taken place in some large country houses, where the hall had become neutral ground in which men and women could meet informally, in outdoor dress, unconstrained by drawing-room manners.[46] This reflects ideas put forward earlier by architects, particularly the gothic revivalists, and indicates an alteration in family relations similar to that which prompted many in the 1960s and 1970s to knock two rooms into one large living room.

After the kitchen, probably the earliest room to be mentioned by function was the dining room (often spelt 'dinning'), which appears regularly in inventories from about the 1750s and occasionally before this. In the largest mansion houses and palaces the dining room was listed by name as early as 1653.[47] At the end of the eighteenth and beginning of the nineteenth century, small houses of four rooms often had a dining room, whereas the drawing room seems to have been confined to the larger houses of the aristocracy, and the contents of bedrooms suggest that they were still used as required for entertaining female guests.[48] It seems likely that many householders kept their rooms multi-functional simply because of the cost and labour of providing heating, and that the season and circumstance determined which room was used when.

Similar in its contents to the dining room was the parlour, which in small houses was often the only formal area in which to receive guests and in large ones functioned as a morning room or family sitting room. The parlour is not included separately in our survey, and deserves more research, especially since the name is one of the few that is virtually never used today, suggesting some definite character of its own which has been rejected wholesale. It may be that the idea of the parlour spread so far down the social scale, remaining in currency in the country far longer than in town, that it became undesirable to anyone with hopes of social advancement.

In a letter of 1762, Sir James Clerk mentions that in his large country house at Penicuik 'Our Usual residence will be in the Parlor … in our Cold Climate a good fire cannot keep a larger room in a tolerable degree of heat'.[49] By the early nineteenth century, in Susan Ferrier's novel *The Inheritance* and in Elizabeth Grant's *Memoirs*, the parlour is mentioned in association with older people, implying that it had become old-fashioned among the gentry.[50] In contemporary inventories of houses of four or five rooms belonging to merchants and professionals in Glasgow and Edinburgh, the parlour is often the only entertaining room. Early this century, architects seriously debated the 'parlour question', which turned on whether to allow the working classes the differentiated small spaces they wanted for social reasons or to force on them the open-plan living rooms architects preferred. These were cheaper to build, easier to heat, and fitted middle-class ideas about how to live.[51] Architects varied considerably in their attitude, and their deliberations had a direct effect on what was provided in the council-house building programmes of the 1920s.

While the 'parlour', sharing functions of several rooms, has disappeared,

27. John Marshall's hall in Edinburgh, from his book, *Amateur House Decoration*, 1883. Clearly he did not have space for his idea of a 'real hall', 'with a cheerful fireplace, and some basket chairs, and a table, and magazines – a place to lounge in and enjoy a little variety of life from the narrow confinement of a room'.

28. A N Paterson in his studio/library at Long Croft, in Helensburgh, Dunbartonshire, in 1908. Paterson was an architect of the generation which concerned itself with the housing of working people. His own house reflects his social status and this photograph promotes an image of a professional man at work, while others of his wife and daughter emphasize their leisure activities.

'drawing room' remains a term used today, though the way of life which inspired its greatest elaboration has largely gone and it is usually named 'sitting room' or something similar, indicating its less formal role. From its introduction in the second half of the seventeenth century the 'with-drawing room' was usually upstairs on the first floor, and at first it was part of a suite of parade rooms which led into each other: dining room, with-drawing room, bedchamber, and closet (pl 157). Later, while the drawing room remained upstairs with the best view of the garden, the dining room, parlour, and main bedroom were more often on the ground floor. Any house large enough to have a drawing room would probably have these other rooms as well. Today the drawing room, refigured into sitting room, is more likely to be at ground level.

The ground-floor bedroom seems to have been a distinctive Scottish feature which continued well into the twentieth century. Several Dean of Guild plans for one-and-a-half storey symmetrical houses in Orkney of about 1912 show the ground-floor rooms comprising a lobby, parlour, kitchen, dining room, and bedroom, with two more bedrooms upstairs in the roof. Information from Orcadians suggests the upper rooms were for children and servants.[52] Is the ground-floor bedroom evidence of a continuing Scottish preference for living on one level, a custom which John Claudius Loudon, a prolific commentator on architectural matters and himself a Scot, deplored as leading to laziness?[53]

Scottish architects were among the pioneers of technological innovations to improve the comfort of the home, such as gas lighting, central heating and ventilation, and sanitation. The spread of any new facility was, however, always governed by the balancing of convenience against economics. As long as servants were available to carry heavy water cans, a plumbed-in bath was not a necessity and householders continued to bathe in comfort in front of the bedroom fire.[54] J J Stevenson, a Scottish architect, in his *House Architecture* of 1880 recommended a bath for every bedroom suite as a labour-saving measure, but the wide adoption of baths and flush toilets and electric lighting in smaller houses had to await the provision of communally organized water and drainage services in the late nineteenth century. Bathrooms were not common until the present century, and they appear at the end of our tour of the Scottish home.

29. A late Victorian billiard room at Kinlochmoidart House, Inverness-shire, photographed in 1985. Strong floors were needed to support heavy billiard tables and lighting had to be carefully placed. These were predominantly masculine preserves and there is a ventilation grille in the ceiling here to get rid of cigar smoke.

Inevitably some rooms must remain unexplored in a book of this size. The library was considered of some importance in cultured Scottish mansions in the late seventeenth century and was often sited distinctively at the top of the house. Billiard rooms entertained countless Victorians, and nurseries remote from the principal rooms kept children in their place, out of earshot. These and other areas dedicated to special uses may be mentioned in passing but cannot be described in detail. Although our visit to the home in Scotland is thus curtailed, we hope to show how important it was and is for the lives of the people, how much the study of the home can tell us about culture and values in the past, and how interesting a perspective this gives on home life in the present.

2 Living in One or Two Rooms in the Country

DAVID JONES

'… here they are, the man, his wife, and a parcel of children, squeezed up in this miserable hole, with their meal and their washing tackle, and all their other things; and yet it is quite surprising to behold how decent the women endeavour to keep the place.'

William Cobbett, 1833[1]

Among the popular attractions of the 1938 Empire Exhibition in Glasgow was 'An Clachan', a fabricated Highland village in the shadow of Thomas Tait's miracle of engineering and modern design, the Tower of Empire. Visitors enjoying the thrill of the new also revelled in nostalgia for a vanishing way of life. By the 1930s, nearly two thirds of Scots lived in towns and cities. A growing number were in smart new council houses such as those in Mosspark just next door to the exhibition site, and few remained in the stone and turf houses which represented 'the traditional Scottish home' so picturesquely.

Before 1891 most people in Scotland lived in rural areas. Their houses inevitably varied considerably according to income, occupation, and where they were. Castles and country houses, generally inhabited by relatively small families, existed in considerable numbers and the great wave of agricultural improvement from the late eighteenth century produced a network of spacious modern farmhouses, at least in Lowland areas. But most country dwellers until well into the Victorian period lived in houses of only one or two rooms.[2]

Because migrant and seasonal labour was prevalent in Scottish agriculture, many of these small dwellings provided the minimum of temporary shelter.

30. The 'clachan', or Highland village, at the Empire Exhibition in Glasgow, 1938. This popular attraction recreated a romanticized version of traditional Scottish country life, peopled by quaintly dressed Gaelic-speaking 'natives'. Rapidly disappearing house types contrasted with the thrilling modernity of 'Tait's Tower'.

One of the most basic was the shieling hut, a simply-constructed cabin for use by women and children while their livestock grazed remote outlying pastures during the summer months, allowing the crops near the settlements to mature while the cattle were away. The imprint of these temporary dwellings can still be seen in upland areas today.[3] Shieling huts, which remained a feature in Lewis until the 1940s, continued ancient patterns of living. Some of the most recent were of corrugated iron, but older examples in Lewis were stone-built domed cells, reminiscent in their 'beehive' shape of the more complex permanent homes at Skara Brae and Knap of Howar in Orkney, structures which are almost five thousand years old. The interiors of shieling huts are distinctive, the dominant feature being the communal sleeping platform occupying up to two-thirds of the floorspace. Along the front edge of this bed was usually a long seat of stone and turf. Food and small implements were kept in wall recesses, while larger items and fuel were stored in a smaller chamber off the main cell.

Sheelins in JURA and a distant View of the Paps.

31. Shieling huts on Jura, engraved by Peter Mazell and published by Thomas Pennant in his account of a journey in Scotland in 1772. Included in this view in front of the Paps of Jura are the domed structures usually made of stone, and conical shelters of wood and turf. Mazell exaggerates the size of the door openings, which did not normally exceed three feet in height.

One of the earliest descriptions of shieling huts is given by Thomas Pennant, who observed on the Isle of Jura in 1772:

> sheelins, the habitations of some peasants who attend the herds of milch cows. These formed a grotesque groupe; some were oblong, many conic, and so low that entrance is forbidden, without creeping through the little opening, which has no other door than a faggot of birch twigs, placed there occasionally: they are constructed of branches of trees, covered with sods; the furniture a bed of heath, placed on a bank of sod; two blankets and a rug; some dairy vessels, and above, certain pendent shelves made of basket work, to hold the cheese, the produce of the Summer.[4]

It is clear that Pennant was looking at huts of different types and that the most common on Jura was the conical turf and branch 'tent'. Similar structures have been recorded in use for other purposes: the 'preaching tent' for minister and precentor when services were held outdoors is well known,[5] but conical huts were also used by forest workers such as coppicers and bark peelers. Stone shielings survived because their construction is more robust than the tent type and at least one is still used for working in the mid 1990s. This 'beehive' hut with stone sleeping platform at Sula Sgeir, Isle of Lewis, is occupied seasonally

32. John Smith of Port of Ness making oatcakes in a shieling on the islet of Sula Sgeir, Lewis, in 1954. Smoke from the peat fire dispersed through a hole in the roof. Four or five men still stay here for about three weeks to catch young gannets for food.

33. Exterior of the shieling at Sula Sgeir, photographed in 1954. Inside are stone seats and a raised sleeping platform. Evidence of similar structures exists throughout the Western Isles, and in Sutherland, Wester Ross, and North Perthshire.

by wildfowlers who catch and process young gannets or 'gugha' for food.

Several features of the housing of migrant workers in the past two hundred years preserve the age-old conventions of the shieling hut and some can be seen in surviving fishermen's huts or 'salmon lodges'. These temporary homes for freshwater fishing teams of up to eight men occur mostly along the riverbanks of the east coast. Slashy Lodge, at the mouth of the Earn in Perthshire, is a typical example.[6]

Although its brick structure dates from the 1920s, the division of space inside remains the same as in the ancient huts of north-west Scotland, with one main room for sleeping and a small adjoining chamber for storing fuel. The beds in Slashy Lodge are wooden cots joined together in a row, but like traditional sleeping platforms they are fronted by a long narrow seat which is part of the bed structure. Bed and hearth are the principal features of the space. Conditions in the Tay and Earn salmon lodges were investigated in detail by Alexander Carmichael of Lochgilphead in 1889 for the Board of Supervision.[7] He highlighted problems of poor ventilation, infestation, lack of privies, and inadequate provision for storage space and disposal of rubbish. Carmichael's report also comments on the transient way of life of the fishing crews: 'The life is a hard one. They are said to be very rough in their habits but as a rule there is nothing in the lodges to civilize them …' There was no movable furniture because, he had been told, 'The men were so rough in their habits that everything of wood would be burned'.[8] The lodges were not homes in which the occupants could be expected to take any domestic pride, but temporary shelters to be vacated at the season's end. Because communal living had been conducted in this manner for generations, the most basic but functional internal fittings had evolved and the need for 'improvement' had not previously been considered. Sea-fishing huts of a similar nature existed where there was no convenient permanent settlement, such as in the more remote parts of the Northern Isles. A Danish visitor to Shetland in 1839 observed:

> Feideland … is a small peninsula united to Mainland by a flat beach … the fishermen from many parts of the country assemble there in the month of May to build stone huts, tightened with moss and roofed with feals [turf sods], or at

best a thatch of straw, and there they remain till the 12th of August, when the fishing season is at an end … The inside of these huts corresponds with the outside. You will find nothing but some beds made of rude boards, nailed together, containing straw and coarse blankets. On some of these lay men, who had thrown themselves down in their clothes and enjoyed sweet sleep. There is, moreover, a hearth round which are hung stockings to dry, and over it suspended a kettle or pot – and this is all.[9]

34. Bothy boys or 'loons' in a bothy at Gagie, Angus, about 1910. All the men's few possessions could be packed into kists of the type seen on the right, here used as a seat. A bothy bench (left) and cot beds were usually the only other items of furniture.

Like many shieling huts these seem to have been built or reconstructed each year by their occupants, and beds were the only items of furniture within. Similar seasonal accommodation existed for other specialized short-term uses: a kelp gatherers' hut with tiered box beds made from fish boxes survives on the island of Ruskholm in Orkney and gold prospectors' huts could once be found at Kildonan in Sutherland.

Year-round accommodation had to be more comfortable, though it was never luxurious for labourers on arable and stock farms. From about the end of the eighteenth century, provision for groups of unmarried male workers was made in large rooms within farm steadings (the buildings devoted to the practical running of the farm), or occasionally in a separate structure away from the steading. In the north east and parts of central Scotland, farm servants ate in the farmhouse kitchen and their sleeping rooms were known as 'chaumers'; but in most eastern parts of the country the young men lived and prepared their own food in a 'bothy', distinguished from the chaumer by its cooking hearth (pl 34).

Typically the bothy was a small building near the byre or stable, lined with deal planking and sparsely furnished with high-sided crib beds, a form or

35. Bothy bed at Mains of Glamis, Angus. This bothy, on a large arable farm near Forfar, has a ground-floor living room with hearth and an unheated sleeping chamber upstairs, fitted out with crib beds and thick, chaff-filled mattresses, each in a separate compartment. It was last occupied in 1963.

bench, and the labourers' own kists. These were plain deal boxes with hinged lids, used for both storage and seating. Although old and unwanted items from the farmhouse were often relegated to the bothy – so its furnishings might include varieties of chairs and even brass beds – most had fixed cots and a minimum of movable seating. Each man had a ration of fuel, milk, and oatmeal. Domestic duties, such as rudimentary cleaning or tending the fire, were arranged amongst the men or ignored. Phrases such as 'panny week', an allotted period for emptying the grate, derive from this system, but towards the end of the nineteenth century 'bothy maids' were increasingly employed to cook and clean. Bothy lads had few possessions and despite hard outdoor work and perhaps comfortless surroundings, enjoyed a relatively carefree existence. Many formed musical bands which performed bawdy 'bothy ballads' from farm to farm, and numerous joke photographs of bothy inmates, particularly from nineteenth-century Angus and Fife, bear testimony to the responsibility-free nature of their communal lives.

Farm bothies and the similar chaumers differed widely in their standard of accommodation. James Robb, editor of *The Scottish Farmer and Horticulturist* recorded several in his *Inquiry* of 1861:

> the bothy in one instance being a room opening out of an outhouse, boarded, with two tidy-looking beds, but no other furniture, but with a fireplace, which, however, did not appear to have been used for some time. The light was good, the ceiling high, and, on the whole, the place did not look so very uncomfortable for a merely sleeping domicile, which it was.
>
> Another, occupied by three men, was about 15 feet by 14, with a roof from 8 to 9 feet high, and a good light. It had two boxed in beds decorated with various articles of dress for man and horse – pieces of harness, Sunday waistcoats, etc., – suspended on nails inside and outside of the bed. For furniture, it had two forms and four chairs, and a blazing coal fire made the place look cheerful.[10]

Women's bothies were generally associated with the fishing industry, particularly fish packing and gutting. Large numbers of young girls lived an itinerant life during the nineteenth and early twentieth centuries, following the herring fleets from Shetland to the south of England. In Scotland, they were accommodated near the processing stations in large huts, frequently of corrugated iron. Unlike farm bothies for single men, the women's huts were furnished with tables and iron beds. Sewing and knitting kit and bandages for

36. Fisher girl in her communal bothy near Stromness, Orkney, about 1900. Women's huts were often decorated with wallpaper and provided with a stove rather than an open hearth.

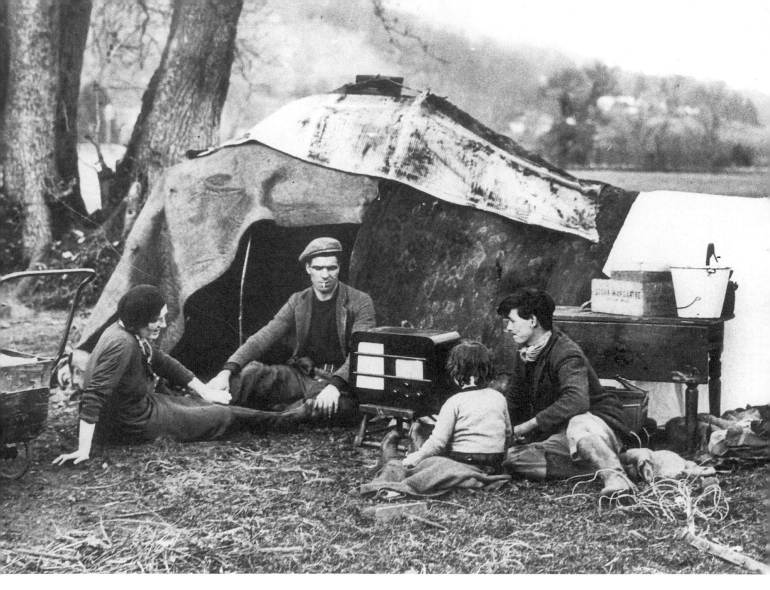

37. John MacKenzie and his family listening to the wireless by their bender near Aberfeldy in Perthshire, April 1939. Benders varied in size and quality of construction and were more substantial in winter than in the summer months.

the women's hands were kept in personal kists. The huts were generally heated by stoves rather than open hearths and the interiors were enlivened by wallpaper and home-made rugs.

Most occupants of small dwellings such as bothies spent much of their time at work or outdoors, using the room as a place to sleep and perhaps prepare meals; but this pattern of living was by no means exclusive to bothy and shieling dwellers. The only truly nomadic population of Scotland were the tinkers, who lived in the same way, in one room, either singly or in encampments. Until the 1850s, when the first wheeled caravans appeared, these travelling people lived in tents called 'benders', a tradition which lasted well into the 1930s. Tinkers travelled in both rural and industrialized areas, setting up camp by roadsides or on the outskirts of towns and villages. Today, travellers are largely restricted by law to controlled sites away from centres of population, where they occupy their own caravans or cubicles provided by local councils, though a few people live in benders still.

From the mid nineteenth century, caravans known as 'living vans' were used to house peripatetic workers on large estates. These spacious horse-drawn vans, similar to those used by road gangs until the 1950s, were used particularly by dykers and shepherds.[11]

Archaeological and other evidence indicates that, as in Wales and northern England, the principal form of permanent rural dwelling house in Scotland until the end of the eighteenth century was the longhouse.[12] In a country where stock farming was the economic mainstay, living in close proximity with one's animals was advantageous for the livestock's security and for warmth. The longhouse provided accommodation under one roof with a common entrance for people and animals (pls 39, 44). The necessities were a hearth and a place to sleep, since much of the farming year was spent outdoors. There were

38. Moirlanich longhouse at Killin, Perthshire, now owned by the National Trust for Scotland. There is evidence of settlement at this site from at least the eighteenth century but this house was built around 1850. Its inhabitants were farmers and their cattle lived within the walls of the longhouse. The thatch was replaced by corrugated iron probably in the 1930s.

39. Inside the blackhouse at 42 Arnol, Isle of Lewis. This rare survival now belongs to Historic Scotland and is open to the public. It has both a traditional Highland dresser and a Lowland dresser bought in Edinburgh just after the First World War, as well as the ubiquitous settle. The space seen through the door is the byre, where the cattle lived.

regional differences, but most were of linear form, with one or two rooms and a byre, a central hearth in the family end and a roof of straw, bent grass, rush, or heather thatch. Many of the materials from which these dwellings were built could be re-used or recycled, emphasizing the impermanent character of the house. Smoke-enriched thatch, for instance, could be trampled into manure in the byre, as could disintegrated sections of turf wall and the chaff filling of mattresses.

The unimproved longhouse in the Highlands and Islands is nowadays loosely known as a 'blackhouse', a term which has been in use probably since the 1850s. A distinctive variant with double-thickness walls survived until recently in the Western Isles. The house at 42 Arnol, Isle of Lewis, now preserved by Historic Scotland, is a good example of this type (pl 39).[13] It is long and low, the walls two metres thick, with inner and outer skins of unshaped stones built around an inner core of earth. The roof of cut straw has hipped, rounded ends. Inside are a stalled byre to the right of the entrance, a fire room and sleeping room to the left, and a barn along the back wall of the house.

Living in the longhouse or blackhouse involved ingenious division of space, frequently achieved by the positioning of large pieces of furniture. Freestanding box beds were grouped in blocks, acting as room dividers and placed so that entry could be made from different sides. There are three box beds at 42 Arnol, two placed lengthways and one put across the large room, forming a wall between the sleeping chamber and the fire room, with its opening facing the hearth.

40. *Interior of a Perthshire Cottage*, around 1850, by an unknown artist. To the right of the fireplace are the tools of a 'souter', or shoemaker.

Like the exterior features of the house, interior furniture and fittings were the result of continuous evolution from distant origins. On Orkney particularly, continuity can be seen between the slab-sided neolithic stone alcove beds of about 3000 BC and the nineteenth-century 'neuk beds' of small farmhouses. The tradition of sleeping in wall cavities, or in freestanding 'closed' or box beds was widespread in small homes in Scotland, rural and urban, until the 1930s.

The furniture in the longhouse in the Highlands was perhaps more fixed than in other regions. A large number of deserted nineteenth-century houses, particularly on the Western Isles, remain complete with abandoned furniture, testimony not only to the strongly implanted tradition of the box bed, but also to the customary appearance of the kitchen dresser. Although a continuous tradition of dressers cannot be claimed, the stone shelves on raised legs which survive in the neolithic houses of Skara Brae and Knap of Howar do bear comparison with Highland and island dressers of the nineteenth and early twentieth centuries. Both seem to have a distinct display and storage function; they share the same position facing a (usually central) hearth; and both have substantial depth when compared with traditional dressers from regions of England. This depth of surface on Highland dressers is connected with the absence of tables, or at least the lack of emphasis on the table, in the small Highland and island house. In the manner of modern kitchen units the tops of these dressers were used as general work surfaces, particularly for baking. Many were designed with a broad overhanging top and a raised lip or gallery which prevents flour or meal from spilling onto the floor. This feature is simply an enlarged version of the traditional Scottish baking board, which has a raised edge on three sides. It seems to have become integrated into the design of dressers at some point during the mid nineteenth century.

Highland dressers have more in common with their counterparts in Ireland than in any other culture, though the shelves and base were in separate sections whereas the Irish ones were joined. Like Irish dressers, they are likely to be individualistic and are often built-in fixtures or, if freestanding, made to the specific proportions of the room. Dressers of the Isle of Lewis and North and South Uist, for instance, have projecting hoods following the slope of the house roof. Like the tops of box beds, these protect the contents of the dresser from drips of water or falling soot. A striking feature of some Highland and Irish dressers is a central wooden-barred cage in the lower stage, for the storage of meat or to house laying poultry.[14]

In their structural details, Highland dressers are also similar to Irish examples in having guard rails on their upper shelves designed to support forward-facing plates and ashets. In the Lowland tradition too, it is rare to find dresser shelves made with beading to support backward-leaning plates, as is common in England. If stored the right way up, dishes and bowls would quickly collect dust and soot, so pottery bowls displayed on Highland dressers were commonly 'whammelled', or placed upside-down on the worktop in stacks, as they were also in Ireland. Wooden trenchers and bowls were used in most areas before the nineteenth century, and there were a few local makers of brown pottery vessels.[15] Glazed white pottery was not widely available in the country until the middle of the last century, when it began to be mass-produced in factories and was cheap enough to be bought by people with little ready money. When used in houses with peat fires it became stained and crazed by smoke, but photographs of laden shelves of dressers indicate how important a feature decorated pottery became (pl 20). It was often sent home by women away for the fishing season.

41. Long settle or 'resting chair' in a Shetland kitchen, early twentieth century. Settles were particularly versatile in the small house because they provided a sociable evening fireside seat for more than one person as well as sleeping space at night.

The position of furniture in the small Highland house was determined by the hearth, the natural focus of life in a country with a cold, damp climate. Many Highland longhouses until well into this century had central hearths, and the furniture was generally arranged around the walls rather than clustered around the fire. Beds, dressers, chairs, and settles all faced inwards to the centre of the room in an arrangement that must have been easier to manage in a multi-purpose room than groups of items taking up floorspace.

In this arrangement, one of the most flexible types of seating was the long seat or settle, on which several people could sit by day and one could sleep at night. Highland and island settles are usually deep from front to back to accommodate a sleeping body and many examples are upholstered with straw matting or provided with cushions to make them suitable for both purposes. It is likely that the wooden settle, with its open framework of back and arms, derives from the earliest of fireside seats, the long turf or stone bench, of which vestigial evidence remains in the turf benches at the edges of sleeping platforms in shielings and the later wooden versions of these in fishing bothies.

There are many names for the settle in Scotland. The most common Lowland term in inventories before the eighteenth century was 'lang saddill'; and 'langsede' remained in use in Shetland within living memory. These were recorded in institutions as well as in houses: they were, for example, specified for use in bedchambers at St Andrews University in 1544, probably for both

42. Cottage of 'improved' design of the nineteenth century at Newton of Wormiston, Fife. Inside there were two rooms, a bed closet, and a small lobby, with a single earth closet outside. The house has now been altered entirely.

43. Box beds in the kitchen of the cottage above. The grandeur of the beds, with their classical decoration, may seem something of a surprise in this small cottage, but is not unusual. Opposite the bed openings was the kitchen hearth. Inside can be seen marks on the bed linings indicating the height of the chaff mattresses used in them, and underneath is storage space.

sitting and sleeping on.[16] In the Northern Isles, and to some extent in northern Scotland, they were known as 'resting chairs', which gives an indication of their dual role. In Aberdeenshire they doubled as tables: the 'deece' or 'dess' settle found in this county is an extraordinary variant, incorporating a falling table leaf hinged to the settle back. The small, centrally-positioned, one-legged table allows one person on each side to sit on the settle and eat from a flat surface. Since tables are usually bulky items which cannot be stored away easily, the deece settle represented a great saving of space in small houses. Interestingly, similar items have been noted in Ireland and in the Basque country, adding to our knowledge of specific furniture traditions (including low stick-back chairs and box beds) which seem to be peculiar to Celtic countries.[17]

In Scotland, there is a richness of Gaelic settle terminology which perhaps reflects the fact that settles were used more frequently, or more recently, on the west coast and in the Western Isles. The most common terms are 'seiseach' and 'being'.[18] These are both used in the Western Isles, where many longhouses had more than one of these seats. The most typical pattern was open-framed, with a long back consisting of widely spaced banisters. The underneath was sometimes filled in with boarding to provide covered storage and this could include a sleeping place for a dog.

Although chairs were not to be found in every small house in the Highlands and Islands, where settles and stools were more common, a great variety of chairmaking traditions existed. The low, stick-back chair of west-coast or Celtic tradition is one of the most prominent, made with either three or four legs, and frequently found with a continuous semicircular row of spindles terminating at the front edge of the seat. These chairs, or 'cutty stools', as they are sometimes known because of their diminutive size, have cut rather than turned spindles and were not influenced by the English 'Windsor' chairmaking tradition. Nevertheless, they provide the basic prototype for eighteenth- and nineteenth-century patterns of turned chairs developed to serve the industrial working populations of Ayrshire and the central Lowlands.[19]

In the northern counties of Sutherland and Caithness, and in Orkney, particularly idiosyncratic regional types existed. The principal components of these chairs are right-angled wooden 'knees' united by horizontal rails or spindles (pl 44). These characteristic sidepieces, made from either one naturally

44. *Caithness Interior,* 1913, by Tom Scott. Cattle can be seen through the door to the byre. On the left is a chair made from naturally bent timber, a distinctive feature of chairs from the northern counties.

bent bough split in two or a matched pair of different pieces of timber, set the chairs apart from most vernacular traditions in the United Kingdom, though very similar chairs have been noted in County Derry in Northern Ireland.[20]

Orkney chairs with woven oat-straw backs, and sometimes hoods, attached to a separate wooden seat frame, are well known today because their making was revived late in the nineteenth century as a picturesque 'folk-craft' which would bring income for the islanders (pl 175).[21] Earlier these were seen by Orcadians as inferior versions of similar chairs made entirely of wood, a material which had to be found as driftwood or imported into the almost entirely treeless island.[22] Chairs and settles in Orkney and Shetland, and probably elsewhere, were made more comfortable with cushions or by hanging a sheep's fleece on the back and seat, providing both padding and insulation.

Isabel Grant, founder of the Highland Folk Museum now at Kingussie, made a collection which represents the wide variety of chair types once found in small Highland and island houses. This, apart from indicating that chairs were by no means uncommon, demonstrates that there was some consistency in construction techniques but very little conformity in final appearance and decoration. Crofters and shepherds in the habit of making and repairing their own tools and implements made their own chairs too, frequently personal versions of either fashionable or vernacular patterns. The large number of miniature or 'children's' chairs surviving in the Highlands has often puzzled historians, but evidence from oral sources and photographs seems to indicate that they were widely used by working adults. Their small size and closeness to the ground made them ideal for many sedentary tasks such as spinning or baiting fishing lines, which could be done outside or in a low cottage room.

45. A creepie stool used as a stand outside 21 North Street, St Andrews, about 1900. Creepies and low chairs are often thought of as children's furniture but were clearly used by adults for a variety of tasks. Here the women are baiting lines in the fishertown area of St Andrews.

While some areas of the Highlands – Perthshire, Strathspey, and Easter Ross, for example – are noted for their timber, and this is reflected in the construction of their regional furniture, other areas have very little. This lack of readily available wood gave rise to a category of 'driftwood furniture', a term now used to denote anything made from found timber, be it a fish box or a usefully-shaped piece of wood picked up in a hedgerow. In many cases the use of found materials, or indeed driftwood from broken-up ships, has had little effect upon the appearance of traditional furniture types: the boarded chairs of Shetland, for

46. Armchair made from kipper boxes, Argyll, early twentieth century. Use of hedge timbers or found materials often caused makers of common furniture to design in a new way and ignore past styles. Here the narrow boards of a dismantled fish box have been put together in an original way around a seat frame which resembles a creepie stool.

instance, are made with conventional joints and have decorative features which reflect the styles of other Scottish chair types. But sometimes the use of found material has caused makers to rethink the design of a piece of furniture and largely ignore past styles. Such an approach is evident in the construction of the kipper box chair from Argyll, illustrated in plate 46. The narrow boards from the dismantled fishbox have been put together in an original way around a seat frame which resembles a creepie stool (see p53). Features often seen on items made from ships' timbers are the enormous boreholes of marine worms and evidence of the former use of the wood in the shape of cutouts and fixings.[23] The use of mixed timbers in items made of driftwood was often disguised with a painted and grained surface.

Ingenuity and hard work shaped the small house in the Highlands and Islands and until the second half of the nineteenth century, when improved transport brought a greater choice of goods, most things in the house were home-made or locally produced. Blankets of wool dyed with natural colours, often black and red, were woven in 'bird's eye' or chequered patterns. Someone sleeping on a settle would simply wrap up in a blanket and lie down, though the occupant of a bed might have linen sheets as well as blankets. Few other textiles would be needed: if a house had windows at all they would be very small, so curtains were not usual, and rugs were not practical on earth floors. Lighting was provided by the fire itself and by small oil-filled cruisie lamps. There was little to give colour to the interior of these houses, and the predominant impression must have been of overwhelming brownness. The atmosphere can be experienced in the reconstructed blackhouse at the Highland Folk Museum in Kingussie, including the all-pervading peat-reek. This must have permeated the hair and clothing of the occupants as well as their possessions in the house.

In the Lowlands, the intensification of farming methods was accompanied from the late eighteenth century by a general improvement in rural housing, but large numbers of people continued to live in one-roomed cabins of various kinds. Richard Ayton, visiting the Solway Firth in 1813, recorded houses little different from the shielings observed by Thomas Pennant on Jura:

At a short distance west of Comlongan I came to the village of Powhellin, which gave me a more complete idea of the utmost rudeness of Scottish cottages than I had yet formed. It contained twelve mud huts, with walls full of grooves and hollows, the effects of the rains, thatched roofs, ready for the scythe, and the same kind of grotesque and preposterous chimneys that I had seen at Annan, – altogether such a cluster of dwellings as a man would not have seen for the first time without surprise in the remotest regions of the uncivilized world. These mud-huts, however, as they are called, in spite of the exceeding meanness of their exterior, are far superior in positive comfort to many stone-built cottages such as one sees in this country and in many parts of England too – cottages with a better name, and of a less *wig-wamish* appearance, but not half so warm and substantial … Mud-huts have the cardinal merit of being perfectly weather-proof. Those at Powhellin have a foundation of stone three feet high, on which is raised a wall two feet thick, composed of clay mixed with straw … The insides of them baffle all description. As each usually contains only one room, in which the family with all their worldly property must somehow be packed, it would be harsh and unreasonable to complain of a want of neatness and tidiness of arrangement; but the dirt that shews itself amidst the jumbled litter of children, dogs, chickens, beds, chairs, old coats, and breeches, and stockings, scythes, shrimp-nets, pitchforks, and spinning wheels, and an incredible number of other materials that are and are not wanted, is quite abominable.

If he had not seen it for himself, Ayton would have assumed the houses were uninhabited lumber rooms: 'That it was a place in which a family, not Hottentots, performed the ceremonies of eating, drinking, and sleeping, one should not have entertained the suspicion of a moment'.[24] He was clearly affected by the apparent disorder inside the huts. The scythes, shrimp-nets and spinning wheels indicate that the home was also a workplace and that its inhabitants were engaged in several different occupations. The ownership of common furniture types, such as beds and dressers, was apparently a luxury available only to those with an assured or stable income.

The 'improved' cottage slowly replaced this kind of mean dwelling and its equivalent regional variants which existed all over the country. Change came first in the Lowlands and the wealthier farming areas in the late eighteenth century, spreading gradually north and west. By 1831 when J C Loudon published the second edition of *An Encyclopaedia of Agriculture*, improvement was noted in Midlothian, Ayrshire, Dunbartonshire, West Lothian, Kinross-shire, Fife, Aberdeenshire, and Nairnshire; while cottages in Dumfriesshire, Angus, Kincardineshire, Sutherland, and Argyllshire were 'by no means improved' or 'nasty and miserable beyond description'.[25]

'Improved' cottages were generally more spacious and solidly built, but continued the tradition of living in one or two rooms, at least until the end of the nineteenth century when country dwellers generally had larger houses than those in the city. In plan the typical Lowland farm cottage of the nineteenth century comprised two rooms flanking a small lobby, but this space was required to perform multiple functions: for instance stored food, such as meal and potatoes, or agricultural equipment might take up a large proportion of one room. A major change was in the placing of the hearth within a chimney.

In his studies of Lowland cottage interiors of the 1820s and 1830s, the Edinburgh artist Walter Geikie provides evidence of the furnishings and use of space inside the improved dwelling (pls 17, 48, 49). Although many of his drawings depict small farmhouses rather than labourers' dwellings, they record accurately the range of things to be found in the better sort of cottage during the early nineteenth century.

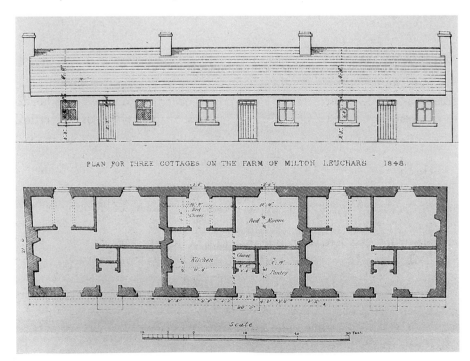

PLAN FOR THREE COTTAGES ON THE FARM OF MILTON LEUCHARS   1848.

Scale

47. Design for improved cottages at Milton Farm, Leuchars, Fife, from *Transactions of the Highland and Agricultural Society of Scotland*, 1848. This was not the most usual arrangement of rooms – there was much experimentation in the nineteenth century to find practical ways of using a small space.

48. Drawing by Walter Geikie, 1830s. Four creepies are depicted in this room awaiting use. The forward-leaning plates arranged on the shelves at the back are likely to be of pewter, and a cast-iron pot hangs from a swee above the fire.

49. Another Geikie drawing of a small Lowland house of similar date. On the left is a Chippendale-style splat-back chair and two brander-back armchairs flank the hearth.

Prominent in these scenes is the small boarded stool or 'creepie', an item of furniture found all over Scotland (and known in Shetland as 'kripi'). The creepie is simply constructed of sawn boards nailed or dowelled together to form a seat, legs, and strengthening side aprons. Shapes cut out of the vertical end-boards define the legs. Geikie illustrated many creepies, sometimes stacked up against a wall (pl 48). It is clear that they were carried about according to need both in the home and at work; and before the advent of fixed pews in the eighteenth century they were taken to church to sit on. However, the creepie was not just a seat but also a stand, as is evident in images of working people. For instance, photographs of fisher folk in St Andrews around 1900 show creepies used outside to support piles of line being baited by women (pl 45).[26]

In contrast with many Highland dwellings of one and two rooms, where the settle and stool were the principal forms of seating, Geikie's sketches show a variety of regional chair types in the small Lowland home. As in Wales, chairs made by country wrights in native woods survived in Scotland throughout the nineteenth century, resisting inroads made by mass-produced designs in cheap mahogany and deal.

The 'Chippendale' splat-back retained its popularity even into the twentieth century, and because there was no widespread tradition of making turned chairs in Lowland Scotland, a wright-made version of an eighteenth-century chair design was most likely to be found in the small cottage. Geikie illustrates several of these, usually occupying a proud position next to the hearth (pl 49). Some more regionally specific types can be seen in the sketches, such as for instance the 'brander back', characterized by its square back which frames a row of plain banisters (pls 49, 51). Its name derives from the resemblance to a brander or gridiron for roasting food over an open hearth. The brander was part of the standard cooking equipment of even the smallest home and one can be seen hanging from the cheek of the Shetland hearth in plate 52. Brander-back chairs were most common in Perthshire and the eastern counties of Scotland.

Most Lowland houses in which there was a steady income had some sort of 'best chair', but the widespread development of steam-powered chair factories and the beginning of mail-order catalogue buying after 1860, eventually brought the dominance of just two popular patterns, the so-called 'Edinburgh' and 'Glasgow' chairs (pl 50). These often appeared alongside each other in nineteenth-century trade catalogues and were made in large numbers for both urban and country markets by firms such as Wylie & Lochhead of Glasgow and Christie & Miller of Falkirk. Until the 1930s, they were also made according to local variations by country wrights across central Scotland from Dunbartonshire to the Fife coast. Plate 52 shows a Glasgow chair in the foreground and the Edinburgh pattern beneath a pile of clothes, sharing room space in a small house in Shetland. These mass-produced items, probably chosen from a catalogue and imported from the mainland, co-existed with older local traditions, such as the oat-straw container being woven by the man in the photograph and the spinning wheel nearby.

Through catalogues and the increasing number of well-stocked shops selling household goods by the end of the nineteenth century, people were able to buy new luxuries. Pottery was more widely available than before from Scottish potteries in Glasgow, Fife, and East Lothian; and cheap Continental porcelains were imported. Oil lamps with glass shades provided a stronger light than the earlier cruisies, and brightly printed biscuit tins were a major source of decoration in the home, placed on the mantelpiece or near the fire to keep dry. The chimney wall was the natural place for numerous items, including salt containers and guns, for this very practical reason.

American clocks seem to have been ubiquitous. These were mass-produced in New York and Pennsylvania with cheap clockwork movements and fancy turning, carving, or printed decoration (pl 52). From another part of the world, seafaring people brought back Russian wooden bowls and dishes, painted red and black and known in Shetland as 'Scovie' ware (from 'Muscovy') and elsewhere as 'Baltic bowls' or 'Riga cups'.[27] In Shetland, plain wooden items from Scandinavia and the Baltic were known as 'Norwakapp', 'Norwaladle', and so on. The 'Norwatrough' was a rectangular dish for communal eating: potatoes were placed on it with fish in the middle, and family members helped themselves with their fingers. Since Shetlanders did not usually have tables in their houses until the end of the last century, these troughs must have been supported on creepies or kists. Containers of steamed and bent birch stitched with birch twine, called 'bøsts' in Shetland, also came from Norway. People in seagoing areas had more variety in their houses than those working the land, partly through having greater opportunity to see different goods but also because they had relatively more cash income.

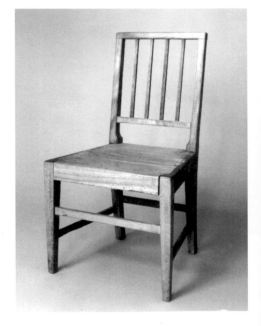

50. *Above*: Designs from Francis East & Co, Dundee. The Edinburgh pattern (top), and the Glasgow pattern (bottom).

51. *Below*: A brander-back chair of ash from about 1800.

52. Shetland kitchen interior, about 1900. It shows from left to right, a kist, a Glasgow chair, an Edinburgh chair, and in the fireplace an iron brander. Above the chairs is an American clock. This photograph illustrates the co-existence of items ordered from mainland suppliers and local products, such as the oat-straw container being made by the occupant.

These foreign goods co-existed with the traditional contents of the home, which reflected the materials available locally and also the working lives of the inhabitants. Implements used in farming or seafaring, for instance, were kept indoors if they needed to be dry or secure, while a decorative feature of many Shetland houses was a ship model, often displayed high up the wall in a case shaped to fit the slope of the roof. Shetlanders often had distinctive 'tattit' rugs on their beds, while 'clootie' rugs seem to have been made in most parts of Scotland. These varied according to what types of old cloth or surplus wool were available; in Shetland, knitted pieces were sometimes used, while in the fishertown of Nairn rugs were made by men of thrums – ends of wool from local weaving factories – sewn onto sailcloth. Other types of cloth were also re-used: flour bags were particularly good for pillow cases and aprons, or could be decorated and made into pictures.[28]

Visible in plate 52 behind the Glasgow chair, is one of the oldest forms of storage furniture to be found in the Scottish home, the kist. This type of lidded chest was a European form widely known by many different names. It was certainly not static: many examples had carrying handles and before coming home may have been used by men as lodging boxes in bothies (pl 34) and sea chests on board ship, or by women in domestic service or following the herring fleets (pl 36). Shetland kists often have a painted ship inside the lid, and in the north east of Scotland they were usually made with deep lids. The interior was fitted with a small compartment known as a 'till', always at the left end, for the storage of small and valuable items. Geikie's sketches demonstrate the versatility of the kist, which was often used as seating, as is clear from its placing next to a table (pl 17).

Box beds, too, had more than one purpose: as well as being used for sleeping they provided storage and sometimes working space during the day.[29] James Robb gives a vivid impression of this multiple use in his description of a labourer's cottage in North Berwick:

> Inside we find the double box bed taking up so great a proportion of the space that three or four chairs, a rickety table, a dresser and a washing tub, crowd the remainder. As occupants of the box beds in one of these houses there were two grown up men … two girls approaching womanhood, an elderly woman, who appeared to be their mother, and three or four children.[30]

The box bed was found in a wide range of households including farmhouses, inns, and fishermen's, miners' and weavers' cottages, but it is chiefly associated with the cottage of the married agricultural worker or 'hind'. The married farmhand in the nineteenth century had to purchase his own furniture, and freestanding box beds were the principal items. James Robb recorded the generally held opinion that ploughmen married too young, before they had saved sufficient to purchase furniture: 'The consequence is that many of them remain for years in debt to country wrights who of course repay themselves for their long outlay by charging heavy prices for the articles.'[31]

In the homes of those who could afford to buy one new the box bed was a prestige item, and indeed many box beds in Berwickshire, East Lothian, Fife, and Forfarshire had a fitting pedigree. Their design, a simple keystoned arch and pilasters beneath a cornice (pls 17, 43) had its roots in Andrea Palladio's *Quattro Libri dell' Architettura* of 1570. This underlines the strong link between Scotland's common furniture and professionally designed patterns. Architectural design sources were prescribed by masters and the Edinburgh Incorporation of Wrights possessed pattern books which members could copy. Records of Mary's Chapel, the headquarters of the Incorporation of Wrights, show that the box or 'closs' bed was one of four standard essay pieces executed by apprentice wrights. For example, on 14 July 1683 the wright Charles George's essay piece was: 'ane Closs bed the lidds to be of raysd work out of the timber it self angled from poynt to poynt with one dorick entablature, to be all done in wainscott'.[32] These architectural patterns were common in the eastern Lowlands.

Other regional patterns existed, but beds with plain panelled doors as opposed to curtained or open sides remained frequent in the Highlands into the twentieth century. As an item of great value for the married worker and his family, the box bed was theirs to decorate and finish to their own requirements. The most important extra, which could be made at home, was the mattress or 'tike', very deep and thick, covered in canvas cloth and filled regularly with fresh chaff. A tike would normally last from three to six months, after which its contents would be burned or taken to the byre to be trodden into manure and recycled. During the nineteenth century, curtains hung from the inside of the bed opening were usual, as was a 'pend' or valance running along the base of the bed, hiding objects stored beneath. When wallpaper could be cheaply produced in the second half of the nineteenth century it was often pasted inside the bed to banish draughts and drips as well as for its decorative effect. The bed interior could also be used for hanging clothes and might have a shelf for a candle.

As in the Highland longhouse, box beds in Lowland cottages and cabins were traditionally used as room dividers. Robb, again reporting on the conditions of agricultural labourers in East Lothian, stated that 'A large number of hinds' cottages in this quarter have as yet only one room for eating and sleeping accommodation of the whole family – two box beds, (joined feet to feet) which are common in East Lothian, being so placed on the floor as to afford space behind for a little pantry'.[33]

Because clothes were few and were usually kept in beds or kists, wardrobes were unknown in small rural houses and chests of drawers were uncommon until the late nineteenth century. Chests of drawers could be found more frequently in the small urban household, but where they did occur in the rural house, one distinctive pattern was dominant: the so-called 'lum-chest'.[34] The type was so idiosyncratic and frequent in Lowland Scotland that it was described as a 'Scotch Chest' when it appeared in English trade catalogues. Its characteristic feature was a deep, square drawer used for storing hats, such as women's mutches or the man's tall 'lum' [chimney] hat, which gave the popular name to these chests. In a small room a lum chest might appear enormous, but the design was adapted for maximum storage capacity in the minimum of floorspace. Height was always favoured over depth so the chest did not project into a room, and the top, frequently five feet or more from the floor, could be used for the display of china and other ornaments.

Except in cases of extreme rural poverty where furniture was not a high priority, at least one item of costly furniture was a general feature of the 'ordinary' household in which the occupants were not always on the move and where a steady income enabled the payment of credit terms. In miners' rows, for instance, proud householders strove to outdo each other in the quality and fashionability of certain items. A West Fife miner, James Rowan, recalls in his account of life from 1919 to 1928 in the Milton Rows, Crosshill:

> One of my special memories is of my mother purchasing a large chest of drawers 'for ben the room'. I believe it was from a firm called Grubb. I clearly remember it cost £12/15/6, for I thought at the time, we would probably spend the rest of our lives, paying off this great financial burden … [Later on] I remember this same chest of drawers stood against the dividing wall of the two recessed beds and there on top of it, sat in all its tangible glory our very first sign of opulence and luxury, a 'Wireless Set'.[35]

Miners' dwellings in rural areas, when planned by the mining companies, were starkly repetitive rows of one- or two-roomed houses. They formed terraces of the typical small Scottish house type known since the late eighteenth century as the 'but and ben'. The 'but' refers to the outer room, usually a kitchen, and 'ben' is an inner, usually a best room. At Milton in Fife, the settlement built by the Wilson & Clyde Coal Company consisted of two separate rows of twelve houses, built directly onto a dirt road to prevent the depositing of rubbish immediately outside. The houses had no sanitary arrangements apart from dry middens between the two rows of houses, where human excrement and household ash was piled up and collected once a fortnight by the 'scaffie', 'who would arrive and shovel this filthy evil smelling mound into his ash cart to drive it away'.[36]

> The front room or 'kitchen' as it was called, contained two beds, set into a walled recess. The beds consisted of a rough wooden frame, on top of which lay wooden planks, this was then covered by a 'straw mattress' which, as the name implies, were wheat stalks packed tightly into a large jute bag. 'Ben the room' [in the best room] was another similar recessed bed. These beds were usually three to four feet above the floor level, and underneath some were stored things, such as, the cradle and the large zinc bath which was an important part of every home.

53. A chest with a large central drawer for a 'lum' hat. These were commonly known as 'Scotch' chests, as is shown in this drawing from an anonymous English trade catalogue of about 1905. Chests of drawers were rarely seen in very small cottages before the end of the nineteenth century.

Above the fireplace, was a swan necked brass fitting, with a single gas mantle. This was the only source of light for the house. The fireplace itself was a deep recess approximately four foot high and four foot wide and two foot nine inches deep. Into this were built bricks at either side, about two foot high, and fourteen inches wide, with a heavy iron grill embedded into the brickwork, and inside this a coal fire was contained, on the brickwork either side, sat the iron kettle, pots and pans ...

Along the front of the hearth was the fender stool, made from two planks of wood, between four and five foot long, and ten inches broad, simply nailed together at right angles, and covered with a piece of lino. On this we children, sat, keeping warm during the long winter nights. The small wooden cradle seemed to be permanently at the side of the fireplace, filled with yet another young brother or sister, before the older child was ready to vacate it.[37]

The Milton Row houses were not modernized until the mid 1920s, when each had a deep sink and brass cold water tap installed at the kitchen window, dispensing with the necessity of carrying water from a communal well. At this date a small water closet was installed outside each house.

Government attention had been drawn to poor housing conditions in rural areas before the outbreak of the First World War, when in 1912 a Royal Commission survey was initiated in response to long campaigning. The resulting *Report on the Housing of the Industrial Population of Scotland, Rural and Urban*, published in 1917, prompted the Scottish Housing Act of 1919, which had the long-term aim of providing 115,000 new small houses in Scotland. These were to be built to an approved standard of living space and sanitation, and financed through government subsidy, rents, and local rates. An additional impetus for improvement was provided by the Tudor Walters *Report on the Provision of Dwellings for the Working Class (1918)*, which recommended a specific minimum standard of three apartments per dwelling unit, supplemented by a bathroom, scullery, and internal water closet. Inevitably, the most pressing need for new housing was considered to be in the cities and the larger country towns, where the majority of the new government-subsidized housing was indeed provided. It was not until the 1930s that the provision of 'rural' council housing, which is such a significant feature of Scottish towns and villages today, really began.

Throughout this century there has been a continual drift of the population away from the countryside and into the towns and cities of the central belt. Only about one in ten Scots now lives in a rural area. Small cottages lie empty or in ruins, and very few people now live in houses of only one or two rooms.[38] Houses which have survived from fifty or one hundred years ago have been modernized by the installation of essential services and in many cases have been enlarged by joining two or more small houses together. This process started at least as early as the end of last century if Nan Shepherd's novel *The Weatherhouse* can be taken as evidence.[39] Since the size of room in the small house in Scotland has always been reasonably generous, and certainly larger than rooms in English cottages, these converted houses now often provide spacious accommodation. Their symmetrical, undecorated, stone fronts can be seen in almost every part of Scotland, with minor variation for regional differences in building materials or weather conditions. A few of the older cottages as shown in the 1938 Glasgow 'clachan' can also be seen in the western and island areas – some preserved as museums, some still occupied, and many more abandoned. Increasing numbers are being restored as holiday cottages, where jaded city dwellers can live out in comfort a fantasy of the simple life in the country.

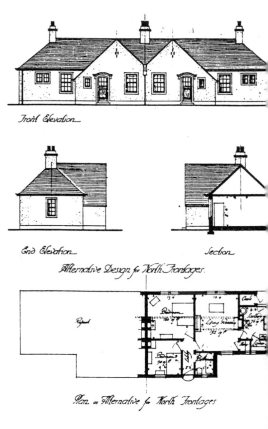

54. Competition drawing of a one-storey cottage by Cullen, Lochhead & Brown of Hamilton, Lanarkshire, 1919. This design proved very popular with local authorities and many were built.

3 Living in One or Two Rooms in the City

HELEN CLARK

'The one-room house is incompatible with a decent or wholesome family life ... the one-room house must go.'
Royal Commission, 1917[1]

In the middle of the nineteenth century well over half the people in Scotland lived in houses consisting of only one or two rooms. Over the past one hundred and fifty years there has been a considerable improvement in the basic requirements of a home, which now include separate spaces for living and sleeping, and the provision of cooking facilities, wash-hand basin, WC, and bath or shower. Fewer than five in a hundred Scots today live in houses of one or two rooms and it is difficult to imagine how large families coped with everyday life in such small places.[2] Oral evidence is used here to convey this experience, which was common for many in the past.[3] This chapter looks at the conditions in which people lived and the solutions they found to problems caused by lack of space.

From 1600 to about 1850, most people in cities and burghs lived in small houses, as did the majority in the countryside. Dwellings of one or two rooms were the norm for working people and for many in the 'middle ranks'. In the course of the nineteenth century, however, the establishment of factories in towns and cities, combined with the effects of the Highland clearances, prompted large numbers of people to leave the land for work in the cities, especially the manufacturing centres of the lowland belt and the west. By 1861 nearly two thirds of the people of Scotland lived in houses of one or two rooms, mostly in overcrowded conditions of more than two people per room. 1861 was the peak, but in the remainder of the century, small overcrowded dwellings remained a significant problem. Although the proportion of Scots living in houses of one or two rooms had fallen to just under a half by 1911, it was still over one quarter of the population in 1951. In Glasgow in 1951, half the houses still had only one or two rooms.[4]

In Edinburgh and Canongate, people lived close together from an early date as a result of the geographical limitations of the city's site. From hearth tax returns of the 1690s it is evident that households were often large and included apprentices, lodgers, and maids along with family members in houses which varied considerably in size.[5] Other records of the seventeenth and eighteenth centuries show that there was a wide social mix within tenement buildings, where aristocrats and gentry often had the best rooms on the first and second floors while tradespeople and craftworkers occupied the less convenient flats and the poorest people had garrets and cellars.[6]

Edward Topham, who visited Edinburgh in 1774 and 1775, wrote that: 'As each house is occupied by a family, a land, being so large, contains many families; … I make no manner of doubt but that the High Street in Edinburgh is inhabited by a greater number of persons than any street in Europe.'[7] Crowded conditions gave the capital a bad reputation, and it was 'made a subject of scorn and reproach' for its 'Stench and Nastiness'.[8] There are numerous descriptions of the disgusting condition of the streets (see p204), but few details about the content and layout of people's houses.

Inventories give some idea. Examples from small houses are generally short and include the basic requirements of fire irons, bed, chairs, table, chest, and press cupboard, plus bedding and utensils. The inventory of William Nisbet, a merchant in North Berwick, indicates that in 1737 he had a chamber, a kitchen, and a shop. In the chamber were a 'curtain bedstead' with 'roaps and roads' (11s) and hangings (6s); 'ane Chist of Drawers' (11s 8d); an 'armed chair and 4 small chairs' (5s 6d); a 'firr table' (4s); a 'Wainscot [oak] table' (5s); a 'firr press' (2s); and probably a 'Chimney, a brass, a Cran and tongs' (6s), the standard fire irons at this time ('chimney' meaning grate and 'cran' a crane, or hinged arm from which to hang the kettle).

Items in the kitchen were similar but of lower value: 'a Closs bed stead' (6s 8d); 'a Curtain bed' (6s); a box bed (4s); 'ane old Chist' (2s 6d); an old table (10d); and an assortment of containers including choppins, mutchkins, cups, and pots, along with trenchers, plates, and candlesticks. In addition there was

55. A flit in St Mary's Wynd, Canongate, Edinburgh, about 1845. People in small houses moved often at this date and had few possessions. These buildings were swept away by the 1867 City Improvement Act.

a considerable quantity of textiles and mixed shop goods. Although the range of possessions is wide, the absence of any mirrors, clocks, books, or other luxury items of the period is noticeable, though Nisbet did have some pottery ('lyme') trenchers and plates. Pottery was not common at this time and these may have been connected with his trading activities.[9] The 1765 inventory of Archibald Clerk, sometime weaver in Leith, lists a similar range of goods at comparable values, with the addition of a small looking glass (1s 8d), and a tea kettle at three shillings, suggesting that tea was by then established among a wide section of the population.[10]

After the development of more commodious housing in areas such as the New Town in Edinburgh and similar schemes elsewhere, the old city-centre houses were divided and subdivided to create smaller dwellings, as people of the 'middle ranks' and skilled artisans gradually moved away. This subdivision of old houses is here described by Dr Alex Wood:

In various parts there are clusters of houses 400 years old; very many are 300 and a still greater number 200 years old. They have belonged to, and been inhabited by, successive classes of people 'til they have passed into the hands of mere jobbing capitalists – 'ruins' lords' as they have been called – who, buying them for an insignificant sum, let them out through the agency of factors to the many debased classes at rents varying usually from 15d to 18d per week for a single apartment. Many of these apartments had no natural lighting. The large rooms of an earlier upper class were divided by wooden partitions into family apartments when the buildings became slums. These inner cages had no direct communication even with the modicum of air and light that filtered in from the arms-breadth wynds [lanes]. The old window of the ancient room remained, but all the light admitted to the inner dens came through that window, across a passage and then through a square hole cut in the partition.[11]

From about 1840, new housing for working people was built in industrial areas of Edinburgh – Fountainbridge, Gorgie, Dalry, Leith, and the Southside – and the Old Town houses entered a spiral of decline. They were owned by landlords unwilling or unable to maintain them and rented by families so poor they took in lodgers even when they themselves had only a single room. Census records for Huntly House, originally three houses in Canongate, show that the

56. Illustration of two families sharing a single room, from *Slum Life in Edinburgh or Scenes in its Darkest Places* by 'T B M', 1891. Each family would pay four shillings a week for 'one room of insignificant size and wretched furnishings, which consist of the beds, a table and a bench or two'.

ROOM FOR TWO FAMILIES IN A LODGING-HOUSE.

population there grew from 220 people in 1841 to 323 by 1881. The Royal Commission reported in 1917 that the practice of subdivision was a widespread and important phenomenon throughout Scottish towns. Pat Rogan, who became Councillor for Holyrood Ward, remembers Huntly House in the 1920s:

> Inside Huntly House it was an absolute warren of houses. They were all living on top of each other. I can always remember this terrible conglomerate crammed into such a small space. A lot of them divided and sub-divided the houses themselves. One simple device was to put a rope across a room and hang a blanket over it and there was another room.[12]

As late as the 1950s, Robert McTaggart, a Sanitary Inspector, remembers pockets of Edinburgh's New Town:

> There were places like Cumberland Street with houses consisting of five, six or even seven-apartment properties. When we went to deal with them we found that there would be five or six houses in what was previously one house. They had common sinks and toilets located in a common lobby.[13]

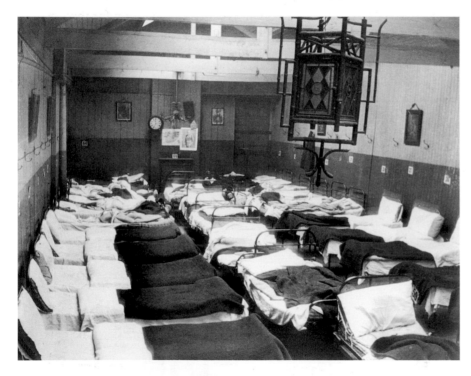

57. McLaughlin's Common Lodging House in Paisley, about 1900. Each bed is numbered and the unmade beds are presumably ready to be let out. The clock stands at 11.35 (am): it was usual for such lodging houses to be vacated during the day.

By the mid nineteenth century it was realized that housing conditions had a direct effect on the health of the inhabitants and Medical Officers of Health were appointed in the major Scottish cities. The first of these, in 1861, was Henry Duncan Littlejohn in Edinburgh. Numerous steps were taken to try to deal with these problems. These included the registration of Common Lodging Houses and provision of a better standard of accommodation in Model Lodging Houses; and the demolition of housing considered unimprovable. Under the Glasgow City Improvement Act of 1866 the Corporation tried to suppress overcrowding by the 'ticketing' of houses. Dwellings not exceeding 2000 cubic feet were measured and a metal ticket, stating the cubic capacity of the room and the number of occupants allowed, was placed on the door (pl 58). Originally 300 cubic feet per person over eight years old was allowed but this was increased in 1890 to 400 cubic feet for adults and 200 for every child under ten years.[14]

58. This ticket was removed from a door in Huntly House, Canongate, Edinburgh. It gives the cubic capacity of the room and the number of people permitted to live there.

Ticketed houses were regularly inspected by the police and sanitary inspectors, who had powers to raid them day or night. Peter Fyfe, the Sanitary Inspector for Glasgow, declared it 'a degrading thing to have any family living under conditions where they are apt to be stirred up at any time during the night by men coming in with lanterns and books and taking notes', and he added:

> If it could be done in any other way, it would be better. If you ask these people how many are in when you call during the day, you get a very large number of false statements; but when you go in at night, between 12 o'clock and 5 o'clock in the morning, the doors are usually closed, and you can count the number of people who are living in these houses. Even then, you cannot always do it, because the one tells the other, and in some streets in Glasgow they are so friendly with one another, that, whenever the night men appear at one end of the street the word passes round right through the street, and by the time they get to the closes further on, the inmates have all got up and are dressed, and your night's work at that particular street has failed. Sometimes the people have got into presses, into barrels, and into enclosed places above the bed – sometimes on the roof, hiding behind the chimney head.[15]

Since virtually nothing was done to provide new housing for those made homeless, these measures simply intensified overcrowding elsewhere. Neither private landlords nor public authorities could afford to build houses at rents the poorest people could pay, and although Edinburgh Corporation in 1867 had limited power to erect tenements and had put up four in Guthrie Street, they were too expensive for those who were displaced and were let to 'artisans of a superior class'.[16] Similarly, co-operative schemes to provide better standards through self-help were feasible only for artisans and better-off working people.

The Housing of the Working Classes Act in 1890 marked the beginning of house-building activity by the local authority in Edinburgh. Several small

59. Tenement plan, Dalry Meadows, Tynecastle, Edinburgh, 1896. Demolition of a tenement in 1978 revealed a time capsule containing this plan of dwellings built under the Housing of the Working Classes Improvement Scheme. An adjacent tenement of the same original plan was renovated in 1983 and the flats now have a living room with kitchen in the bed recess, a bedroom, and a shower room. The single-roomed houses were knocked through to form larger units.

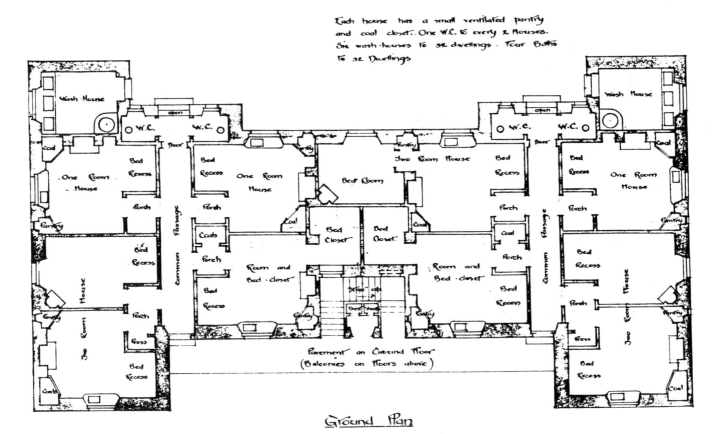

improvement schemes were carried out, but did little to ease the acute housing problem. After many years of campaigning by Medical Officers, social reformers, trade unions, politicians, and other groups, a Royal Commission was finally set up in 1912 to investigate. Its report, delayed by the War but also given impetus by the desire to provide houses 'fit for heroes', catalogued the appalling conditions in which many Scots lived, and made it clear that the state would have to assume responsibility. The Addison Act of 1919, implementing the findings of the report, imposed a duty on local authorities to provide adequate houses and also for the first time offered help with building costs.

Although only the earliest council schemes came up to the standards desired by the local politicians and architects, providing houses of four and five apartments, by 1931 so many three-apartment houses had been built that the census report was able to record a substantial improvement in housing in general and a decrease in the number of one-roomed houses.[17] Overcrowded slum dwellings remained a problem until well into the 1950s, and, especially in Glasgow, fuelled the drive to demolish the old tenements and replace them with modern housing, often in the form of high-rise flats (pl 8). These were built until the early 1970s, when it was recognized that many of the demolished tenements had been of architectural merit and could have been renovated for modern use, especially as many people still wanted to live in this type of house. Since then, the emphasis has been on rehabilitation and rebuilding of property. Private-sector growth was encouraged from 1980.[18]

Looking back from the end of the twentieth century, it is hard for us to imagine what it was really like for families living in the crowded conditions described above. Many people at the time also found it difficult to comprehend, and Glasgow University students laughed in disbelief when told in 1884 that forty one out of one hundred families in their great city lived in houses of only one room.[19] Realising that 'percentages, though an accurate, are a feeble mode of expression for such facts regarding men and women like ourselves', Dr John Russell in addressing a wealthy middle-class Glasgow audience in 1888 took a more imaginative approach. None of his listeners was safe from his appeal:

> You mistresses of houses, with bed-rooms and parlours, dining-rooms and drawing-rooms, kitchens and wash-houses, pantries and sculleries, how could you put one room to the uses of all? You mothers, with your cooks and housemaids, your nurses and general servants, how would you in your own persons act all those parts in one room, where, too, you must eat and sleep and find your lying-in-room and make your sick-bed? You fathers, with your billiard-room, your libraries and parlours, your dinner parties, your evening hours, undisturbed by washing-days, your children brought to you when they can amuse you, and far removed when they become troublesome, how long would you continue to be that pattern husband which you are – in one room? You children, with your nurseries and nurses, your toys and your picture books, your space to play in without being trodden upon, your children's parties and your daily airings, your prattle which does not disturb your sick mamma, your special table spread with a special meal, your seclusion from contact with the dead, and still worse familiarity with the living, where would you find your innocence, and how would you preserve the dew and freshness of your infancy – in one room? You grown-up sons, with all the resources of your fathers for indoor amusement, with your cricket field and football club and skating pond, with your own bed-room with space which makes self-restraint easy and decency natural, how could you wash and dress, and sleep and eat and spend your leisure hours in a house of – one room? You grown-up daughters, with your bed-rooms and your bath-rooms, your piano and your drawing-room,

A STARVING SEAMSTRESS AT WORK.

60. Seamstress at work, 1891, from *Slum Life in Edinburgh* (see pl 56). Sewing was an exceptionally poorly paid occupation. The original caption for this plate describes the seamstress 'toiling in hunger and squalor … glad that by so doing she could keep her bairns with her in that dilapidated and almost furnitureless shelter'.

your little brothers and sisters to toy with when you have a mind to, and send out of the way when you cannot be troubled, your every want supplied, without sharing in menial household work, your society regulated, and no rude rabble of lodgers to sully the purity of your surroundings, how could you live and preserve 'the white flower of a blameless life' – in one room? ...

How would you deport yourself in the racket and thoughtless noise of your nursery, in the heat and smells of your kitchen, in the steam and disturbance of your washing-house, for you would find all these combined in a house of – one room? Last of all when you die, you still have one room to yourself, where in decency you may be washed and dressed and laid out for burial. If that one room were your house, what a ghastly intrusion you would be! The bed on which you lie is wanted for the accommodation of the living. The table at which your children ought to sit must bear your coffin, and they must keep your unwelcome company.[20]

This is a far cry from the reports of charity workers and philanthropists who referred to the inhabitants of the 'rookeries', 'warrens', 'honeycombs' and 'congeries of dens', as if describing the habitations of animals.

When trying to picture life in one or two rooms, it is important to remember that the home extended beyond the walls into the lobby, the stair, and neighbours' houses; even to the street and parks, picture house and public house. It was at the centre of a network of sites. People were not at home all the time. Workers could be on different shifts, so beds might be used night and day by several people. Children were often outdoors:

> You were never in anyway. When you say you lived in a room and kitchen, your Mum and Dad lived in a room and kitchen but you played out in the street, summer and winter, you didn't come in 'til bed-time. And you had your clubs and the Band of Hope. Your father would be at his work or at the pub.[21]

Going into the house, people were often struck by the darkness and gloom. Older tenements were frequently so close to each other that light was limited, and new buildings put up in the garden grounds of existing tenements created the infamous 'backlands', with warren-like passages and closes. The internal layout, too, could be entirely dark and unventilated, as in the typical 21 Middleton Place, Glasgow, where a 'T'-shaped passage gave access to each one- or two-roomed house. It must also have been foul smelling, since one privy or dry closet served thirty-four houses with a population of one hundred and thirty people.[22]

Darkness was clearly a hazard in many divided houses even into the 1950s, when stair lighting would be standard in purpose-built tenements. Robert McTaggart, a Sanitary Inspector for Edinburgh Corporation, visited these for his work:

> If you imagine walking into any large house, you go into a hallway and there are rooms leading off. Well, that hallway would be the common lobby and you enter your house from that. The common lobby was dark. Maybe in one corner would be the old fireclay sink with a tap above it. I've seen me knocking on the doors in the dark and you'd find you'd been knocking on the toilet door, it was so dark.[23]

Typical purpose-built working-class Glasgow tenements of the end of the nineteenth century were of a standard design, with a house consisting of a 'room and kitchen' at each gable end and a 'single end' – a one-roomed house – in the centre. Designs varied in other cities; sometimes the single end was at the gable.

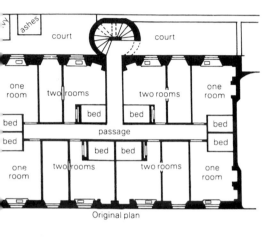

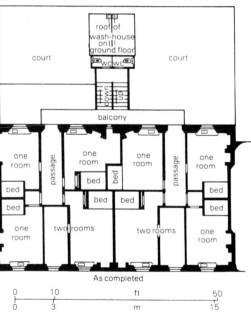

61. Plans of 21 Middleton Place, Glasgow, with a T-shaped passage (above) and as improved (below). Outside privies were replaced by shared WCs on stair landings and a washhouse was provided. The T-shaped passage was removed and the two-roomed houses enlarged, but some houses were reduced to one room as a result.

Some single ends had a tiny internal lobby of maybe four feet square with a press on one side. If the house was of two rooms, the lobby could be 'L'-shaped and about 3ft 6in by 4ft wide. Off it there were doors to a press (cupboard), 'the room', and kitchen, and perhaps an internal WC. The lobby was a lasting memory for some children:

> The long narrow eerie length of corridor was known as the lobby … dimly lit during the day and pitch black at night, this passageway was that territory which every tenement child knew to be haunted – not only by all sorts of bogey-men, but also by the phantoms of mice, rats and cats which had died down in the 'Dunny'. The lobby especially at night was an awesome and forbidding place where even the bright golden-light of a carried candle could do little to dispel the terrors of a child.[24]

The layout of the Glasgow tenement kitchen is detailed by George Rountree in *A Govan Childhood* and in Jean Faley's *Up Oor Close*, and was remarkably consistent through a range of tenements of different size and status.[25] Usually the window was opposite the door, with the range on one side wall and a dresser and coal bunker on the other. The 'hole-in-the-wall' bed was in the same wall as the door, at right angles to the fire. In the window stood the sink, known in Glasgow as the 'jawbox', 'jaw' being an old Scots word meaning 'to pour abruptly' (pl 62). Sinks in nineteenth-century tenements were of black cast iron, and those in newer buildings were white glazed ceramic, boxed in by a cupboard which stretched the length of the window recess. The single tap was a brass swan's neck shape, known as a 'crane', supplying cold water only.

Some standard items of rough furniture were built in. The 'dresser' was a two-door cupboard where pots could be kept, with two drawers above. The bunker had a hinged lid and held two hundredweight bags of coal. In Edinburgh and Dundee the bunker was often built into the window recess next to the sink. Some 'improved' kitchens had double sinks, known as a sink and tub: a wringer could be attached to a piece of wood between the two, and the tub had a lid for use as a worktop.

62. Tenement kitchen of a 'room and kitchen' in Glasgow, 1946, showing a typical layout. Note the gas pipe for lighting above the fireplace and the range, which probably dates from 1900 or even earlier.

63. *Left:* Irene Daniels cleaning out the range in her kitchen in Beith Street, Partick, Glasgow, about 1940. The time is 6.27am.

64. *Right:* Irene Daniels sweeping the hearth of her now improved kitchen in 1956. The gas pipes have been removed but the electric wires to the right of the fireplace have just been papered over. It is clear from the comfy chair in both these photographs that the kitchen was used as a living room.

Along the wall opposite the fireplace ran two shelves for storing pots and bowls or for a display of wedding china. Shelves were often decorated with strips of lace paper or lengths of crochet. A press cupboard for food was set into the wall between the fireplace and the sink.

The most important feature in the house was the fireplace. Food was cooked and water heated on the fire, which provided the main source of heat and a focus to the home. From the seventeenth to nineteenth centuries, cooking was done on an open fire. Fireplaces began to be fitted with cast-iron hobs from the late eighteenth century and with waterheating units and ovens from the early years of the nineteenth, but people in small flats would rarely have a new range and photographs from around 1900 often depict grates which date from decades earlier (pl 77).

A cast-iron kettle and broth pot usually stood on the hobs. In some fireplaces there was a gas ring or small gas stove where food could be cooked more quickly. At the end of the last century and up to the 1930s and even later, the most usual type of range seems to have been the coal-fired, polished steel model with heavy doors hung on distinctive strap hinges (pls 63, 94).

Keeping the fireplace gleaming was often a chore for the younger members of the family on the universal cleaning night:

Friday night was Brasso night. You didn't get out to the dancing 'til the brasses were done. Blackleading was done on a Friday night too. Once a week you got a packet of black lead. You broke it up and mixed it with water. Then you put it on with a brush, let it dry and then you polished it. A velvet square was used for burnishing it.

> My dad got this burnisher made. It was leather backed with steel hoops all
> sewn together on the leather. You used to burnish the knobs and go along the
> front of the range. When you finished, they looked like chromium.[26]

The fender could be of steel, cast iron, pressed sheet brass, or copper, and
was often placed over a decorative enamelled metal sheet made to look like
tiles.[27] Some fenders had low corner boxes for kindling and brushes, which also
provided seating by the fire. On the mantelpiece could be found brass
ornaments and a pair of 'wally dugs' (see pls 62, 67). Mantelpieces often had
hooks for hanging cooking implements and a rod along the fireplace was used
for drying clothes.

People's household possessions depended often on their area of work, as
Marion Smith, born in 1906 in Springburn, Glasgow, describes: 'As my father
was a brass moulder, the mantelpiece, above the stove, was gleaming with brass
adornments, all made in the works. This was one of the perks of the trade.
Everybody made things in the works.'[28]

An essential piece of furniture was the kitchen table of scrubbed deal (pine).
This was used for eating, food preparation, working, and even for minor
surgical operations such as tonsillectomies.[29] There would be various chairs and
stools, although sometimes not enough for all the family to sit at once. Food
was often served in relays, and children might stand to eat, or kneel round a kist.
'Father' always had his seat at the table and by the fireside.

Any type of furniture could be found in the kitchen if there was room for
it. The room and kitchen of a spinner in a Glasgow mule factory in 1833 had
a table, chairs, chest of drawers, mahogany bedstead, a china cabinet, books, and
a longcase clock, an important status symbol for an operative family.[30] Davie
Duncan described a kitchen in an Aberdeen tenement nearly one hundred
years later:

> I remember the brass double bed in the corner, beside the window; the
> mahogany ogee chest of drawers, the wooden shelf (fixed on the wall at the door
> side) laden with pots, pans and kettle plus various other objects; the ochred walls
> and dado of varnished wallpaper. The lino on the floor was patched and worn.[31]

The bed in a recess or 'hole in the wall' was a distinctive feature, mentioned
in evidence to a Royal Commission in 1885: 'In Scotland they have a bed recess
in the kitchen, they cannot do without that, a Scotchman always likes to lie in
the kitchen, and of course that saves fires. They are near a fire in the winter time.
It is the favourite bed in the house.'[32] These beds were built in on side battens
about two feet six from the floor, leaving space below for storage of a kist or
tin bath or for a 'hurley bed' on wheels which was 'hurled out' at night.
Children often slept in this. Curtains hid the space below the bed and were
sometimes hung up behind to prevent marking the wall. 'It's the same as today
with a valance, it's what we called a 'pand' on the bed. It was on a stretchy wire
and Mum had another on the back of the bed recess on a wooden stick.'[33] The
word 'pand', meaning bed hangings, is found in seventeenth-century inventories.[34] Long curtains could cover bedding and clothing kept on the bed during
the day and enclose the sleepers at night. Sofa and chair beds served as useful
furniture during the day and other beds were disguised in the form of cabinets
and chests to save space.

The 'room' of a room-and-kitchen house had many functions – as a
bedroom, a best room for celebrations, and when needed, a place for laying
out the dead before a funeral. Many 'rooms' of nineteenth-century houses
contained a 'bed closet' with a bed hidden behind a closed door (pl 66).[35]

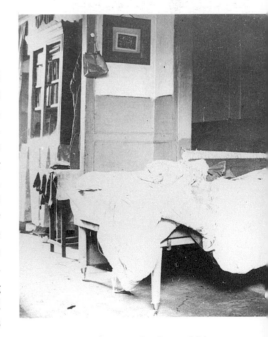

65. A hurley bed on wheels could be
pushed out of the way under the high bed
in the kitchen closet. This photograph is
from a series kept by the sanitary officers in
Paisley.

66. Closet bed in the parlour of a flat in Paisley, about 1900. Someone appears to be asleep inside this 'cubicle of consumption'.

These were usually unventilated and caused concern over the risks of contracting tuberculosis. Glasgow Building Regulations of 1900 specified that they should be open in front from floor to ceiling and three quarters of the length, and an Act of Parliament in 1913 outlawed enclosed beds altogether, to the approval of the Burgh Engineer, who now had the power to prevent these 'cubicles of consumption', though many must have continued in use in Glasgow and elsewhere.[36]

The room, which was sometimes also known as the 'parlour', often had a small fireplace in which a fire was lit only on special occasions, as Joan Williamson recalled: 'Oh just high days and holidays or when it was really cold. You stayed in the kitchen until it was time for bed.'[37] Furniture in the room varied according to the size of the space and family income. It might contain only beds, or could include a bedroom suite and easy chairs, a bookcase, a china cabinet, or a sideboard.

In a small space there was little room for possessions:

I must have been about six when we moved across the street to a bigger house. It had two rooms. It also had a lobby and a very clean lavatory on the half-landing of the stairway.

You really had to see a removal from a room and kitchen house in a Glasgow tenement to realise how few goods and chattels people owned. They usually filled a coal-cart with room to spare for the bird-cage and the two rolls of linoleum.

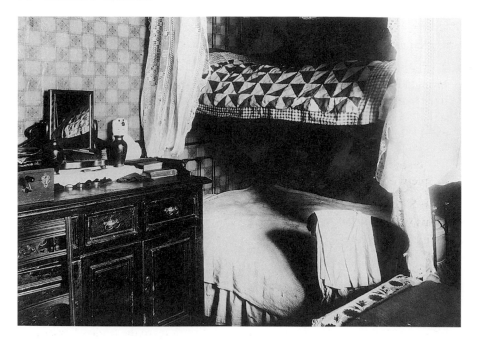

67. A rare photograph showing tiered beds in a kitchen recess in Forest Park Place, Dundee, about 1929. This practice does not appear to have been usual, whereas bunk beds are commonly used today when children are expected to have a bed each. Patchwork quilts were also unusual in Scotland but 'wally dugs' were favourite ornaments.

As far as I remember our wealth of furniture and fittings, carefully scraped and saved for over years, was a wardrobe, chest of drawers, two tables, four chairs, a medicine cabinet and a couple of dozen odds and ends like Dad's tool box, a shaving mirror, crockery, cutlery and ridiculous things like a goldfish bowl and Aunt Marian's soup tureen.

Everything had its place in our house. You would *never* find the hammer anywhere but in the kitchen dresser drawer, Uncle Roddy's wartime photograph but in the bottom drawer of the wardrobe, the washhouse key but on the nail behind the kitchen door or my schoolbag but hanging on the adjacent hook. Even in the busiest, most disordered house in the street there were limits to carelessness because there was simply no room for chaos. There was the benefit of familiarity and speed about a wee place with few possessions.

No hunting in attics for sledges, cricket bats or old model railways was ever necessary because there was no attic and no old things. Spring cleaning was easy and simple. Books were got from the local library; toys were swopped with other children or destroyed at the end of the 'season'; newspapers lit the morning fires or protected the freshly-washed kitchen floor; the few 'survival' documents like birth certificates, insurance cards, the rent book and the Co-operative dividend book were all safe in mother's large handbag in the wardrobe. No wonder we never heard of a burglary in a tenement house. It wasn't worth it.[38]

Town dwellers could buy food when required, so there was no need for a well-stocked larder. Food was kept in a press or in wire netting on the windowsill. One-roomed houses were almost inevitably crowded, however, and a plan and description of 1931 indicate how difficult they could be (pl 68):

This room was so packed with furniture that it was almost impossible to walk across the room to the window. The family consisted of man, wife and six children – boys aged 12, 3, 1 and girls aged 5½, 2 and 1 month. The walls were very dirty and verminous. The ceiling sloped to the window; there was no place to put clothes other than on the back of the door or piled on the coal-bunker. The man was a miner, unemployed, who had lost his work through the pit being closed. The children's bed had been pushed one foot under the parents' bed owing to lack of space. They and three other families shared a lavatory and sink.[39]

68. Plan of an attic in Clyde Street, Edinburgh, from *Behind Princes Street, A Contrast*, a report by Irene Barclay and Evelyn Perry, 1931. The difficulties of living in such a space are easy to see.

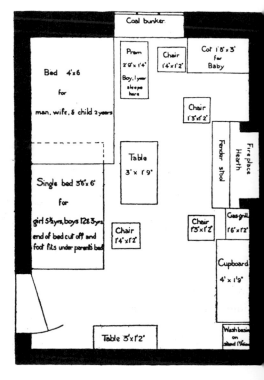

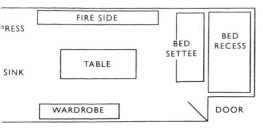

69. Plan of John Sinclair's single end at 38 Glover Street, Leith. The room was occupied by seven people in the 1930s.

Living in a small space required the constant moving of furniture. Many struggled against enormous odds to keep their houses clean:

A typical single end that's how people lived, they cooked, slept, entertained and brought up a family. There was a single end next to us and there was six people lived in it, and yet when you went in the place was immaculate; the chairs were scrubbed, the table was scrubbed – no tablecloth – scrupulous. The grate was clean and there was a gas ring, right enough, for cooking and a fire and a black sink – black iron – a bunker at the side and one window and, of course, one bed recess and another bed and a bed-chair which I remember. That's how people were living – I don't know how they did it.[40]

John Sinclair had a single end at 38 Glover Street in Leith, where he lived with his wife and five children in the 1930s (pl 69). Four slept in the bed and three in a bed-settee pushed in front of the door at night. Four of the children were born in this house.

One of the worst landlords was the Railway before it was nationalized, a single-end and the rent was 5/-. We got new furniture from Grants in the High Street – a bed, a wardrobe, table and four chairs and took them into the house. And we discovered there were bugs in the house. I went up to the landlord's place and spoke to him through a small window. He near enough accused me of taking them in. I explained to him that the furniture was brand new. I couldn't possibly have. I had to strip all the wallpaper off, seven layers of it and paint it with a light green. Then the Corporation came along and sprayed the lot. When we moved to a Council house I had to get the 'buggy van' to take my furniture away and get it fumigated.[41]

Keeping on top of bugs was a perpetual problem, as Pat Rogan remembers:

Until the arrival of DDT the bulk of these houses were infested with bugs, fleas, scabies and lice. People would buy Carbolic Acid from the chemist, add it to hot water and wash everything down. If of necessity people had to call in the aid of the Sanitary Inspector, because the house was particularly buggy, the usual thing that was recommended was to remove pictures from the walls. Now most houses in those days had pictures of Granny and Grandpa and if they were Irish

70. The 'buggy man' disinfecting an Edinburgh house in about 1935. Bugs lurked in corners and behind picture rails, and getting rid of them was a messy and time-consuming process.

there would be pictures of Parnell and Emmett. And every picture that hung on the wall was a harbour for bugs. The sanitary man would say, 'For the love of God burn them!', which was sacrilege to them![42]

In the new houses built from the 1920s preventive action was taken: a picture hook donated to The People's Story Museum arrived with a note saying, 'We could not use this when we were moved from the Canongate to Prestonfield as there were no picture rails in the new houses which could encourage bugs'.

Joseph Paterson here describes measures against bugs in Dundee:

They used to paper the walls with flour paste, which is a source of food for vermin. And consequently most people preferred ochre. It wasn't like yir emulsion paint nowadays, you lean'd against it, it came off, you know you got covered in – yir back was a' brown, it was a sort of powder like. And it's ridiculous when you think on it, people used to go down to the Sanitary Department because, for to borrow a whitewash brush to do their house.[43]

Typical decoration of the house between the wars would be whitewashed ceilings and papered walls in the room and papered or painted walls in the kitchen. Yellow ochre was sometimes applied to the walls to keep down bug infestation and woodwork was painted dark brown or varnished (pl 72). Floors were often laid with linoleum or oilcloth, with small rugs by the fire or bed.

Beating the rugs was another chore given to the children, as Betty Hepburn recalls: 'You just had wee rag rugs and linoleum. You took them down to the green and had to wait 'til the washing was in. We were given the beater and told to get out. There wasnae any need for a vacuum cleaner because you didnae have carpets'.[44] Joan Williamson remembers the move up from a rug to a carpet: 'Most people didn't have a carpet until the 50s and 60s when you were able to afford a four by three [yard] carpet to fit your room, with a surround to polish up. If you got a four by three carpet, you decided you were going to get a vacuum cleaner as well. You weren't goin' to go on your knees for a four by three carpet'.[45]

71. An outside shared sink in Edinburgh, 1959. By this date few people had to put up with such facilities (see p75).

Brown Ochre on the crumbling walls
To keep the bugs at Bay,
A Family of Nine in two small rooms
Yet another on the Way
A Crippled Hero of the Kaiser's War
Soon to fade away,
A Pregnant Spinner Wife
who earns the only Pay.

72. *Brown Ochre on the Crumbling Walls*, painted from memory by Joseph Paterson of Dundee. Mr Paterson also wrote the poem with this image.

Many families did not have a separate sink in the house until well into the twentieth century. Shared access to a source of water supply and sanitary conveniences was commonplace. In 1914, about a third of houses in Edinburgh and in Glasgow had no separate WC. In both cities, over 90 per cent of one-roomed houses shared a water closet.[46]

WC stacks at the back of tenements date from the passing of the 1892 Burgh Police Act, which made internal sanitation compulsory and replaced the dry closet or privy in the back court (pl 74). These water closets were frequently placed on the half landing (pl 73). By 1946 in Edinburgh there were sixty houses where dry closets were still in use and of all houses, one in ten still had shared water closets. Even in 1967 there were 2354 houses in the capital with shared lavatories.[47]

The main problems of this are graphically described by Ralph Glasser in *Growing up in the Gorbals*, a vivid account of his childhood in Glasgow:

On the common staircases, six or eight flats shared two lavatories, each tucked into a tiny intermediate landing between two floors. You had to hold its decrepit door shut with your foot or wedge it with a lump of wood. And when the flush system did not work or the soil pipe was blocked, which was often, the floor was soon awash and the overflow spread freely down the main staircase. Going to the lavatory we had to remember to carry a supply of newspaper, not only for use as toilet paper but also to clean the soles of our boots of excrement and urine before going back into the flat.[48]

73. Boys on a tenement stair in the Gorbals, Glasgow, photographed by Bert Hardy in 1948 for *Picture Post*. The original caption was 'Where the young can sit and read'. Stairs were an important play area for children.

74. Back court and washhouse in Springburn, Glasgow. The tenements have brick stacks built on the back to house the shared WCs on the stair landings. Such stacks were erected in great numbers after the passing of the Burgh Police (Scotland) Act in 1892.

Most people who grew up having to use a shared toilet remember the wait and the hazard of being 'caught short'.

There were striking differences in the provision of shared sinks in Edinburgh and Glasgow in 1915, when almost all Glasgow houses of one and two rooms had their own sink, whereas in Edinburgh only just over half the number of one-roomed houses had a separate sink. This probably reflects the higher proportion of made-down houses in Edinburgh.[49] By 1946 in Edinburgh, 98 per cent of all houses had individual sinks, but there were still 198 houses with shared sinks in 1967.[50]

More than a third of houses in 1946 had no bathroom,[51] and even by the 1961 census, one quarter of houses in Edinburgh had no fixed bath. Water could be collected from the common stair and taken into the house, as Stella Stewart remembers:

> When I was a child in Brown Street we had no water in the house. We had to go to a tap that was in the hallway outside the stair. There was a sort of sink. I don't know what it looked like because it was pitch dark and you could never see it because there was no natural light and no gas light. We used basins to carry the water. My mother heated water on a fire on a range.[52]

In the tenement at the David Livingstone Centre at Blantyre, there is a 'jawbox' at the top of the stair. It has no tap, only a hole where the dirty water could be poured to drain away down the outside of the building and onto the ground below, very like the facilities in castles much earlier.

Whether the water supply was outside or inside the house, water had to be heated on the fire before washing could be done. Cathy Lighterness describes washday in Newhaven:

> My mother did the washing in the house, on a Monday. You'd come back from school and find the house full of washing. She heated the water on the gas ring and filled the tin bath which she had on two chairs and the wringer standing up. They'd be hung out to dry. We had a rope between our window across the way.[53]

This was made easier if the kitchen was fitted with a sink and tub and wringer.

In some towns, tenements were built with washhouses which could be used on a rotational basis by the tenants (pl 74). Doing the weekly wash in the washhouse was a regular feature of tenement life in Glasgow. It was a backbreaking job, difficult to imagine today with the convenience of washing machines. The procedure is described in detail in *A Govan Childhood* and *Up Oor Close*. Rotas sometimes broke down and were a cause of bitterness and strife within the block: 'They had their days in the washhouse, and that caused bother, "That's my line, it's my day!" It got tae fisticuffs, and knives tae cut the ropes!'[54] The 'washie' had another function for small boys in Glasgow, as Roderick Wilkinson describes:

> The 'Washie' was a domain in itself for the children in our street. Every back-court had a small, flat-roofed building consisting of a wash-house and a midden built side by side. And it was this flat – well, nearly flat – roof that lured the boys to crew the pirates' ship, defend the Foreign Legion fortress, man the stockade against Indians – or just to get up higher than anybody else. You could do almost anything on a Washie except play on top of it when your mother was washing clothes inside it – not because it annoyed her but simply because the smoke belching out of the clay chimney-pot blackened your face and choked you. And the concrete roof got too hot for your feet. Washies in full power were formidable places.[55]

75. A single end at the David Livingstone Centre in Blantyre, Lanarkshire. The bed was fixed at a height to allow for the storage of a kist or hurley bed below. Livingstone's birthplace is open to the public as a museum.

76. The 'hole-in-the-wall-bed' in the kitchen of a room-and-kitchen flat at 468 Springburn Road, Springburn, Glasgow, painted by Andrew Lillie, who was born in 1911. A much more cheerful and bright image of a tenement interior than is usual, though it clearly makes a point about the work involved in keeping it like this.

The Royal Commission in 1917 reported that washhouses were built onto tenements in Paisley, Motherwell, Kirkcaldy, Arbroath, Port Glasgow, Bo'ness, Selkirk and Clydebank. There were none in Leith and only a few in Edinburgh in the newer tenements.[56] Here, drying space was provided in shared back greens, and in certain public parks and open spaces the drying and bleaching of clothes was allowed. Large public washhouses, called 'steamies' in Glasgow and 'washhouses' in Edinburgh, were set up from the end of the nineteenth century to meet the needs of people in overcrowded conditions, without running water or room to do a wash. Their closure led to one of the biggest public demonstrations Edinburgh has seen: 'It was far superior to daein' the washin' in the hoose ... You went oot at seven o'clock and you came back at nine with a beautiful wash, washed, dried, and mangled, just ready to be put away.'[57]

Apart from a good clean wash, the washhouse provided a social centre for women in the local community: 'You used to get a rare blether and hear all the local gossip. And you knew everybody that went at the time, it was like a club really.'[58]

The Co-op also provided a laundry service. A bag wash could come back damp or dry. Wherever the wash was done there was always the problem of

77. Washing in these conditions was heavy work. This room was in a property in Calside Street in Paisley, closed by the sanitary officers in 1903. The range appears to date from the early nineteenth century and the wooden tubs are of the traditional type, though the galvanized bucket is a newer addition.

getting it completely dry. Clothes would be hung on the pulley, on the clothes horse or the mantelpiece rod, or on a line out of the window. The next stage was to iron or mangle them. Women often took in this type of work.

Until the provision of public baths, personal washing and bathing was carried out in the house. Washing was often done in cold water, as described in this extract from Dundee:

> We were never bathed cause we didna hae a bath, we got washed in the sink in cald water, that's true, ye got standin' in this sink an' the water jist came oot the well, that's true, freezin', eh, ha ha ha, ye never got bathed until, em, oh we were a bitty aulder and she got a big zinc bath.[59]

Washing and shaving took place at the kitchen sink or in a bowl of water collected from an outside tap. Some habits learnt as children lasted a lifetime, as Joan Croall describes:

> One thing I've noticed, my husband he was brought up in a room and kitchen and it annoys me. To this day, he never uses the sink in the bathroom and if I'm doing anything in the kitchen, he'll come and say 'Can I get a wash?' His brother was over from Canada staying with us and he did it as well.[60]

In some families, bathnight was on one regular night during the week. The bathwater would do for all the children, who would take it in turns to bath as they got older. Betty Hepburn describes how this was organized: 'There were five of us and my mother used to say "lantern lights are on tonight!" There's your penny and away you go [to the pictures] and the girls all had a scrub. The boys got their wash when we went to the Brownies.'[61]

In some families 'A laddie and a lassie went intae the bath the gither. There werenae any sex in they days!'[62] Many claim to have been unaware of sex until they got married, but the main criticism of one-room living in the official reports and public opinion was that adults and children of both sexes shared beds. In 1885 the Reverend Hannan felt that living in fewer than two rooms 'must tend materially to immorality',[63] and the Medical Officer for Health in Glasgow in 1913 referred to 'a kind of pressure that goes on in our two apartment houses. It is not legal overcrowding, it is sexual'.[64] The Inspector of the Poor for Glasgow gave evidence of 'a case here where the stepfather of a girl of eighteen years of age is the father of her child'.[65]

Incest presumably went on in houses of all sizes, but it did occur as a result of bed sharing in small houses. Ralph Glasser in his autobiography, *Growing Up in the Gorbals*, describes how his friend, Alec, while talking of going with a prostitute, wonders:

> 'if it wid be different fuckin' her than blockin' ma sister.' I should not have been shocked but I was, and I must have shown it, or at least that I was surprised, perhaps by the slightest shift in my step or a questioning turn of the head, for he looked at me in astonishment. 'Yours've done it wi' yew surely?' I shook my head, not sure what words would fit. 'Come on!' he said, disbelieving, 'Yewr sisters must've shown ye whit's what? Ah'll lay ye odds o' a hundred tae one ye'll no' find a feller, who's go' an older sister, who's no' been intae'er – aye, many, many times, sleepin' in the same bed night efter night! Hiv ye really no' done i'? Ah'll no' tell on ye mind!' 'No, it really is true.' I searched for a bland excuse. 'Maybe it was because they were so much older than me.'[66]

He describes the arrangements at home, where he shared a room with his sister:

> In the tiny room I shared with her, hardly bigger than a bathroom in a present day council house, father rigged up a dividing screen that folded away during

78. Jocelyn Hepburn in her fireside bath at Stewart Terrace, Edinburgh, in 1952. This kind of enamelled tub would be kept under a recess bed until wanted and then filled with water heated on the range.

the day; on one side of it she slept in a chair bed – a wooden armchair that opened out into a single bed, its three cushions of velveteeen cord laid end to end as a mattress – and on the other I lay on a narrow flock palliasse on the floor.[67]

Even with a variety of beds made from chairs, sofas, and mattresses on the floor, bed sharing was an inevitable, natural part of life for families living in small spaces:

I stayed at my aunt's once, she had ten in the family. The boys were at the top and the girls at the bottom. No-one ever thought anything about sleeping with anyone else. You didn't have a goonie or pyjamas, just your vest and pants. You just got up and dressed yourself, there was no embarrassment.[68]

If there was one baby already in the cot or pram, other pieces of furniture were used, as Betty Hepburn remembers: 'The house I went to, they had twelve in their family. They used to empty the stuff in the corner out of the drawers and the drawers made three cots. They lived alright and they all grew up into healthy people.'[69]

Some people have rarely had the opportunity to sleep alone. Joan Williamson went from sharing a bed with her sisters to sharing one with her husband: 'I never had a bed to masel' until I lay in hospital having my daughter. It was the first time. And then I couldn't sleep.'[70] Although bed sharing was warm it was not always comfortable. Richard Goodall describes sleeping with his brothers, three to a bed:

These beds had no mattresses: they were straw, what they called 'Dunkey's Breakfast'. That's what they called it. One person slept at the bottom and two at the top so there was many a night when your toes happened to be in the mouth of one of your brothers.[71]

Sex between adults took place in the same room or bed where children were sleeping. Ralph Glasser mentions this in *Growing Up in The Gorbals*:

To enable a coupling to take place in a semblance of privacy behind the curtain, the woman would step out in her shift, snatch a blanket off the bed and wrap the child in it and lay him on the floor boards near enough to the cooking range for him to get some radiated warmth from its banked-up fire.[72]

Even though space in the small home was restricted, resourceful children found places to play:

We had a room and kitchen. In the kitchen was a bed recess. One of my earliest memories is having a concert on the bed, with the curtains and everybody had their piece. I used to sing 'I'm a Little Dutchman' and do a clog dance.[73]

Molly Weir in *Shoes Were for Sunday* remembers the coal bunker being a favourite hiding place in a game of hide and seek, which was lost when the bunker was filled up with coal.[74] In a confined space there was no room for children to run wild. 'It was instilled in us – to be quiet and you always got a whack if you overstepped the mark', or you would be made to stand on your own in the room when the rest of the family was in the kitchen.[75]

Children were sent out to play on the stair, street, backyard, or green as there was not enough space in the house. Today it is often thought that there was less need in the past to worry about child safety, but it was a cause of concern. Davie Duncan, writing of his childhood in Aberdeen in the 1920s, recalled a man attempting to assault him in the dark WC by his tenement entrance,[76] and social reformers reported on the everyday dangers to health and safety:

The mother must choose between cooping up her young children in a small space where they may be interfering seriously with her household occupations, or letting them go out into the yard or the street where they can no longer be under her supervision … The yards attached to the tenements are not desirable playgrounds. They are frequently small, airless, and pervaded by the odour of ashpits or insanitary closets and the larger part is sometimes railed off for clothes lines.[77]

Men also found a break from the confines of the home. For many it was going to the local public house:

Saturday night was the night they went out to the pubs … They'd been arguing in the pub, so when they came home they'd be arguing … And many, many a time we wouldn't get much sleep, because of the arguments and that had gone on because of the drink. Sometimes he came in early with a drink in him. And many a night, rather than argue, my mother would kid on that she was away out and shut the door. He never found her hiding place yet. In all these years she used to stand at the back of the curtain in the room until she thought he was sleeping. Then she would come in beside us.[78]

Children grew up with an awareness of different aspects of life and came into direct contact with birth and death. Most people died in their homes. The body was laid out and kept there for about three days until the funeral, even if the house consisted of one room. After the funeral, friends and relatives came back to the house for tea and sandwiches. Women were excluded from the actual burial. Elsie Tierney remembers the death of her grandmother in Newhaven:

79. *First Encounter with the Inevitable* by Joseph Paterson of Dundee. A young Polish neighbour of Paterson's died and was laid out by her poverty-stricken mother as if for her first Communion.

My Granny had a lot of rheumatism before she died and had to keep her feet up in bed. When she died, they had to break her legs and put a wringer on top to keep them down. She was laid out in her coffin on three chairs and my mother slept in the room with her. We went to my Auntie's. They had an awful job gettin' my Granny down the stair.[79]

Joseph Paterson of Dundee depicted and described a memory from his childhood of when a young neighbour died at home of TB (pl 79):

she was only 14! She was emassiated, ye know, thin. I used to run along an jist barge in there and she'd be in bed on her own. And that's how poor that room was! There was the bare minimum – a bed, couple o' chairs, a wee kitchen table, a fire, a ring, and whit have ye. And it was tiny ...

I was playing out, my mother picked me up. She says, uh, 'you of all people should see this'. So she brought me in and here's Mary lying on the bed like that – oh, beautifully dressed. It was the first time I'd ever seen a dead body ... It was a south facing window, and the light coming through – this was the family crucifix ... a lovely sculpted brass figure of Christ. Oh I was shivering a bit because the light from the window hit the brass and it reflected up into her face and – oh yellow ken, what.[80]

It was common practice for children to be sent to stay with neighbours on the stair or relations who lived close by, as Betty Hepburn describes:

There was one wifie on our stair, she did anybody that died, she laid them out and the other one delivered the babies. The rest of them on the stairs would say, 'Send Jeanie to me, or Johnny to me' and they looked after the kids until it was all over.[81]

It was this tightly-knit sense of community, the open doors, the support of neighbours, and mutual responsibility for the children that many people missed when the old communities were broken up and people rehoused. It is this aspect of life that they mention with nostalgia, even though they would readily admit that life was a constant struggle. Hardship and necessity threw people into a reliance on each other and a real sense of comradeship. Councillor Pat Rogan does not underestimate the conditions in which people lived: 'This idea that "we may have been poor but we were comfortable and cosy", it's just not true. Their life was hell – it was a constant daily grind against dirt and disease.'[82]

For many people, the memory of the outside toilet and lack of space is still vivid and there is no rosy view of the past:

I would never live in those days again, never. The houses were all crammed together and built close together and maybe one lavatory for maybe a whole stair. It was terrible. It was terrible living long ago. Talk about the good old days. They say, 'would you like to live them again', I say 'no, never again'. Never, nothing would make me live in the old days again. I've seen too much of the poverty, you know.[83]

And when people were moved to the new housing schemes, 'It was paradise! For my sister and myself to share a bedroom just for our two selves, we thought this was heaven. There was a bathroom and electric light.'[84]

Some people, however, missed the way of life they had left behind. Joan Williamson remembers the move out to Gorgie and the move back again:

We lived at that time in Newport Street in a room and kitchen with outside toilet shared with another three families, so you can imagine how we felt when we heard we were moving to a three-bedroomed house, living room, kitchenette and bathroom in Gorgie Road right opposite Saughton Park.

Nos.125 & 126, HOUSE AT 8, FULLARTON STREET. NEW HOUSE. CORPORATION SCHEME. HOUSING REPORT, 1929.

Nos.127 & 128, HOUSE AT No.39, OVERGATE. CLOSED by ORDER. HOUSING REPORT, 1929.

Mum never settled in the house, she missed the town and all her friends so because of that and other problems she decided to get an exchange. We moved back in 1941 to a room and kitchen with gas light and toilet outside, the house was never empty, we were back to where we started.[85]

Although most people stayed in their new council houses, many moved back into town. The new schemes tended not to provide pubs, shops, or meeting places, and people missed the sense of belonging and friendliness of the communities they had left. This is best put in the words of Betty Hepburn:

You were never alone when trouble came along, no wondering who was going to feed the kids and bed them down if you had to go and look after one of the family overnight. If you were short of cash or food someone always helped you over the rough patches and that was no compensation for extra bedrooms and a bath. I was very happy in my tenement home. There is a lot to be said for the tenement. No-one would be left on their own to die.[86]

80. Contrasting interiors in Dundee in 1929. The upper photographs were clearly taken to express pride in the achievements of the corporation in providing improved housing. They both seem to depict the same room, which though smart and clean was still cramped. The arrangement of the chairs in front of the bed is particularly striking.

4 The Kitchen

ANNETTE CARRUTHERS

'In the modern small house, where, so often now, the housewife does all the domestic work, the kitchen has become the hub of the home.'

M S Briggs, 1937[1]

Architects' plans for 'improved' cottages in the mid nineteenth century often include a 'living room' rather than a kitchen,[2] and previous chapters have shown that the kitchen in small houses was used for working, sleeping, washing, playing, and a multitude of other activities. In larger dwellings (the more usual sphere of the architect), the functions of the kitchen were focused on cooking and cleaning, which were themselves separated into distinct spaces: food preparation areas, larders and other stores, serving rooms, sculleries, laundries, and drying rooms. Sleeping accommodation for servants was also an important feature of the kitchen over much of the period under review, disappearing only during the past hundred years. The decline of domestic service in the present century, accompanied by developments in technology and changes in social behaviour, have brought new attitudes to the kitchen in relation to other rooms in the house and to its claim on household expenditure.

Numerous factors influence the appearance and working of the kitchen, which has always been circumscribed by practical needs. The size of the house and number of people living in it, their work and leisure activities have a direct effect on the type of kitchen wanted. Social attitudes, size of income, and availability of labour dictate whether the house is run by the householder and family or is staffed by servants. The more people there are involved in domestic management, the more space is needed for them, though servants have often found themselves squeezed into the smallest places.

The preparation and cooking of food is the major activity in the kitchen and its equipment and arrangement are much influenced by the availability of foodstuffs and methods of keeping and using them. Before the adoption of refrigeration (introduced for domestic use early in the twentieth century but not widespread until after the Second World War), other methods of preservation were relied upon, including salting, smoking, drying, pickling, and bottling. The development of passable roads from the late eighteenth century and the spread of the railways from the 1830s began the change from reliance on seasonal and local produce to the present-day availability of almost any food one can imagine, at any time of the year. Sea trading brought foreign foods to island communities and coastal ports and cities, but until the nineteenth century, most Scots lived on the range of local resources which could be farmed or found naturally in this northern climate. By the middle of the century there would have been a big difference between town and country. Scotland is not known for its town markets, but in urban areas provisions were more readily available to those who could pay for them and hot food could be purchased in the streets. In the country, by contrast, especially in remote areas, householders had to lay down stores for the winter. To some extent this remains true in places which are regularly cut off by snow.

Large parts of Scotland have abundant supplies of peat for fuel, though this too requires forethought: the digging, drying, and stacking of peat for the winter is a labour-intensive summer occupation. The change in the Lowland areas from peat to coal had a dramatic effect on the form of fires and altered the range of possibilities for the cook. A similarly momentous changeover to gas and electricity in the early twentieth century has made it possible to cook in a much smaller space than before, and so allowed the development of the 'kitchenette'. The introduction of bottled gas and its spread since the late 1930s has brought instantly controllable cooking equipment to all parts of the country if required.[3]

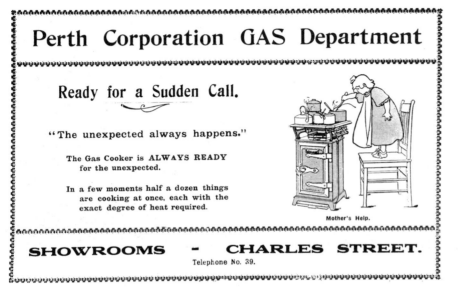

81. Advertisement from 1914. The design of this cooker was clearly based on that of coal ranges and stoves, though much smaller. Its size and the fact that it did not have to be lit all day meant it could be used in a smaller space.

82. Small girl using a washboard in the 1950s or 1960s in Shetland. The packet of soap powder gives evidence of the spread of consumer commodities but the wooden tub is of a type used for centuries.

Most people also now have access to clean piped water, though country areas are often still served by wells with unpredictable water flow, as holiday-makers in farm cottages can discover. The provision of mains water by local authorities in the late nineteenth century revolutionized the kitchen and its equipment, saving much tiring fetching and carrying. Instantly available water, combined with a source of power, enabled people to use washing machines and, more recently, dishwashers – though such changes are also intimately bound up with changes in how people wish to live: they do not simply result from the innovations of technology.

In all parts of the world a major influence on the form of building in which the kitchen is contained is the material from which it is built. The hazards of spitting fat and rising sparks made it sensible to site the kitchen away from the main body of a house constructed largely of wood or other combustible materials. In Scotland, with its abundant building stone, this has not been a major factor and the kitchen could be included within the house itself, though some early hall houses and castles had separate buildings for cooking.[4] From an early date the kitchen's usual position was in the vaulted basement rooms of castles and tower houses and it later remained in the basement or ground floor of most dwellings. This was the practical place for bringing in stores and removing waste, and especially for carrying in heavy water and fuel. In households large enough to include a dining room, the obvious site for the

83. An Orkney kitchen, about 1900. Although this is a posed photograph taken for sale as a postcard, it depicts the type of arched fireplace found in Scotland from at least the sixteenth century. Such an enclosed 'inglenook' provided a warm space for activities other than just cooking.

kitchen is nearby, but some architects and owners were more concerned to prevent the spread of kitchen smells than to ensure the food was served hot, and the location of the kitchen in relation to other rooms varies over time.

In the years around 1600 only a very small minority of people lived in houses with a separate kitchen. Even by 1691, hearth tax returns show that the average number of hearths per house was less than two, and analysis of these returns suggests that in rural Scotland – Highland and Lowland – there was normally one 'mansion' house on each estate, while most other dwellings had only one hearth. The mansion house might have between two and fifty hearths and the manse and the small laird's house around four to six, but even relatively wealthy tenants and small proprietors often had only one or two. It is difficult to tell what the position was in the towns because of the diverse trades carried out in different areas, but figures for Perth in 1694 suggest that only professional people, dyers, and merchants had three hearths or more and most tradesmen had fewer than two.[5]

Houses with enough hearths to imply a kitchen separate from the living room therefore belonged in the 1690s only to the aristocracy, professionals, small lairds, ministers, and merchants. They were most numerous in areas such as Fife, Lothian, and Perthshire, with rich farming land and good trading ports or other means of communication. Many were likely, therefore, to be fuelled by coal rather than the peat used in isolated and upland rural areas, though Lady Grisell Baillie's household accounts in Edinburgh and Mellerstain, Berwickshire, include payments for both fuels from the 1690s to about 1740.[6] Coal gives a much fiercer heat than peat, and requires a metal basket or something similar to raise it above the floor, providing an updraught. Apart from the fire implements, however, there can have been little difference between the equipment of the separate kitchen and that of the living-room-kitchen of the smaller dwelling, though it might have been on a larger scale and would include a few items, such as roasting spits, for which there was no requirement in the smallest houses, where people lived largely on porridge and potatoes.

An inventory of 1653 of the Earl's Palace at Kirkwall in Orkney lists in the 'Kitching' a 'Great pair of Iron lying Raxes' (the supports on which spits were stretched), two spits, five pewter dishes, two 'Pye Platters', a bolster and pillow, a great iron kettle and a small copper one, a brass skimmer, a copper dropping pan (probably for dripping), an old broken brass pot, and a 'dressing boord'. Nearby was a 'Bruehouse' containing cisterns and a copper vessel, while the brewhouse at the House of Birsay at the same time contained various vats and 'punshons' (probably large pottery bowls).[7]

All interior fittings at the Earl's Palace have disappeared, but most of the building stands, making it possible to see how the vaulted basement kitchen, with its arched fireplace and surprising lack of an oven, relates to the nearby storerooms, the well, and the Great Hall on the floor above. Much of the food prepared in the kitchen was eaten in the hall, where another impressive fireplace may have been used for some cooking or reheating. The 1653 inventory shows that by this time the palace also had a 'Dyning Roume' (also spelt 'dining') next to the hall, with more comfortable furnishings, including Arras hangings and a 'Turky' carpet.[8] Dinner at this date would have been taken in the middle of the day, at least partly because the kitchen, with its few and small windows, would have been too dark for satisfactory cooking later on. Artificial light, in the form of candles and rushlights, would not only have increased the household expenses but would add to the heat and smoke of already difficult working conditions in the kitchen.

Large houses, castles, and palaces, like the Kirkwall building, usually had similar arrangements of basement kitchen and storerooms, though a few had the kitchen on the same floor as the hall.[9] Some were in an entirely separate building, as at Stirling Castle, where kitchen and bakehouse occupied underground rooms away from the main body of the King's Palace. These were probably built in 1542 and demolished in 1689, and comprised two large vaulted spaces with paired fireplaces and baking ovens.[10]

In the largest houses, such as the House of Binns in West Lothian, from which an inventory of 1685 survives, stored provisions would be divided into numerous rooms: the 'corne house'; the 'Girnell House' (granary); a cellar; 'Wyne Cellar'; and the 'Laidner', in which were kept barrels of herring, butter, and vinegar. Livestock belonged in the 'dowcat in the Yaird' and the hen house, while stored utensils for food preparation, serving, and washing appear in the 'Brewhouse', the 'Pantrie', and the 'Washing House'.[11]

Major items in the kitchen itself were the fireplace fittings, the furniture, and a variety of implements. It is an extensive list and probably represents a fairly typical selection of the equipment of a large house, though considerably more than most people had:

A chimnay with a gallows with 3 cruiks at it. An iron baik. A pair of lying raxes [andirons]. 2 speits with horls at the end of them [the end bent over]. 2 irons above the braise [chimney-piece; in this instance a stone arch] for laying speits on. Ane Jack [roasting-jack]. 2 iron chayns for the jack. A salt barrell. A salt backet. A draping [probably dripping] pan with a standing brander [gridiron] to set it on. A pair of taings. A handle for the jack. 2 brass pots & an iron pot. Ane iron pot for pick [pitch]. 2 pair pot clips [hooks]. 3 brazen pot lids. 3 brass pans. 3 iron ladles. A flesh crook. 13 peuther plaits & an eg plaite with a salt [salt-cellar] in it … 2 Ambries with a faulding lang setle [a wooden bench]. A calve [chaff] bed. A feather bouster. 2 pair of bed plaids. Ane old grein rug. A Scots covering unlyned rid & yellow. A seed box with a cover. A chappin knyfe. A timber plait. A kitchin table with a firme [form]. 2 water stoups. Ane backet. 2 clogs. A felling aix. A graiter of whyte iron. 2 frything [frying] pans. 2 branders. A fire shooll. A coall ridle. A hand barrow. 2 large capper kettles. A water stand with 3 iron girrs [hoops], & 2 iron handles. A sloped hand barrell. 4 dozen timber trenshers. A pair of hinging raxes.[12]

Clearly, one or more of the servants slept in the kitchen. Ambries (or aumries or aumbries) were wooden cupboards, sometimes with ventilated doors or sides, for the storage of food and dishes. Kitchen tables were probably made of fir (pine) – as they have been traditionally to the present century – and rarely survive because they were utilitarian items subject to rough treatment. Clogs were protective overshoes for wearing when the floor was wet or for going outside, and would be of wood and metal or of leather. Shetlanders wore imported Dutch clogs made entirely of wood into this century.

84. Illustration by David Allan for *The Gentle Shepherd* by Allan Ramsay, published in Edinburgh in 1788. The freestanding fire grate must be for burning coal since it is raised on feet. Such big round pots were used for Scotch broth or similar stewed dishes. The birds in the roof may include pigeons, or 'doos', as well as chickens.

The gallows with three cruiks was a hinged metal arm for hanging pots or kettles over the fire, and would be in use all the time the fire was burning. Large, round-bellied cooking pots enabled the cook to make stews and broths, or, with skilled management, to heat a variety of separately bagged foods in a common boiling stock. Elizabeth Grant of Rothiemurchus describes this practice in 1804 in the gentrified 'but and ben' of the Duchess of Gordon:

> a kitchen was easily formed out of some of the out offices, and in it, without his battery, without his stove, without his thousand and one assistants and resources, her French cook sent up dinners still talked of by the few remaining partakers. The *entrées* were all prepared in one black pot – a large potato *chaudron*, which he had ingeniously divided within into four compartments by means of two pieces of tin sheet crossed, the only inconvenience of this clever plan being that the company had to put up with all white sauces one day and all brown the next.[13]

Whether or not General Dalyell at The Binns had such a cook, the three brass pans and two frying pans in his kitchen suggest that elaborate dishes could be prepared, and there was clearly adequate provision for roasting meat, fowl, or fish. Coal was used at The Binns, but in houses with a peat fire, the area in and around the chimney would be used for preserving foods by smoking (pl 83).

Other utensils and containers in the kitchen and associated rooms at The Binns were made of pewter and wood. Simple pewter plates and dishes from this time survive in quite large numbers, but wooden trenchers, barrels, buckets, tubs, and measures are less common because they were easily damaged and subsequently thrown out. It seems likely that they would have been little different from those seen in Walter Geikie's drawings of one hundred and fifty years later (see pls 17, 48, 49), and indeed, from items excavated from Iron Age sites in Britain.[14] Bone, horn, and stone items, and brushes and besoms made of twigs and heather have also disappeared. An inventory of 1691 lists a 'birse bissome' and a 'birse switcher for hangings'.[15] Baskets too were common, made of woven willow or bound straw. All would be of pale natural colours and there was little in the kitchen to brighten it.

If any baking was done at The Binns, it must have been in the brewhouse, where an oven and 'peill' (or long-handled shovel) were listed, and a 'baik house table with ane iron skraiper'.[16] Larger households, such as Stirling Castle and Hamilton Palace, had a separate bakehouse producing oatmeal and wheaten rolls, but most people had oatcakes made on a girdle hung over the fire, and bought what leavened bread they could afford if they had a baker nearby. The accounts of the Earl of Angus when in lodgings in Glasgow in 1608 indicate the consumption of bread in prodigious quantities.[17]

Brewing, in contrast, was an essential activity in most households, if only because the available water was not usually fit to drink untreated. Brews of various strengths were often taken in combinations unappealing to modern tastes, such as milk and ale mixed with spices to make 'posset' or 'caudle'. The 1691 inventory of the possessions of an Edinburgh Writer to the Signet (lawyer) mentions 'ane large possett dish of Loame at £1.4.0' – possibly a blue and white tin-glazed pot from England or the Netherlands.[18]

Wine and spirits from France, Germany, and Spain were imported by the wealthy and kept in barrels until transferred to stoneware flasks or the bulbous dark green bottles which came into use around 1650 and by 1750 had slimmed down to the cylindrical shape we know today. Spa water also features in the accounts of Lady Grisell Baillie, perhaps imported in the Rhenish stoneware bottles decorated at the neck with a bearded face (pl 85). An Orkney inventory

85. A stoneware 'gray beard', probably from Frechen, near Köln in Germany, and found in the sea off Eyemouth, Berwickshire. These were imported in the seventeenth and eighteenth centuries.

of 1747 includes in the wine cellar 'four gray beards. one of them with mineral watters'.[19]

The drinks we take for granted today were unknown in Scotland until about the 1680s. Coffee and drinking chocolate arrived via the Netherlands and were in use before tea, which seems to have appeared in the 1690s. In 1702, tea was a novelty even for the wealthy Duchess Anne at Hamilton Palace and in the same year, Lady Grisell Baillie in Edinburgh bought a 'tee pot'.[20] For many decades tea was so expensive that while the water might be boiled on the kitchen fire, the actual preparation of the beverage would be carried out in the parlour or bedroom, and the precious leaves were kept in a locked box.

Food for immediate use was prepared on the kitchen table but anything requiring cooler conditions, such as dairy products, would have a separate area. In country places, much of the dairy work of making butter and cheeses was carried out in summer shielings (see p38).

Working in the kitchen in the seventeenth and early eighteenth centuries was not easy. The fire was often smoky and difficult to control and the dinner was in danger from falls of soot. Water usually had to be carried in from outside, soap and other cleaning aids were made at home, and the largest households were very large indeed, requiring enormous quantities of food. This may be one reason why dinner consisted of few courses with a wide range of dishes, since it must have been difficult to time things to be ready exactly. Cooks employed by Lady Grisell Baillie between 1715 and 1718 rarely stayed longer than two months, though it is not known whether this was because of their inadequacies or the demanding nature of their employer.[21] Cooking was clearly a skilled job, and cooks who stayed were well paid.

Lady Grisell Baillie's 'Derections for the House Keeper' written in 1743 indicate how much activity was going on in the domestic offices, and Elizabeth Grant of Rothiemurchus in her *Memoirs* describes the work of a 'busy guid-wife' some sixty years later:

> such spinnings, and weavings, and washings, and dyings, and churnings, and yearnings, and knittings, and bleachings, and candle makings, and soap boilings, and brewings, and feather cleanings, never were seen or written of even in these days.'[22]

It was the task of Lady Grisell's housekeeper to keep the maids 'at their spinning till 9 at night when they are not washing or at other necessary work', and 'the dairy maid, house maid and kitchin maid always to spine when they are not otherways necessarily imployd which they will often pretend to be if they are not diligently lookt after and keep to it.'[23] Spinning wheels must have been kept in or near the kitchen (preferably near a window) for such times. The making of cloth was of great importance in the home and Lady Grisell's instructions on keeping the cleaning clouts well wrung out to prevent them rotting are perhaps a reminder of the preciousness of textiles at this time. Chemical cleaning agents make it easier to avoid fetid floorcloths today.

Cloth was not the only thing kept with care. Numerous inventories list items which were broken or repaired, but still in service.[24] Metal pots were mended by local blacksmiths or travelling 'tinkers', whose name came from the 'tink' of the hammer on metal. More precious items of silver or glass were kept in cupboards in or near the kitchen in small houses, or in the 'womanhouse' or servants' hall of larger ones, and were carefully counted back in after use. Household goods were relatively more expensive than today and more difficult to acquire, so they were carefully preserved.

86. Bottling in the cellar, a sketch by John Harden, 1804. Wine is being transferred from the wooden barrel to dark green glass bottles.

Reading Lady Grisell Baillie's detailed accounts, which include payments to servants of different status, her directions to the housekeeper and butler, and her recipes and menus, one gets a feel for the complexities of running a large household in the early eighteenth century and the management skills involved. In smaller houses with fewer staff the job appears less demanding, but a good housekeeper (whether paid or the mistress of the house) could make the difference between comfort and mere survival.[25]

In the houses of minor lairds or wealthy merchants, in country or in town, a common arrangement was for the kitchen and parlour or business room to be sited on the ground floor, with the dining room and bedroom upstairs. As the eighteenth century progressed, however, people of the middle ranks were able to afford houses with more rooms. In Edinburgh's New Town there was no need to squeeze into a small space. Within the uniform terraces was a range of options – flats off communal stairs or complete houses on three or four floors

87. A page from an inventory of 1807, giving a fairly standard list of the items found in the kitchen at this date. The house belonged to an Edinburgh textile merchant and manufacturer and had, in addition to the kitchen, a parlour, two bedrooms, dining room, and closet.

– all with a separate kitchen and usually a dining room or parlour and a drawing room for entertaining.

The development of the New Town coincided with changes in technology and production in Scotland, given impetus by the amount of competitive new building that was going on. Manufacturers in the Falkirk area made new types of kitchen grate. These had cast-iron panels on either side of the fire basket, providing convenient resting places for kettles and pots. They appear frequently in the inventories of bankrupts, indicating that they were the property of the tenant and not of the landlord of the building. By the 1780s, inventories often listed 'grate' rather than the earlier term 'chimney' (meaning hearth rather than the ventilation shaft). This suggests a rapid spread of cast-iron products, but not enough inventories have been sampled to allow firm conclusions.

Although the fittings of the National Trust's Georgian House kitchen in Charlotte Square came from elsewhere and the room is displayed to show the maximum amount of equipment rather than exactly how it would have looked in use, it does indicate the spaciousness of New Town basements and the division into separate areas for different purposes. Such changes took place in all of Scotland's cities and must also have affected the planned towns and villages built in the late eighteenth and early nineteenth centuries.

Apart from the fireplace, it would seem from inventories that there was little change in the basic kitchen equipment in the eighteenth century from that in the 1653 and 1685 lists quoted above (pp86–7). The hinged crane remained to support kettle and pot, and a pair of tongs was kept nearby for rearranging the coals. An increasing number of roasting jacks for turning meat above or in front of the fire make their appearance in more modest houses of the eighteenth century.[26] Unfortunately there is very little visual evidence to go on. Painters such as David Allan or Alexander Carse depicted scenes in rural cottages, but town and city kitchens do not seem to have interested artists – they were evidently unsuitable backdrops to scenes from poems by Burns. In addition, the fittings of kitchens wore out more quickly than those in other parts of the house or were replaced with newer technology, and it is difficult to know exactly what eighteenth-century kitchens looked like – or whether there was much difference between Scotland and England, where more images survive.

In new houses, kitchens were probably neatly built with plastered walls and stone floors[27] and their cleanliness depended on the diligence of the householder. Older properties must have been almost impossible to keep clean. Elizabeth Grant, describing her family home in the Highlands as it was around 1800 (a house with a state bedroom with green silk damask bed), mentions that 'A kitchen built of black turf was patched on to one end'.[28] Changes made in 1803 included its demolition, 'much to the satisfaction of my Mother and Mrs Lynch, who declared no decent dinner could by possibility be dressed in it. It was indeed a rude apology for a set of kitchen offices. A mouse one day fell into the soup from the open rafters, a sample merely of an hundred such accidents.'[29] A further step towards making the place fit for a gentleman was the removal in 1808 of the poultry house and washing shed with all its 'pots, tubs, baskets and kettles'.[30] A few years later, it was the fashion of the day to move the fruit and vegetables to 'an inconvenient distance from the Cook, the kitchen department of the garden being considered the reverse of ornamental.'[31]

There is more evidence on kitchens from the beginning of the nineteenth century in several paintings of household servants which include glimpses of furniture and useful articles (pl 89). Walter Geikie's drawings of small houses give a good idea of the general contents of the room in the 1820s and 1830s

88. Detail of *The New Web* by Alexander Carse, 1813. The fire basket is placed within a chimneypiece as an improvement on the arrangement seen in the David Allan drawing of twenty-five years earlier (pl 84), but the cooking is still done in a single pot. On the floor is a flat iron, which must be connected with the part of the painting omitted from this detail, where a tailor is cutting cloth.

89. *Servants at Dalkeith House* by John Ainslie, 1832. A variety of wooden and wicker wares can be seen here in what appears to be a vaulted room, probably in a basement.

(pls 17, 48, 49) and inventories of larger houses of three or four rooms include very similar goods. Items most commonly listed were of brass, copper, tin, cast metal, and wood, so the colouring in the kitchen was still muted, though brighter pottery and stoneware was becoming available from early in the century. Apart from the expected kitchen chairs, fir tables, servants' beds and bedding, and frequent mention of 'wheel and reel', there is also the occasional bird cage, and now and again, a 'fowling piece' or a sword.[32] The financial value of kitchen contents was always low in comparison with other rooms.

Goods which begin to appear in the kitchen include 'smoke' and 'bottle' jacks (devices for turning meat while it roasts), and increasingly from the 1830s, 'grate with oven'.[33] An object mentioned frequently in Scottish inventories is the 'bachelor's oven', which must have been a roasting screen of sheet metal, sometimes listed simply as 'tin oven'.[34] This could be placed in front of the flames with food inside it for cooking. Kitchen grates were becoming more complex, combining the open fire with water-boiling containers and ovens which had new methods of distributing heat more evenly. As entertaining at home was increasingly used by middle-class merchants for business purposes, there must have been added demand from cooks for suitable facilities. Alternatively, the fact that cooking was easier to control may have influenced this fashion for inviting dinner guests and providing more elaborate meals.

Improvements to kitchen ranges took place slowly from around 1800 following ideas put forward by Benjamin Thompson, 'Count Rumford', an American inventor who found that fires draw better with narrower chimneys and cooking ranges are more efficient if the fire is enclosed.

A fine example of a kitchen with a wide selection of the equipment available when it was fitted up in the 1820s is at Callendar House in Falkirk. Here, in a double-height space designed to disperse the heat, a large open fireplace has huge spits before it, turned by a smoke jack in the chimney: vanes inside the chimney were moved by the updraught and rotated the spit by means of pulleys and chains. A movable screen for warming plates can be shunted in front of the open flames when required. One wall has a built-in bread oven and a hot plate

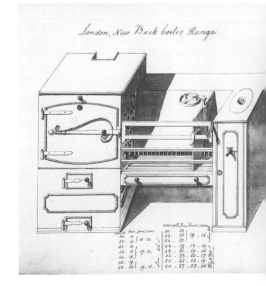

90. The Carron Company in Falkirk must have supplied countless builders with cast-iron ranges, but this appears to be the only early design in the firm's drawing books at the Scottish Record Office. It dates from 1820–40 and has an oven on the left and a water heater with a tap on the right.

91. Kitchen at Callendar House, Falkirk, a fine example of a country-house kitchen from the first half of the nineteenth century, now open to the public. Experiments with candles in the lamps shown here on the walls to left and right have proved how difficult it is to get enough light for working.

for keeping finished dishes, while the opposite, window wall has a cast–iron bench range eight and a half feet long. Originally half this size, it was extended in the 1840s when gas was introduced to the house for cooking, and bears the mark of Gray & Son, Makers, Edinburgh. The long wooden bench next to the stove was probably originally longer and cut down when the gas was installed.[35] In the centre stands a table of pine, on which the cook prepared the food, and shelves have been reinstated on the walls where it is presumed they were formerly. All the washing of kitchen dishes was done in a scullery next door. Such a kitchen might have been a pleasant place to work when the conditions were right, but could be filled with smoke if the wind was in the wrong direction. It was probably too hot in the summer and dark in the winter, in spite of new forms of colza oil lamps developed in the 1780s and the increasing use of gas lighting in Scottish houses from the 1820s. The dinner hour was getting later by this date, perhaps partly because these new sources of illumination made it feasible to cook and eat without daylight.

Few homes were of the size of Callendar House, but in the nineteenth century vast wealth was spent on building rambling country houses which could only be run by large numbers of servants. Fasque, in Fettercairn, for instance, altered by John Gladstone from 1829 onwards, had a spacious kitchen, sculleries, larders, still rooms, housekeeper's room, butler's pantry, servants' hall, dairies, laundry, washroom, boot and knife room, lamp and oil rooms, and bakery. Until 1914, at least fifteen servants were employed. Similarly, at

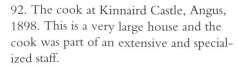

92. The cook at Kinnaird Castle, Angus, 1898. This is a very large house and the cook was part of an extensive and specialized staff.

93. A laundrymaid at Kinnaird, from the same album of photographs. Ironing must have been one of the most unpleasant household tasks at this time, with no temperature controls on the irons and lots of frilled petticoats and nightgowns to deal with, as well as tablecloths and linen towels.

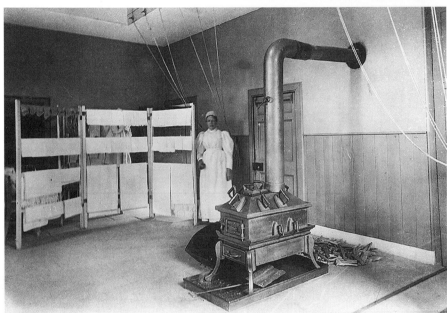

Kinnaird Castle in Angus, a large kitchen was supported by ancillary rooms, including an impressive laundry depicted in a photograph of 1898 (pl 93).

These kitchens and 'offices' were normally sited to face north or east to be cool, or around a courtyard. They occupied space that was unsuited to reception rooms and were out of sight of polite company, continuing the process of 'improvement' noted by Elizabeth Grant early in the nineteenth century, banishing the practical functions of the house backstage. Robert Kerr, a Scottish architect of great influence through his numerous books and articles, had this to say in 1873:

> the offices as a whole ought to be kept strictly separate from the family part of the house. This is one of the most conspicuous characteristics of a well-planned house for the residence of well-bred people – the sight, sound, and, we must add, smell of the servants' working apartments are perfectly shut out. It does not follow that the mistress of the house is to sacrifice one whit of her personal supervision; but when she crosses the boundary she shuts the door.[36]

The desire to prevent cooking smells pervading the reception rooms meant that the kitchen was often a long way from the dining room.[37]

In the 'gentleman's house', the rooms of male and female servants were well segregated and the housekeeper's room was placed so that she could keep an eye on the staff, while the butler's pantry was usually where he could see anyone approaching the house. This was the age of Isabella Beeton and rules of domestic management, and numerous publications explained the rationale behind such arrangements.

After the First World War few such houses were built because they were no longer economic, but in their heyday at the turn of the century, they were very grand indeed. Some architects, such as Robert Lorimer, gave particular attention to domestic arrangements, providing well-planned suites of rooms fitted with the best modern equipment. At Hill of Tarvit in Fife, for instance, the separate laundry had the type of heated rolling racks also found in public washhouses of this date. The kitchen here and in other Lorimer houses, such as Monzie in Perthshire and Ardkinglas, Argyllshire, is built of glazed bricks, as is the palatial kitchen of 1901–5 at Manderston in Berwickshire.[38] Ardkinglas and Manderston were both supplied with electric power, and a freestanding imported French range at Manderston must have been the height of luxury. The gothic vaults and marble columns in the dairy at Manderston also reflected the extravagant fancy of such a house.[39] Picturesque dairies were more often shown to visitors than utilitarian kitchens, though Susan Ferrier in *The Inheritance* of 1824 mentions a tour around a castle to see the 'Dutch tiles of the dairy, the hot and cold pipes of the washing-house, the new invented ovens, the admirably-constructed larder, the inimitable baths, with all the wonder-working, steam-going apparatus of the kitchen.'[40]

Smaller houses did not have the range of rooms dedicated to single functions, nor the large and expensive fittings, but their inhabitants shared the architects' growing interest in hygiene in the kitchen. 'Sanitary' wallpapers with a glazed wipeable surface provided a cheap alternative to ceramic tiles and a range of tiled patterns was available, suitable for kitchen or bathroom.[41]

94. Absorbed in his Meccano, this unknown boy sits in a Paisley kitchen in 1927. Behind him is a tile-effect wallpaper of the kind that was very popular in kitchens. On the range, which probably dates from around 1900, are three kettles of water, keeping warm for when they are wanted.

95. Cooking 'puddens', made of sheep's intestines with various fillings, on a stove in Shetland in the 1930s. One-pot cooking remained popular in country areas into the twentieth century.

96. Rose Brown in a Shetland kitchen in 1915. The dresser is of a Lowland type, imported by a retailer or purchased direct by mail order, and the jars on the left appear to be of Keiller's marmalade.

Tile-effect wallpapers appear frequently in photographs of Scottish kitchens in the twentieth century (pl 94), but it is also clear that kitchens were often plain (pl 97).

The central feature continued to be the range, fuelled by coal in most parts of the Lowlands and in coastal areas. Peat-fired stoves were also made and the portable 'Scotch' stove became a feature of manufacturers' catalogues in the nineteenth century and was widely used in the country. Gas cooking stoves were installed in the Edinburgh house of Sir John Robison in the late 1830s as a result of his passion for technology and ventilation, but these were very unusual, and must have been specially made.[42] Gas was not promoted as a fuel for a mass market until the 1880s, and was not in widespread use for cooking until early in the twentieth century. A Carron Company catalogue of 1892 includes some gas-fired ranges and a few models which used both gas and coal, but most of the products were open or closed coal-fired ranges. By 1906, a similar catalogue illustrates mainly closed ranges, in which the fire was contained within the iron casing.[43]

Furniture and fittings were usually of deal, often painted to match the walls. An inventory of 1891 details the contents of Burnside, Auchtermuchty, in Fife, the eleven-roomed house of Mrs Bonthrone, and the list of kitchen equipment is very brief:[44]

Kitchen	
Cooking Stove and Copper	1.12.6
Three Chairs @ 1/-	-.3.-
Two Tables @ 2/-	-.4.-
Dresser	-.4.6
Crockery &c. on Shelves	-.5.6
Three Dish Covers	-.8.6
Sundries	
Electro Plated Tea Service	2.7.6
Do Cake Basket	1.5.-
Toast Rack	-.2.-
4 Decanter Stands at 2/-	-.8.-
peuter Tea pot	-.3.6
Five Cut Decanters @ 2/-	-.10.-

Presumably the kitchen stove was not the latest model since its value is less than a sewing machine in a nearby room and not much more than the silver-plated cake basket.

Within the kitchen, the arrangement of furniture must have varied from house to house, but in Glasgow tenements and probably in flats elsewhere, there was virtually a standard layout, conforming to that described above in very small dwellings (pp66–7). By the late nineteenth century, many of the smaller items found in the kitchen – crockery, cooking tools, cleaning supplies, and popular foods – were mass-produced and sometimes colourfully packaged. Staple foods and drinks were usually bought from local grocers or manufacturers, often in containers of glass or stoneware marked with the local producer's name. Alternatively, especially in maritime areas, these bottles and jars might contain commodities brought into Leith or Glasgow, packaged there by grocers in the vicinity of the port, and then sent out to other parts of the country. The Bod of Gremista Museum in Lerwick, Shetland, for instance, contains a number of marked Leith-bought stoneware jars.

A rare photograph from the beginning of the twentieth century, taken at 16 Leamington Terrace in Edinburgh, shows a rather bare room with few such

97. Mrs Mather in the kitchen at 16 Leamington Terrace, Edinburgh, about 1900, apparently preparing tea. Since they were at the back of the house and at ground level, kitchens often had bars on the windows, adding to the bleakness of the surroundings.

goods. It would appear from her clothing that the figure in the photograph was Mrs Eva Mather, who lived here with her husband and seven children. The family's two live-in employees at the 1891 census were a nurse and a general servant, so Mrs Mather may have had a cook who came in daily or possibly did most of the cooking herself. Most middle-class houses and flats at this time still had a small room near the kitchen in which the maid slept. Often this would be simply a recess in the kitchen itself with a bed built in. These are now described by estate agents as 'dining recess' or 'breakfast area', since they are just big enough for a small table and benches.

Although concern was expressed from the turn of the century about a shortage of reliable servants, census figures show that in Scotland domestic service remained a large employer of women until the Second World War. The percentage of women in service went up in the 1930s and even people who lived in small bungalows were able to afford a maid of all work, who might no longer live in.[45] Few people, however, could retain the armies of staff required to keep up the old style of upper- and middle-class living, and emphasis in advice books on architecture and decoration was on how to save unnecessary labour by arranging the kitchen in a more practical way. Most of the early ideas on planning the kitchen to avoid unnecessary walking across wide spaces came from America.[46] A transatlantic influence can be traced in the fitted kitchen of Gribloch at Kippen in Stirlingshire, a house built by Basil Spence in 1938–9. This modernist country house commissioned by John and Helen Colville was, according to a 1951 article in *Country Life*, 'a brilliant example of the fruitful pooling of ideas between clients and architect'.[47] Mrs Colville was American and expected a labour-saving kitchen, even though the house was planned for a staff of at least five servants. During the 'servantless years of the war' the family found the tiny kitchenette next to the dining room invaluable.[48]

The kitchen itself was a substantial space with cabinets built in by a local joiner and large metal windows, giving a light and airy atmosphere. A solid Esse stove from the Falkirk company of Smith & Wellstood had an extractor above, and the floor and work surfaces were covered with lino, presumably from Kirkcaldy. The only decoration was in the delicately patterned curtains, perhaps made of the oiled silk which appears in books of the period as suitable

98. The kitchen at Gribloch, Stirlingshire, 1938, as published by *Country Life*. With its cream-painted cupboards and red lino floor and work surfaces, this must have been warmer-looking than it appears in a black and white photograph. The adjacent pantry was cream and green.

for kitchens. Was the room always as pristine as it appeared in *Country Life*? With so many cupboards, everything seems to have had its place.

Next door was the pantry, in which were a silver safe, warming cupboard, sinks and dishwasher, and a dumb waiter to the floor above to serve the nursery and bedrooms. Nearby were two stores, a game larder, the laundry, a staff hall, and the Butler's room, though it seems that there never was a butler after the war.[49]

Unusually, the kitchen was at the front of the house where it could be seen by approaching visitors, and it has a wonderful view. This was partly because the front is on the cool north side, but perhaps also indicates changes in the early twentieth century. As books and magazines spread the notion that the 'servant problem' was worsening, architects and employers felt the need to improve conditions for domestic workers to attract and keep them, especially in houses like this in the country. 'Maids' rooms' became slightly more spacious than hitherto, and advertisers played on the idea that servants would be more likely to stay if they were given labour-saving equipment to assist their work.[50] There was also an increasing emphasis in advertisements, and in the papers and journals that carried them, on middle-class women doing more household work themselves and taking pride in it.

One way of persuading women to accept their role in the kitchen, especially just after wartime when many had acquired a taste for work outside the home, was to emphasize the importance of hygiene and the woman's responsibility for her family's health. While this was connected with advances in knowledge about germs and bacteria, it arose initially from concerns at the start of the century about the health of men available to the army for the Boer War, and resulted in numerous classes to teach domestic science and parentcraft to girls. By the 1920s and 1930s, such ideas were well established. The ideal of the small, separate, and spotlessly clean kitchen reflected society's need to coax women out of the drawing room into the kitchen, attaching more status to the kitchen by connecting it with modernity.

Gribloch's kitchen fittings represent an extreme of design in the 1930s, specially made as in other architect-designed houses, and there can have been very few kitchens in Scotland of this type. At Dean Castle in Kilmarnock, for instance, expensively renovated in the early 1930s, the kitchen fittings were modern versions of traditional equipment, in contrast with the sleek new approach at Gribloch. Most people in smaller houses would still be using the stone sink under the window with a wooden draining board (as at Dean Castle),

99. Mrs Irene Daniels toiling over the washtub in the kitchen of her house in Partick, probably 1940s. The washing behind her is hanging from a line stretched above the mantelpiece. For another view of this kitchen see pl 63.

100. *Opposite:* Triplex grates were advertised in Dundee at least as early as 1936 but were clearly still regarded as the modern alternative to the range nearly twenty years later when Dudley Watkins drew this 'Broons' cartoon for the Dundee-based paper *The Sunday Post* in 1954.

For cosy, comfy, couthie heatin'—the auld-style range just can't be beaten !

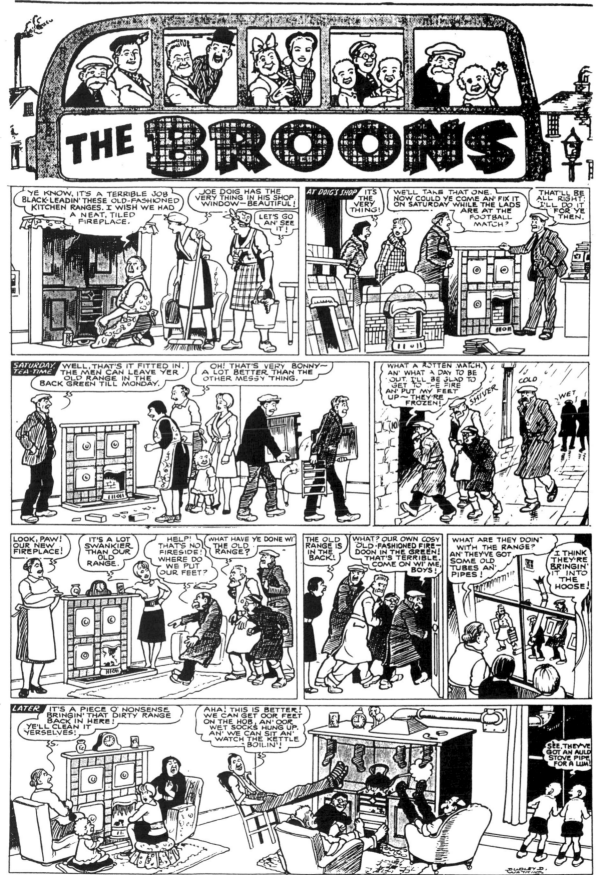

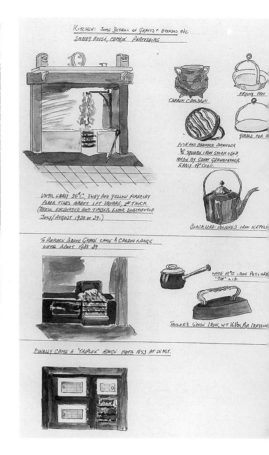

101. *Above:* Sketches of changes to Smiddy House in Comrie, Perthshire, painted in 1992 by Mr James Hardie, who had lived there.

102. Thomas Justice of Dundee was selling a version of a kitchen cabinet in 1913. This 1927 advertisement was clearly aiming upmarket. It is rather unusual to have a man depicted in the kitchen at all, let alone in a dinner jacket.

the pine kitchen table, and the wall–mounted shelves. One innovation of the period (familiar to anyone who has lived in a bedsit or shared flat) was the freestanding kitchen cabinet with storage cupboards for food and a flap which can be lowered to provide a working surface. But it was the range which was the most likely piece of kitchen equipment to be replaced, and by the 1920s there was more choice. A 'Triplex' range might be fitted (pls 100, 101), occupying the chimney space of the old-style open range and using fuel more

103. A 'pre-fab' kitchen in Edinburgh, 1940s. The design of compact units to fit into a small space influenced post-war kitchens in Britain.

104. Another view of the same kitchen, leading into a corridor with a hanging washing line and a foldaway ironing board. It was more usual for council houses of the 1930s to have a gas cooker and there must have been some reason for installing the coal-fired range here.

efficiently, but it was also now possible to have a freestanding cooker heated by gas or electricity. Thermostatic controls were introduced on gas cookers in 1922 and on electric ovens in 1931. Before this, such cookers must have been almost as complicated to control as the ranges they replaced, and baking in particular was clearly skilled work.

An additional force for change in the Scottish kitchen in the 1920s and 1930s was the extensive programme of council-house building as a result of the 1917 Royal Commission report on the housing of the 'industrial' population of Scotland. Gradually as more houses and flats were built the majority of the population could expect a kitchen separate from the living and bed rooms. Although early plans for council houses show fairly large living rooms with substantial fireplaces containing ranges and a small scullery for wet tasks, the fact that the scullery often housed a gas cooker (sometimes on hire from the local council) points to a change. While the living room was still used for eating and other family activities, the cooking was increasingly done in the small space which became known as the 'kitchenette'. During and after the Second World War, the development of compact kitchens for 'pre-fabs' also had an influence on what people expected.

Recent books on the history of housework and domestic design have shown that for middle-class women in the twentieth century the idea of labour-saving devices and the easily run 'servantless house' was an illusion, and the 'housewife' had to take on a wider range of activities.[51] For working-class women, however, the fact of a separate space for food preparation, cooking and washing, apart from the living room in which all other family activities took place, must have made a different kind of change. Did it alter feelings about the home?

Although women are still expected to take general responsibility for the family diet and health, the kitchen has changed again in its layout and decoration in the past thirty years, returning more to the idea of the family living room than the austere workplace (though there is the choice between 'farmhouse style' and 'the appliance of science'). Apart from the obvious influences on design of nationally available magazines, shops such as Habitat and IKEA, and depictions on television, this must be related to women's changing role in the workplace and their expectation of more domestic responsibility from men. If women are no longer accepting the part of sole guardian of the family's health and provider of meals, the kitchen as separate female space is no longer appropriate. It is notable that men are more likely to share food shopping and cooking than cleaning, so the kitchen has become more of a focus for family life. It now often houses a television, telephone, and the paraphernalia associated with pets, as well as the expected kitchen goods.

In addition, the dining area which in the 1950s and 1960s was often a screened part of the living room, is now frequently a semi-separate area of the kitchen, indicating a more casual attitude to family meals and entertaining. How much is this the result of improved steam- and smell-extracting equipment, and how much the consequence of an appreciation of the aesthetic qualities of useful kitchen goods (along with the money to buy things which are not strictly utilitarian)?

It is extremely difficult to know how eagerly innovations in domestic technology and design were embraced in Scotland in the twentieth century, since statistics on the consumption of household goods are difficult to track down. Occasionally 'time-capsule' kitchens with all their fascinating original equipment are discovered, but from magazines and trade catalogues and from observation in people's homes, it is clear that gradual changes have taken place similar to those seen in Britain as a whole. Fitted units with wipeable surfaces in new, colourful materials such as Formica became more usual from the 1950s and almost universal by the 1980s. Linoleum has given way to vinyl floorings, and Kirkcaldy's extensive factories have contracted in size, though both lino and vinyl continue to be made in the town. Stoneware sinks have been replaced by enamelled metal or stainless steel, and more recently, plastics. And cookers have changed from heavy cast-iron equipment with dark mottled enamelling to much lighter, usually white, supposedly easy to clean models, or built-in ovens and separate hobs, tied into a fitted system. Food is rarely packaged by local grocers but is processed in bulk and distributed to national networks of shops; and microwave ovens have encouraged the purchase of ready-made dishes. Refrigerators became much more common after the Second World War and by 1969 nearly half of Scottish households had one.[52] At the same date, nearly two-thirds had a washing machine, a figure which increased to 90 per cent by 1994.[53]

Study of the subject is at an early stage, however, and no-one has yet, it seems, done any research along the lines of, for instance, work in Canada to discover why Canadians preferred twin-tub washing machines when Americans had turned to automatics.[54] Are there different patterns of ownership in Scotland in comparison with England or Ireland? Does the high incidence of washing machines reflect the large percentage of Scots living in urban flats? Do Scottish householders buy the same designs of kitchen as their European neighbours now that much fitted furniture is imported from Germany, or do they favour certain types? How many Scots still eat porridge? Does anything Scottish remain in the Scottish kitchen?

5 The Hall and Lobby

DAVID JONES

'We usually found many people in the hall when we came in for breakfast, tapping the barometer or looking out through the glass doors at their other barometer, the Black Isle, seven miles away.'

David Thomson, 1987[1]

Perhaps the most public space in the Scottish home, the lobby or entrance hall is frequently the only room to be seen regularly by casual visitors or passers-by. It is the link between interior and exterior and forms an introduction to the rest of the house.

The hall and lobby were once rooms of quite discrete function. In Scotland, as in the United States, 'lobby' has come to be the generally accepted term for a ground-floor reception room entered either through an outer vestibule or directly through the front door. The predominance in Scotland of this name is indicated by the influential anonymous Scottish architectural pattern book *The Rudiments of Architecture* of 1773, which includes 'lobby' but not 'hall' in its 'Builder's Dictionary' appendix. It equates lobby with 'antichamber', defined as 'an outer, or fore-chamber; a room in noblemen's houses where strangers stay till such time as the party to be spoken with is at leisure.'[2] Robert and James Adam, in their *Works in Architecture*, published between 1773 and 1822, concern themselves chiefly with their designs executed in England, in which they use the term 'hall', but it is interesting to note that the familiar 'lobby' appears in the details of such Scottish commissions as the Professor's apartments in the new college buildings at Edinburgh University.[3]

To take the late seventeenth-century Scottish country house as a starting point, the lobby first appears as a central feature of the new symmetrically planned mansion houses introduced on a significant scale in Scotland by the architects Sir William Bruce and James Smith in their designs of the 1670s and 1680s (pl 106). This new sense of order represented a departure from the marked irregularity of castles and tower houses. It was ultimately derived from the Roman ideal of harmonic, balanced proportion in housebuilding and the subsequent interpretation of Roman ideas by architects such as Andrea Palladio in sixteenth-century Italy. The lobby was of great importance in this plan, being the first and central room of the house. It was, as the Adam brothers later described, 'a spacious apartment, intended as the room of access where servants in livery attend'.[4] The fashion was eventually to filter down the architectural scale to smaller houses in cities and country towns. It was also translated to upper floors in the flatted tenements of larger cities.

The term 'hall' is of much older pedigree in Scotland, referring originally to a principal living chamber, usually found on the second floor of castles and tower houses built before the later sixteenth century, and then situated, English-fashion, on the ground floor in some houses of this type built in the

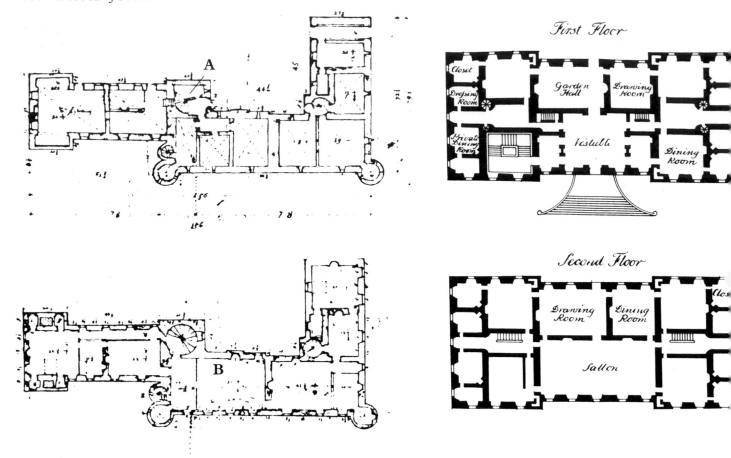

later sixteenth and the seventeenth centuries. Although the vogue for ground-floor halls emerged at this early date – there is a sixteenth-century example, for instance, at Huntingtower in Perthshire – the Scottish tradition of the second-floor hall continued throughout the seventeenth century. Kinnaird in Angus, surveyed with a view to modernizing the plan in 1697 (pl 105), had what was a fairly typical arrangement of vaulted basement below a Great Hall on the second floor with a screens passage at one end where the servants waited during service of the meal. The hall was used as a communal dining room for the owners, their guests, and retainers. There was no formal entrance lobby to the house, which was entered via a small compartment housing a turnpike (spiral) stair, leading in turn to a sequence of larger rooms.

The custom of upper-floor living survived in the new houses built on the classical plan, in which the principal living rooms were invariably on this storey, and this arrangement persisted into the twentieth century in larger urban houses; but the idea of an upstairs living room called a Great Hall did not enjoy such continuity. Living in the classically planned house was less communal, and mixing of the social classes was restricted to the downstairs lobby. Strangers were received here and the private areas of the house were clearly sealed off by a series of doors.

One of the few seventeenth-century houses for which it is possible to analyse the original architectural drawings in conjunction with early inventories of the household contents is Panmure in Angus (built from about 1666 and now demolished). The plan gives evidence of changes in ideas: the principal and central chamber on the first floor (raised ground storey) was a dining room, in effect serving the purpose of an English 'great hall'. There was what approximated to a formal entrance lobby between dining room and front door, but this

105. *Left:* Details from a survey plan of Kinnaird Castle, Angus, by Alexander Edward, 1697. The visitor would have entered directly into a small compartment on the ground floor containing a staircase (A) and then proceeded to the next storey, where the Great Hall (B) could be entered. There was no ground-floor lobby or vestibule.

106. *Right:* Plan of Kinross House by Sir William Bruce, 1694, as illustrated in *Vitruvius Scoticus*. Here the visitor entered a small porch and then a great lobby or 'vestibule'. To the left was a waiting room and then a great stair to the next floor.

space was simply described as a 'vestibule'. It was furnished with a large oak table, a clock in a painted case, two other tables, and four chairs. The room described in the 1695 inventory of the house as 'the lobby' was in fact a small space in between the dining room and the staircase chamber. On the upper storey, or 'principal floor' there was another, even larger, eating room called the 'Great High Dinning Roume', which again recalled the function of a great hall, but this time in the old Scottish tradition because it was situated on an upper storey. It was entered through a 'high lobbie' which opened off the staircase from the floor below, and was furnished with 'a wanescott chist of Drawers, a large oak square folding table, three litle carpet work chairs wt. green baiz covers.'[5] This furniture does not appear to have been made specifically for the lobby and may have been less formal than that in the vestibule. It could have been brought in from elsewhere in the house: the drawing room, for example, contained seventeen carpet-work chairs with green baize covers, which suggests that those in the lobby might be from a set of twenty.

It is interesting to observe the transition between the disappearance of the great hall and the emergence of the lobby in the groundplans of the earliest classical country houses. For instance, several of James Smith's designs of the 1690s - for Craigiehall, West Lothian; Raith in Fife; and Newhailes, Midlothian - have turnpike stairs which look as if they should lead up to a great hall as they would in an older house; but these stairs are squeezed in to the right of a formal lobby space with doors leading off to the main rooms. Smith's later designs experiment with larger central staircases and associated lobbies.[6]

Undoubtedly the most magnificent country-house lobby of its period is the architect William Adam's showpiece, designed in 1726, at Arniston, Midlothian (pl 108). This double-height chamber is of great size (partly because it occupied the position of an open courtyard of a previous house on the site), and it was intended as the impressive starting point of a formal sequence of rooms culminating in the State Bedroom. In what was known as the 'state apartment', the lobby assumed a new importance in the early eighteenth-century country house as the grand entrance to a processional route which led through the relatively public dining room to the successively more private withdrawing room, bedchamber, and closet.

Appropriately, the lobby at Arniston is richly styled as a rectangular atrium with an upper gallery around three sides. Giant Corinthian pilasters support groin vaults and a framed ceiling panel. The plasterwork, an exuberant composition of scrolling foliage, birds, and fruit, is by Joseph Enzer, a stuccoist employed by Adam at various important commissions, including Yester in East Lothian and House of Dun in Angus (pl 133).

The lobby at Arniston is well documented and thus provides an excellent example of a combination of different named craftsmen's achievements in stucco decoration, smith work, and furniture. Apart from the plasterwork by Enzer, who was working at the house between about 1730 and 1735, accounts survive for 'chimney furniture' (grate and fire irons) and for a 'Mahogany Clock Case carved and guilt' (sic) supplied in 1738 by the fashionable Edinburgh cabinetmaker Francis Brodie.[7] This clockcase (pl 107), which echoes the arcaded design of the architecture of the room and is fitted into the balustrading of the upper gallery, is the single surviving piece of documented lobby furniture by Brodie. Lobby clocks are known in other William Adam houses and remained after this period as a standard feature, most commonly as longcase or table clocks with eight-day movements. The lobby was the obvious place for

107. Mahogany clock case 'carved and guilt', supplied for the lobby at Arniston House, Midlothian, by Francis Brodie in 1738. The case, arcaded to echo the classical architecture of the room, houses a sixteenth-century movement from the old house on this site. Francis Brodie was the leading Edinburgh cabinetmaker of this period.

108. Entrance hall at Arniston, designed by William Adam in 1726, a particularly lavish example of a central lobby in a newly-built great house, marking the beginning of a sequence of state rooms.

a clock because it could easily be seen by all in the household (few of whom would have personal watches until the early twentieth century) and could conveniently be consulted by those entering and leaving the house. By the late eighteenth century, most country towns had an established watchmaker who as well as making timepieces might make barometers, which were also hung in lobbies, again for obvious practical reasons. They not only provided information useful to anyone leaving the house, but fitted neatly in the often narrow wall spaces left between the doors to different rooms.

Although proper specifications for lobby furniture were not printed until the first Scottish cabinetmakers' price book appeared in 1805,[8] formal suites of unupholstered chairs with solid mahogany seats and backs decorated with family coat of arms and motto appeared in regular use in the 1750s. Among the best-documented examples of the period are the '8 mahogany chairs' which were supplied at £1 10s 0d (£1.50) each to the Earl of Dumfries by the Edinburgh cabinetmaker, Alexander Peter, in July 1759. These survive in the lobby of Dumfries House in Ayrshire.[9]

An adventurous type of lobby furniture which gained popularity during the eighteenth century was that which could be employed both inside or outside in the policies or gardens of a house, emphasizing the role of the lobby as an 'inside-outside' space. Pairs of wooden settees were used for this purpose.

109. Wooden settee with a 'gothick' fretted back, one of a pair at Hopetoun House, West Lothian. They are attributed to the Edinburgh Upholstery Company, 1755–9, and were originally painted white.

Examples of these survive at Hopetoun House, West Lothian (pl 109), and can be attributed to the Edinburgh Upholstery Company, a co-operative partnership of cabinetmakers who provided a large stock of fashionable furniture from their warehouse at Carrubber's Close, High Street, between 1754 and 1759. A Hopetoun inventory of 1768 records in the lobby:

> 2 large marble tables in mahogany frames
> 2 white painted wooden settees
> 4 chairs of ditto
> 2 hair matts
> 2 straw matts[10]

It also mentions '16 pictures panell'd in, 8 bas relievos ditto and over 30 marble busts and statues on pedestals etc'. Since a favoured decoration for the walls in a hall at this time was stone-coloured paint with lines to imitate ashlar (fine-cut rectangular building blocks), the 'inside-outside' nature of the space would be further emphasized and the effect of the room with the white furniture and sculptures would be striking.

In what was a large room, the Hopetoun inventory lists a typically spartan selection of furniture for an eighteenth-century country house of this type, especially since the seat furniture was probably moved in and out according to the season. The tradition of wooden settees which could be carried outside seems to have continued into the nineteenth century. An Arniston inventory of 1850 mentions a 'large spar bottomed [planked] seat' in the lobby and a subsequent undated inventory records this same seat placed outside the door.[11]

Stick-back or 'Windsor' chairs also played this peripatetic role. Johann Zoffany's conversation-piece portrait of *William Ferguson introduced as heir to Raith* of 1769, set in the parkland surrounding Raith House outside Kirkcaldy, shows grey-painted comb-backed chairs which were very probably taken from the lobby of the house.[12] White-painted chairs of this kind are mentioned as part of the lobby furnishings at Paxton House, Berwickshire, in an inventory of 1828;[13] and Durie House, Fife, had a set of low stick-back chairs of a distinctive Scottish pattern which could be carried outside for use in the garden. These were photographed in use in about 1901. They were suited to this dual purpose because they were formal enough for the hall and light enough to carry.

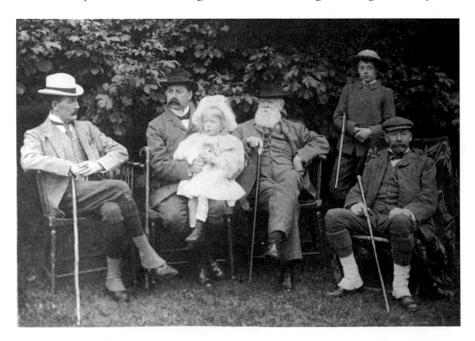

110. Members of the Christie family sitting outside on chairs from the lobby of Durie House, Fife, in about 1901. The use of stick-back chairs such as this in Scottish country-house lobbies dates back to the eighteenth century.

If we move from the large country house to the smaller town house, a pattern book such as *The Rudiments of Architecture* of 1773 charts very well, in its range of both conservative and progressive designs, the evolution of lobby spaces and the position of stairs in this type of house. In Edinburgh, great importance was attached to the lobby in the design of houses in the New Town. This first room provided an opportunity for a display of fashionable but dignified taste before the visitor was shown by a servant to one of the main reception rooms. Perhaps to emphasize the roominess of these houses, in direct contrast with the often cramped, multi-storey accommodation of the Old Town, lobbies in the new houses were almost always separate rooms, with staircase compartments to the back. They were also large: the average size of lobbies in the Moray Estate houses built to James Gillespie Graham's designs between 1822 and 1830 was 9ft x 20ft (2.75m x 6m).

The interior decoration, and indeed the overall design of the lobby was not necessarily the concern of the principal architect. A look at the houses in Royal Circus and North-West Circus Place, Edinburgh, designed by William Playfair in 1820, reveals that while the exterior elevations are designed as one and conform to the same architectural language, the lobbies, which were not executed under Playfair's supervision, are interestingly varied. Some have coffered ceilings, others have vaults or shallow domes, and some have elaborate screens of columns which follow either Grecian or Roman architectural orders. Plasterwork is similarly diverse, lending different themes to lobbies by the addition of classical details, such as the Parthenon frieze, or 'gothic' fan-vaulted ceilings with hanging pendants.[14]

Few Edinburgh New Town entrance halls were without a formal suite of lobby furniture. Remnants of these suites survive, but for evidence of the full specification in an early nineteenth-century town house, part of William Trotter's estimate for furnishing Number 3 Moray Place, Edinburgh in 1831 or 1832, is worth reprinting. It was prepared for Sir Duncan Campbell of Barcaldine, an Argyllshire landowner:[15]

LOBBY

A Handsome mahogany Lobby Table on truss legs 5 feet long
4 Handsome Mahogany Lobby chairs richly carv'd
2 Hemp foot matts
A Mahogany Hat Stand with brass rings & pan & brass branches
A Great Coat stand to suit wt. the above
Painted floor cloth to plan
Brass plates
Carpet for Stair canot be calculated not knowing the number of steps
Brass Rods and butts
Drugget cover as above
A Lobby Table for Inner Lobby to fold down

When William Trotter became sole proprietor of his old company (previously Young & Trotter, then Young, Trotter, & Hamilton) in 1805, the firm developed a virtual monopoly in furnishing the Edinburgh New Town: its only serious rivals were Morison & Company and Bruce & Burns. Trotter specialized in letting furnished town houses, which must have been equipped to a standard formula little different from that in the estimate quoted above, which lists the items needed in the whole house. While a grip on the domestic market was assured by his close personal associations with the architects of the new urban scheme, such as James Gillespie Graham, and by the convenient location of the firm's wareroom at the east end of Princes Street, William

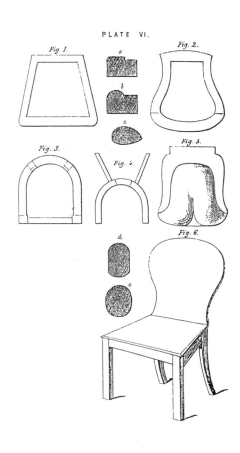

PLATE VI.

Fig. 1.   Fig. 2.

Fig. 3.   Fig. 4.   Fig. 5.

Fig. 6.

111. *Opposite:* Stone floor painted in imitation of marble pavement in the lobby of Dunninald House, Angus, about 1824.

112. *Opposite, bottom left:* Lobby chair from a set supplied to Trinity House, Leith, by William Trotter of Edinburgh in 1818.

113. *Opposite, bottom right:* Specification for hall or lobby chair with 'sweep'd back', from *The Edinburgh Chair-maker's Book of Prices for Workmanship*, 1825.

114. An early nineteenth-century lobby table in a St Andrews town house. It is narrow so that the door could be opened easily and visitors could enter without obstruction, pausing to leave their gloves or calling card on the table top.

TRUSS LEGS.

Cutting out, shaping, and clamping a truss leg, three inches thick, and preparing ditto for carving, when introduced into sideboard or lobby tables, extra from a plain tapered leg	0	3	0
Each half inch extra in thickness	0	0	6
When ditto is sunk pannelled on the sides, with raised scrolls, each side	0	2	0
A sunk pannel in front with reeded toe	0	1	6
Working a double ogee in front and round the toe, extra from flat pannel and reeded toe	0	1	0
A Square block for ditto to stand on, with a plain hollow round ditto, each block	0	0	9

115. Specification for 'truss legs', a feature of Scottish lobby tables after 1820, from the supplement to *The Cabinet-maker's Book of Prices*, Edinburgh 1825. The design of these scrolled legs was developed from Roman stone sarcophagi and was thus suited to the formal, sometimes funereal, tone of the town-house lobby.

Trotter's pre-eminence in public commissions, such as the furnishing of Register House and the Signet Library, was achieved through political activity: he became Lord Provost of Edinburgh in 1825. The firm's lobby furniture was predominantly in the Greek Revival style but items were also made in gothic, Tudor, or Elizabethan tastes. The furniture was manufactured at the company's Princes Street works, which had its own extensive timber yards and a large upholstery department.

The principal item in the furnishing formula was the 'Handsome mahogany Lobby Table on truss legs', which is a distinctive Scottish type. Whilst being a useful and dignified focus in the room, this type of narrow-topped table was designed to stand closely against the wall so that it would not obstruct the entry of groups of guests. Its top might have taken a clock or provided a temporary resting place for items brought by visitors, such as calling cards or gloves. Early lobby tables had plain tapered or turned front legs (pl 114) but fashion after 1800 decreed more decoration. Distinctively scrolled and carved 'truss legs' (pl 115) appear in this later period and are used on a number of other furniture types developed for specific requirements in the Scottish house, which were set down in the country's first cabinetmakers' price books. These were published in Edinburgh in 1805 and 1811, and in Glasgow in 1806 and 1809. The lobby table had a direct parallel in early nineteenth-century France where cabinetmakers such as Georges Jacob made almost identical types with scrolled front legs terminating in small blocks.[16] The origin of this design is clearly neoclassical and may derive from Robert Adam's borrowings from tombs in the Pantheon at Rome, which featured similar truss supports.

To turn to seat furniture, oval-backed or waisted lobby chairs, similar to designs published by Chippendale and other English makers in the 1750s and 1760s and to those by Alexander Peter at Dumfries House, appear to have been favoured in early nineteenth-century Edinburgh. It is possible that the 'richly carv'd' examples in Trotter's estimate for 3 Moray Place were intended to be similar to the pattern shown in plate 112, a chair from a set of six supplied by Trotter to Trinity House in Leith in 1818.[17] The backs of these chairs are unusual in that they are carved with a coiled rope and anchor between two truss scrolls, a reference to the maritime connections of the building for which they were commissioned, the headquarters of a charitable foundation for merchant seamen. A more commonly seen decoration was a carved or painted coat of arms or heraldic device, which boasted to all who entered the lobby that the owners were people of pedigree.

In 1825, *The Edinburgh Chair-maker's Book of Prices* set down specifications and a sample design for 'Hall chairs'.[18] The suggested design, illustrated in plate 113, had what was described as a 'sweep'd back', a waisted shape which corresponds with the chairs at Trinity House. Like the earlier hall chairs, these had solid wooden seats and were usually made of mahogany, though oak was also commonly used in the early nineteenth century: both woods were resistant to damp clothing. The chairs were not intended to be relaxing, and indeed the desired effect of these formally furnished lobbies was discomfort. It was only servants and people on business who would be kept waiting: welcome visitors would be shown into the parlour or drawing room.

At most times of the year the lobby would be chilly as well as uncomfortable since the floor was usually of stone flags: being exposed to the outdoor world, it needed to be easily washable. By the mid seventeenth century, a fashion for black and white paved floors was established in Scotland. In Fife, for instance, Leslie House and Wemyss Castle had notable lobby floors laid in chequer patterns in 1670 and the one at Leslie has survived.[19] Both patterns and materials were in this case Dutch: the marble squares were shipped from Holland to east-coast Scottish ports and laid by local craftsmen. Handsome variants on this theme continued to be executed throughout the eighteenth century, becoming particularly common in town houses (pls 116, 117). Where decorative stone-flagged floors were not laid, painted floorcloth planned to the

116. *Left:* A mid eighteenth-century black and white marble pavement in the lobby of a town house in St Andrews. Such paving was fashionable in Scotland by the early seventeenth century and was used until the late eighteenth, when it began to be replaced by painted floorcloth and, later in the nineteenth century, linoleum and encaustic tiles. Double inner doors with outer 'storm doors' beyond form a small protective vestibule.

117. *Right:* A view of the same lobby looking towards the stair compartment.

room appears to have been a regular feature in lobbies. The backing material was sailcloth, or 'duck', which was produced on a large scale in Scotland's maritime ports such as Leith and Kirkcaldy and could be supplied in large seamless pieces. Bold pavement designs were made for the neoclassical lobbies of early nineteenth-century Edinburgh New Town houses, a pattern which has sometimes been continued when floorcloth has been replaced by linoleum or other materials. Few original painted lobby floorcloths survive, but some painted stone floors remain in relatively unworn condition in country houses. Dunninald in Angus, for instance, has a lobby floor painted in imitation of marble pavement which dates from 1824 (pl 111). Few if any of the numerous hair or hemp mats and rugs which appear so frequently in inventories are likely to survive today.

Trotter's estimate for Duncan Campbell specifies 'A Lobby Table for Inner Lobby to fold down'. This second lobby contained the stairs, and it is almost certain that the folding table was the Scottish type usually found in antechambers to dining rooms. This had a single broad flap which could be supported on a fly leg, and was designed to take serving dishes and other items being transported to and from the dining chamber. There is a good documented example by Alexander Peter at Dumfries House in Ayrshire.[20] Smaller versions of this pattern were used in kitchens where space was at a premium.

Among the expected lobby items in Trotter's estimate are 'hemp foot matts' and matching hat and coat stands. Not mentioned, though they were often supplied by cabinetmakers, is a lantern. Lobbies had distinctive light fittings with glass-panelled sides which were designed to protect the candles from draughts when the door was opened and to prevent grease dropping on the people below. The candles were superseded in the late eighteenth century by Argand lamps, which burned oil, but these were still encased in glass.

To provide a welcoming feeling of warmth for visitors, it was customary for the main lobby in an Edinburgh New Town house to be heated by a cast-iron stove projecting from a niche in the wall opposite the lobby table. These were manufactured in pedestal, vase, and pillar designs by the Carron Company of Falkirk, which employed company designers William and Henry Haworth to provide ornamental patterns in the neoclassical and gothic tastes (pl 118).[21] Again, few remain in town houses, many of which have been converted to offices in the twentieth century. Niches survive in Robert Adam's Charlotte Square town houses of about 1792, and both niches and later stoves can be found in houses on the Moray Estate of 1822–30. Examples are rare in other cities such as Glasgow or Aberdeen, where once they may have been common, but some original lobby stoves remain in country houses such as Midmar, Aberdeenshire, and Foulis Castle in Ross-shire.

It is perhaps also important to note that part of the effect of the lobby in the grandest houses was achieved through the deployment of servants in impressive livery. In Susan Ferrier's 1824 novel *The Inheritance*, an old gentleman finds himself 'in the hall surrounded by a train of servants', at whom he scowls in his usual manner; 'but they were too well-bred to testify either mirth or surprise … and in spite of himself, he was ushered to the saloon with all the customary demonstrations of respect.'[22] In the heyday of the country house in the mid nineteenth century, footmen could be matched in pairs for appearance (like horses) but might have little real work to do.[23] And even in smaller houses, where the servants were usually female (and had a great deal of work), it was of importance that the person who opened the door and escorted the visitor to a reception room should be neatly dressed and behave in a correct manner.

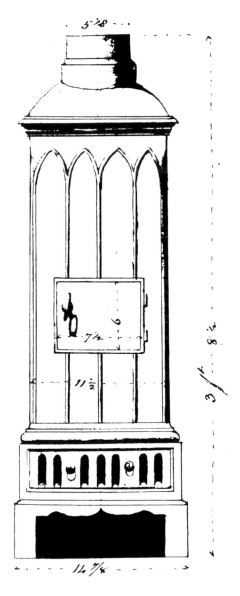

Gothic Stove

118. Design from the Carron Company sketchbooks, 1805. Cast-iron pillar stoves were designed to fit into round-headed stove niches provided in town-house lobbies, most particularly in Edinburgh.

119. Watercolour of about 1812 showing 'Randolph's Hall' at Darnaway Castle, Morayshire. Between 1798 and 1812 the house was completely rebuilt, retaining this late medieval hall as its centrepiece. The furniture is a very early antiquarian collection of Scottish pieces, which perhaps set a precedent for such a display in a hall.

Returning to the subject of the hall, this time in the eighteenth-century country house, we find that acknowledgement of the English fashion for ground-floor 'great halls' was to be repeated in the newly-built castle at Inveraray, Argyll, executed to the designs of the London architect, Roger Morris, between 1745 and 1760. A 90ft (27.5m) high central space was constructed with pointed gothic-revival windows and an emphasis on the semicircular northern end. This was reminiscent of the dining function of a medieval great hall, but the northern apse led on to a long gallery, and the main reason for the room's existence was display. This was a 'gothick' hall, in the eighteenth-century antiquarian sense, a symbolic entrance hall with formally arranged trophies of arms high on its walls and architectural detailing which was distinct from the classical vocabulary of the rest of the castle interior. It has been observed that this type of central top-lit chamber of very large proportion has a number of precedents in the great halls of a group of English sixteenth-century houses including Mount Edgecumbe in Hampshire, Michelgrove in Sussex, Lulworth Castle in Dorset, and Wollaton Hall in Nottinghamshire.[24]

The great hall at Darnaway, Morayshire, is more important as a historical revival because it represents a remodelling of an original Scottish late medieval hall structure and contains a very early antiquarian collection of Scottish furniture. Darnaway Castle was entirely rebuilt around the fourteenth-century 'Randolph's Hall' by the architect Alexander Laing between 1798 and 1812. The old hall, which was raised on a basement in Scottish fashion, had its floor lowered, windows enlarged, battlements added at roof level, and exterior walls refaced to become the centrepiece of the new classical house, set behind a completely new lobby. Its most spectacular feature was the hammer-beam roof of 1387 which, with minor additions, was retained in its original form. A watercolour of about 1812 (pl 119) shows the room furnished with arms, family relics, and a collection of oak furniture including 'Randolph's chair', which was believed to date from the fourteenth century and, indeed, appears to be sixteenth-century or earlier.

Darnaway's hall and its assemblage of ancient furniture was an important precursor of the medieval-revival hall in castle-style houses but it was

120. J Valentine's photograph of the hall at Sir Walter Scott's Roxburghshire house, Abbotsford, in 1878. By the early nineteenth century it had become fashionable to have a mock-medieval 'great hall' placed English-fashion on the ground floor. This meant that the room could be used for reception and dining, as well as serving the function of an entrance lobby.

exceptional in being a remodelling of an original fourteenth-century structure. More typically, the early nineteenth-century plan was to place the hall, English fashion, on the ground floor, most usually at the entrance to a house where it could function as a lobby. This was the scheme adopted by Walter Scott at his new house, Abbotsford in Roxburghshire, executed by the Manchester architect William Atkinson between 1816 and 1823.

Scott's hall was placed in the centre of the east range, between a staircase lobby and an 'armoury', with doors leading into the dining room and library. Its focal point was a massive gothic chimneypiece copied from stone seats at Melrose Abbey but domesticated by a 'Delft'-tiled insert. Its chief ornaments comprised armour, weapons and 'spoils of animals' – deer antlers and antelope horns mounted on wooden panels. Scott's hall was small enough to use in the medieval manner but in modern comfort. His memoirs record, for instance, that his family sometimes dined there.[25] Valentine's photograph of 1878 shows a very eclectic interior including Scottish, Continental European, and oriental arms and armour, animal trophies, cast-iron cooking pots, and portrait busts (pl 120). Because individual chairs were generally thought to have been scarce in medieval halls, seating for visitors was provided here by a hall bench. Its bobbin-turned legs are a characteristic early nineteenth-century Scottish feature and the arms – scrolls on turned stumps – correspond with a pattern in *The Edinburgh Chair-maker's Book of Prices for Workmanship* of 1825.[26]

Although Abbotsford was very much a hybrid creation, there can be no doubt that the cult which quickly grew up around Scott and his Borders home started a trend in 'castle-style' houses throughout Scotland. The 'medieval' hall required some sort of historical theme to give it antiquarian authenticity and Scott provided a fund of ideas. A set of relics which he adopted with particular enthusiasm were the wooden portrait roundels from the King's Presence Chamber at Stirling Castle. These renaissance-inspired medallions of about 1540, which portray historical figures such as Margaret Tudor and King James V, were becoming better known at the turn of the century, but they were first popularized in print in 1817 as a series of engravings entitled *Lacunar Strevelinense, A Collection of Heads Etched and Engraved after the Carved Work which formerly decorated the Roof of the King's Room in Stirling Castle*.[27] Scott consulted this and reproduced images from several of the roundels as stained-glass window panels, but others obtained plaster casts of the heads in much the same way as collectors of classical marbles made casts of their finds. These impressions were sometimes grained to imitate the original oak and used as wall decoration in antiquarian rooms. A good example can be found at Tayfield

121. One of a series of decorative roundels copied from the sixteenth-century Stirling Heads from Stirling Castle. These were used as decoration in the staircase hall at Tayfield House, Fife, inspired by publication of engravings of the heads in 1817 and by their use by Sir Walter Scott at Abbotsford.

122. Entrance hall and staircase at Mount Stuart, Isle of Bute, photographed in 1904. The Third Marquess of Bute took great pleasure in architecture and deliberated carefully over whether this hall should be fitted in marble or granite. It was clearly not intended to be a comfortable 'living hall'.

House in Fife, where casts of the heads line a first-floor hall of early nineteenth-century date (pl 121).

The medieval-revival entrance hall then, was very much a nineteenth-century phenomenon which developed to become an essential part of the 'baronial' house executed by architects such as David Bryce. Because many Scottish castles had never had such rooms, they were added, or alternatively entrances were re-aligned, so that vaulted basement chambers could be converted into new halls and decorated with the paraphernalia of a militaristic past. One of the best examples of such additions to an older castle is at Blair in Perthshire, where the seventh Duke of Atholl employed Bryce to provide a new double-height hall in 1872. This survives in its original state, with a combination of elements which betray the evolution of this new type of room. A minstrels' gallery and a concentration of mounted arms which signifies the Duke's possession of a private army, is combined with a suite of eighteenth-century lobby furniture, indicating the room's other function as an entrance vestibule.

Experiment with mixed architectural forms and styles in the late nineteenth century introduced new themes for hall and lobby decoration whilst blurring the distinction between these rooms in country houses and public buildings. The first illustration of this can be seen in the colossal French Gothic hall by Robert Rowand Anderson at Mount Stuart on the Isle of Bute (1878–86), which was repeated in a similar design on a smaller scale at the Scottish National Portrait Gallery, Edinburgh (1885–90) to provide a public lobby with access to picture galleries at either side. Both the Mount Stuart and the Portrait Gallery halls have elaborate mosaic decoration and 'zodiacal ceilings' painted with constellations of gold stars on a blue ground.

A second clear example of similarity between the private and public lobby is the grandiose marble hall by the Paisley-born architect, William Young, at Gosford House in East Lothian. In its architectural sources, size, and use of materials this palatial room of 1891 has a direct parallel with another of Young's works, the lobby at Glasgow City Chambers of 1888. Both designs use great scale to impress, quote from a medley of Italian Renaissance sources and make sumptuous use of highly coloured marble and alabaster.

Young's marble hall at Gosford is also interesting in that it incorporates an informal living area furnished with soft upholstered chairs: this space was used for sitting and, indeed, taking afternoon tea. In this respect it is an example of the 'living hall' which became fashionable in Scottish country houses in the early years of the twentieth century. An early example, which highlights the piquant contrast between urbane country house interior and the wildness of the Highland landscape immediately outside, survives at Ardtornish in Argyll. This was a spacious late nineteenth-century 'living hall', designed by Alexander Ross of Inverness between 1884 and 1891 (pl 124). When remodelled by John Kinross of Edinburgh in 1908–11 (pl 125), the room's comfort was markedly increased by the addition of soft upholstered furniture, smaller tables, a draught screen, revolving bookcase, and improved lighting. In a country house such as Ardtornish, which had a men's billiard room and smoking room, bachelor apartment, and ladies' boudoir, segregation of the sexes could be relaxed only in such neutral space as the living hall. This was an area to which women of the house would arrive back from country rides or boating expeditions, or bring flowers from the nearby gardens, to meet men returning from their outdoor pursuits, which of course included hunting, shooting, and fishing. However, one of the most important functions of this room in Scottish country houses was, and indeed is, to provide a place for dancing. The carpet can be rolled back

123. A grand ball held in honour of Queen Victoria in the 'Banner Hall' at Taymouth Castle, Perthshire, in 1842. One of the major functions of the hall in large Scottish houses was to provide a suitable space for dancing.

124. Hall at Ardtornish Tower, Morvern, Argyllshire, as built to designs by Alexander Ross of Inverness, 1884–91. The visitor to this West Highland mansion entered a small lobby and proceeded through double doors to this grand hall, which, with its informal collection of furniture and servants' bell pulls flanking the fireplace, was clearly used as a living space by the occupants.

125. The same hall, as remodelled to designs by John Kinross of Edinburgh and furnished by Scott Morton & Co, 1908–11. It looks much more comfortable with the addition of soft upholstered furniture, smaller tables, a draught screen, bookcase, pictures, and improved lighting.

to make a large uninterrupted space, and service stairs open into the hall, allowing food and drink to be supplied conveniently from the kitchens below. But perhaps the hall at Ardtornish was found to be too cold for general living, for a subsequent furnishing scheme reintroduced an element of formality. The sofas and 'occasional' furniture were replaced with exhibition-quality mahogany ribband-back chairs and a serpentine commode, which were ranged around the edges of the room. These new items were made by the Edinburgh manufacturers, Morison & Co, who specialized in formal 'parade' furniture of this type. The effect is one of extravagant proportion and glamorous quality of furnishings, the purpose of which seems to be simply introductory display.

A contemporary of John Kinross, the architect Robert Lorimer, excelled at designing informal living spaces, allowing imagination and expedience to govern the siting of halls and lobbies in his houses. For instance, Ardkinglas in Argyll of 1906 (pl 228) has two halls, upper and lower: the upper one has a loggia with views over Loch Fyne and the lower is ingeniously lit from an open court at the side. Lorimer was also very keen on designing modern conveniences such as lavatories and WCs, which opened off halls, as well as the fittings that went in them (pl 229).

The suburban houses of Scottish towns and cities provide plenty of visible evidence of the taste and wealth of the growing middle class in the nineteenth century. Their lobbies were intended to indicate, in just the same way as those in the large country house, the elegance and quality of the occupants within. One of the first furniture pattern books to inform and reflect this bourgeois taste was *The Cabinet-Maker's Assistant* of 1853, published by Blackie & Son in Glasgow. Taking the reader round an imaginary house room by room, the 'Assistant' stipulated the correct tone for each area and specified the appropriate furniture. In public rooms, the commentary declared, bright colours, gilding, and pictures may be used, but 'these are either entirely excluded from the approaches to these apartments or else used very sparingly. Sculpture, articles of taste and *vertu*, of quiet and unobtrusive colouring, are employed as hall decorations'.[28] This seems a striking survival of the eighteenth-century idea of the stone hall with sculptural decoration as exemplified by Hopetoun House, and some traces are seen even later in photographs of 16 Leamington Terrace in Edinburgh taken around 1900 (pl 126).[29] The lobby, or 'hall' was, according to *The Cabinet-Maker's Assistant*, intended to be a sober and dignified space with a range of furniture which should be strictly limited to: lobby table, chairs, a long seat, a clock (either longcase or bracket), and a hat and umbrella stand. Designs for lobby tables, chairs, and long seats were shown in rococo-revival and Elizabethan styles, to be executed in oak.

The traditional set of lobby table and chairs was beginning to disappear in the 1860s, although inventories demonstrate that this conservative formula survived into the twentieth century, particularly in Edinburgh New Town houses and in the larger houses in country towns. A few can still be seen today. The new arrival which supplanted the lobby table, especially in the expanding suburbs, was the combined hall stand. In the same way that the combined sideboard table in the dining room of the 1770s had joined all the functions of the separate parts of an ensemble – serving table, cellaret, cutlery storage, and basin – into one article of furniture, the hall stand of the mid nineteenth century integrated into one item the lobby table and coat, hat, and umbrella stand, and introduced a new feature, a mirror. This last was an obvious improvement since the lobby was the ideal place for anyone coming in or going out to check their appearance. Plate 126 shows a stand of this type in the lobby of the Mather household around 1900.

It is not surprising, however, that a comparison of the contents of roughly contemporary late Victorian lobbies reveals that whereas some, like the Mather family, had opted for a single multi-purpose stand, others kept an accumulation of old and new objects with different uses. For instance, the lobby and staircase of a Mrs Bonthrone, shopkeeper, of Auchtermuchty in Fife, contained in 1891 a varied collection comprising in the 'Lobby room', a 'Wardrobe, Folding Table, Three Chairs, Waxcloth & Matts'; and in the 'Low Staircase', an eight-day clock, waxcloth and mats, carpet and rods, lobby table, and umbrella stand.[30]

126. A member of the Mather family outside the lobby at 16 Leamington Terrace, Edinburgh, about 1900. A combined hall stand has taken the place of the traditional lobby table, the floor is laid with encaustic tiles, and the stencilled walls are hung with pictures.

127. Cast-iron umbrella stand by the Falkirk Iron Company. The design was evidently one of the firm's successful lines since it was registered in 1866 and was still in production in 1910.

Umbrella stands, as opposed to combined hall stands, were amongst the earliest of items to be added to the conventional formula of lobby table and chairs. They became common in the early nineteenth century, particularly in urban households, and were one of the first types of domestic furniture to be mass produced in cast iron, which was also used for lobby chairs. Plate 127 shows a typical example of the type to be found in the lobbies of mid nineteenth-century homes and institutions throughout Scotland. The design for this was registered by the Falkirk Iron Company in 1866 and was evidently one of the firm's more successful lines because it was still being carried in its catalogue of 1910.[31] This stand, with decorated back and removable double water pans, could be ordered in gold-painted (as illustrated here) or bronzed finish. The Falkirk Iron Company was one of several Scottish iron-founding companies, including Carron and Walter Macfarlane & Co of Glasgow, which manufactured cast-iron umbrella stands on a large scale. The umbrella stand is also interesting as an indicator of the status of the umbrella in Victorian society. Umbrellas often had handles mounted in silver or of carved ivory and their fabric could be refurbished when it became shabby. The disappearance of the

128. Trumland House, Rousay, Orkney, about 1900. On the table are a telephone and post box, some of the accoutrements of the country-house hall which can still be seen in many surviving houses. General Burroughs reads his paper in what looks like a morning room or parlour.

umbrella stand from the lobby must be related to the decline of the umbrella in the twentieth century. Similarly, the hall stand has virtually vanished since the Second World War, partly because people no longer wear hats regularly.[32]

Other typical features of the late Victorian and Edwardian hallway or lobby which have now largely gone are the 'sanitary' wallpapers with glazed wipeable surface, often printed in patterns of a large scale suited to the height of staircase walls,[33] and the door curtains, or *portières*, which appear in old photographs. Things that remain in use are those which are more durable, such as terrazzo-tiled floors as seen in plate 126 and stained-glass panels in front doors or hall windows; or items which are convenient to use in a room which is not occupied by people for long periods. Few hallways still have the dinner gongs, weighing scales, and post boxes often seen in large country houses, but many people keep the telephone here, usually with a table and chair and something to write on.

The nineteenth-century cottages of two rooms or more which are found throughout Scotland on farms and in country towns and villages, provide clear evidence that the lobby was also of functional importance in the small house. The lobby in the two-roomed cottage was not an area for display, but a useful space, and this is reflected in the colloquial term 'trance', the essential meaning of which is 'a passage within a building'.[34] This exactly describes the purpose of the room, as a space connecting the two main rooms of a cottage.

Architecturally, this arrangement has several advantages. Firstly, it provides an introductory barrier within the confines of a very compact area, avoiding the unsatisfactory practice of stepping straight from the outside into a living room. Secondly, it gives extra protection against the weather and against dirt being brought into the kitchen or best room. And, perhaps most usefully, the wall needed to form the lobby creates an alcove space behind, which can be used for storage, or, more commonly, as a bed closet entered from one of the main rooms. This type of lobby, which appears in most improved farm cottages built or rebuilt after 1850, has distinctive associated features, one of which is the double outside door. Such doors, with two narrow leaves opening inwards, allow the lobby to be of minimum depth, thus maximizing the usable space within the cottage. Perhaps because so much of the occupants' working lives was spent outside, the existence of a transitional space has been of great importance in the small Scottish house. The lobby could be used as a place to put things before they were taken outside and was clearly an area where outdoor clothing could be kept at hand. But, even in the smallest house, the lobby was an essential means by which a householder could maintain standards of propriety, privacy, and communal friendliness. To leave one's outer door open was a means of welcome, and an indication that one was at home.

The social importance of the lobby became apparent to architects and planners only after moves were made to dispense with it in designs for public housing after 1919. Early schemes, such as that for the Logie estate in Dundee, omitted a lobby in designs for new two-roomed dwellings and had to be modified as a result of public criticism. Potential occupants argued that a lobby afforded privacy for the 'working man' because it allowed for rooms branching off it to be self contained. Tenants were not used to walking through one room to reach another and were not prepared to accept this layout.[35] With increasing economy in housebuilding and the widespread adoption of English house styles in recent years, the outer vestibule as seen in plate 129 has now all but disappeared, and there has been a tendency for entrance lobbies, now merged with stair compartments, to become long and narrow and to be called the 'hall'. It is noticeable, however, that where lobbies are not provided, house-holders often build on a porch outside their front door.

The flat is altogether a different case and in cities where this has been the predominant housing type, it is evident that most dwellings, however small, were originally built with a lobby. This can be seen, for example, in the one-roomed flat or 'single end', where the end wall would consist of an alcove or 'set-in' bed and a small lobby providing just enough space for the front door to be opened (pl 61). There are interesting regional variations in the layout and fitting up of entrance passages and rooms in the Scottish urban tenement. The process of entry is usually the same, inviting the visitor to pass through a close, up a stair onto a common landing, and then through the front door into an internal lobby or passage of some sort, but there are important differences of detail. In Aberdeen, for instance, the stairs are commonly timber and the closes are similarly lined; in Glasgow, tenement blocks are well known for their decorative tilework, a feature which has given the name to the city's 'wally closes', while in Edinburgh, wall decoration is most likely to be a plain painted surface and the close is not generally open (as in Glasgow) but has a door at ground level.[36] On the west coast, for instance in Dumbarton, Glasgow, and Paisley, coal bunkers are a common feature of lobbies, while in other cities they are not. Although the term 'lobby' cannot be said to have been used in Scotland with infallible consistency, it does seem to have been applied with most clarity to the entrance room or space in the urban dwelling such as the tenement flat. More investigation could be made of this and other aspects of the tenement, which is such an important part of the Scottish building culture and not just a feature of cities such as Glasgow. It would be particularly useful to compare the planning and room use of Scottish tenements with that in other countries such as Russia or the USA, where formal planning has been of similar importance and where the lobby has enjoyed a similar status in people's homes.

129. Mrs Lovat Langridge of Cupar, Fife, in her vestibule, 1995. In Scotland the outer door of the lobby is usually kept open as a means of welcome and an indication that one is at home.

6 The Dining Room

IAN GOW

'The best ornament for a dining-room is a well-cooked dinner.'

Mrs Loftie, 1878[1]

In 1814, Elizabeth Grant of Rothiemurchus, seventeen years old, was invited to her first adult dinner by her kinsman, the Marquess of Huntly, at Kinrara. Later she recalled that the prospect 'frightened me out of my wits':

> In the ordinary run of houses, Company was any thing but pleasant. Every body seemed to assume an unnatural manner ... All were put out of their way too by a grand fatigue day of best glass, best china, best linen, wax candles, plate, furniture uncovered, etc., making every thing look and feel as unlike home as possible. It was not a welcome we gave our friends, but a worry they gave us. In great houses there were skilful servants to take all this trouble and to prevent any mistakes or any fuss; in lesser houses it was very annoying, I must say.[2]

In the event her worst fears were realized: on reaching the 'sweets', having sat dumbly through dinner between two 'gentlemen sportsmen', she found to her consternation that she did not have a fork to eat her jelly with. Lord Huntly then focused the entire party on her plight by loudly berating his butler for his neglect of Miss Grant.

One did not have to be young to be intimidated by the Scottish dining room. The 33-year-old James Hogg, the Ettrick Shepherd, found himself ill at ease during dinner at Inveraray Castle in 1803: 'I was so proud that although I did not know how to apply one third of the things that were at table, unless I called for a thing I would not take it when offered to me.'[3]

The dining room in Scotland was an invention of the Baroque, and if the room was a theatre of artificiality, its stage was the table itself. The performance was governed by etiquette and convention but these could suddenly change, requiring constant vigilance on the diner's part.

Interior decoration of the past is usually discussed in purely stylistic terms today. As far as the dining room is concerned, inasmuch as its form altered with changing dining customs, it can be viewed in terms of the architecture of the dinner table. It is worth emphasizing that we know almost nothing of Scotland's past dining habits and whether they had any distinctive characteristics. There are few visual records of Scottish dining rooms before the nineteenth century. Although this has recently become a field of considerable interest to social historians, attention has not unnaturally settled on the well-documented royal court, which reflected Continental etiquette.[4]

The importance of the dinner in Scottish life, however, is not in doubt. A formal meal was the centrepiece of any entertainment the purposes of which might embrace political or business aspirations, the desire to put guests under

a social obligation, or the need to marry off a string of daughters. Indeed the Calvinist colour of the Established Church of Scotland had left the dinner table the only form of self indulgence that could be enjoyed and admitted to socially. A housewife's ability to carry off a dinner advertised a family's general well-being and prosperity. As Elizabeth Grant wrote of her mother: 'She kept a clean and tidy house, and an excellent table, not doing much herself, but taking care to see all well done.'[5]

There is no reason to think that Scots were out of touch with the London-based court or Continental customs. The hosts of both Elizabeth Grant and James Hogg were Highland chieftains, whose lands lay in remote spots, but there was no whiff in their early nineteenth-century households of cosy feudalism and the baronial hall. The dining room of the Duke of Argyll at Inveraray was in the most sophisticated London taste (pl 130) and could bear comparison with the Prince Regent's interiors at Carlton House – all the more startling when contrasted with Argyllshire rather than St James's Park.

The furnishing of rooms with flunkeys added to the unsophisticated James Hogg's difficulties at Inveraray, where he found himself unable to tell servants from masters. But impressive appearances, reflecting the Scottish love of display, were not always what they seemed. As Elizabeth Grant recalled of dinners at neighbouring Castle Grant, there was 'a footman in the gorgeous green and scarlet livery behind every chair, but they were mere gillies, lads quite

130. Although the new dining room at Inveraray Castle, finished in 1784, was situated in a remote area of Argyllshire, it was decorated with metropolitan sophistication by the French painters Guinard and Irrouard le Girardy. The Scots were to have a predilection for decorative painting in their dining rooms.

untutored, sons of small tenants brought in for the occasion and fitted into the suit that they best filled'.[6]

Although the dining room had inherited some of its functions from the baronial hall, of which the best survivor in Scotland must be at Darnaway Castle (pl 119), as a specialized room it probably developed only from the middle of the seventeenth century. It did not stand alone but was the most important component of the 'state apartment' or 'following of rooms' that occupied the lion's share of a house and was reserved for the guest of highest rank. The origins of this apartment lay in royal and papal etiquette and the components were fixed, allowing little scope for innovation. Much about this subject remains obscure. Confusingly, the royal model did not include a dining room, possibly because it was considered of symbolic importance for the king to dine in public as in European courts. The custom was to set up a trestle table under a canopy of state where he sat, practically enthroned, on a carpet. Although Scotland had no resident court after James VI's translation to London in 1603, it does not mean that there was no public dining, if by proxy. The inventory prepared by James Steuart, 'Keeper of the King's Wardrobe in Scotland' from 1714, includes 'One foot Carpet used to lye under the Commissioner's feet, when he Dines in publick (or in State) much spoiled and torn.'[7]

It is possible that the lack of a resident court after 1603 favoured the rise at the end of the seventeenth century of the distinctive non-royal format of the Scottish state apartment, with its dominant 'great dining room'. This can be thought of as a chain of rooms between two staircases. The formal purpose was promoted by purely architectural effects. The suite was approached by a great stair leading to the *piano nobile* or principal floor, usually on the first floor enjoying impressive vistas across formal gardens. The first room was the great dining room, of a size to reflect its importance: a double cube, often breaking up into the roofspace, was the norm. This was followed, through doors impressively lined up, *en enfilade*, by a square withdrawing room to which the principal guest and exalted fellow diners would retire after dinner. The withdrawing room also served as an antechamber to the state bedroom, beyond which lay the dressing room and closet served by a back stair, not solely used for service, as the phrase 'back stairs diplomacy' reminds us. As successive rooms became more personal to the exalted occupant, progress through the suite became an index of the attendee's rank.

To squeeze the required number of rooms into the confines of a new-built classical house taxed the ingenuity of Scotland's architects, as William Adam's great survey of our national architecture, *Vitruvius Scoticus*, begun in 1726, reveals. It also shows that it was possibly easier to stuff the state apartment into the irregularities of a converted ancient castle. In decoration, Charles II had established the norm through the interest he took in the rebuilding of his Palace of Holyroodhouse after the Restoration, although its taste really reflected that of his Secretary of State for Scotland, the Duke of Lauderdale. It was Lauderdale who brought the English plasterers Houlbert and Dunsterfield to execute the Palace's sumptuous fretwork ceilings. The rooms of the King's apartment were panelled in oak and his Surveyor, the architect Sir William Bruce, favoured a very architectural treatment – a chimneypiece of exotic imported marble flanked by pilasters, obeying the classical language of architecture.

This look was soon copied in the state apartments of Scotland's castles and country houses, although few were able to attract craftsmen of the same calibre as Holyroodhouse. Some of the effects achieved by the imitators are distinctly rustic in comparison with the suave baroque of the King's bedroom, finished with its complement of decorative painting. The grandest state apartment in a country house was at Hamilton Palace, where the architect James Smith, who had worked at Holyroodhouse, created an even more eloquent effect than the gentleman-amateur Bruce, as a result of his superior grasp of architectural profiles. At Hamilton there seems to have been deliberate uniformity throughout the suite, with little distinction in the detailing between dining room, withdrawing room, and bedroom. The pace of the rooms may have been varied originally by the subjects of the tapestries which occupied the wallpapered panels shown in photographs.

Sadly, no Scottish dining room from this period retains its original furnishings. There was, anyway, little that was distinctive. The standard chair was made to suit equally standard 'Turkey work', like the set which has been preserved miraculously at Holyroodhouse since 1668.[8] These were succeeded by the more fashionable high-back caned chairs which survive in quantity. Although it should be treated with caution, a 1911 photograph of the Great Dining Room at Smith's Melville House in Fife may help us to imagine how these rooms might have been.[9]

Some inventories mention two tables in this room but it is impossible to determine if these were to cope with different numbers of diners or were used at the same time for reasons of etiquette. Two tables would certainly have dictated the typical 'double cube' format of the Scottish great dining room, although the need for service circulation space around a single table might have been reason enough for this room's greater size in comparison with the adjoining square withdrawing room and bedroom. Some great dining rooms have two fireplaces, as at Dalkeith House in Midlothian, which again might reflect the practicalities of usage as much as the architect James Smith's, obsession with symmetry.

131. Although this 1911 photograph of the Great Dining Room at Melville House, Fife, shows a self-conscious sense of period antique furnishings and a Victorian chimney-shelf, it perhaps gives an impression of the original effect of this room completed in 1703. The caned chairs, large oval gate-legged table and portraits are all characteristic of formal Scottish dining rooms at this period.

If no dining tables can be documented from this period, their form might be indicated by the Council Room table at Heriot's Hospital, with its oval top with flaps on gatelegs allowing it to be folded away against the wall. An amazing concertina flap table of about 1740, photographed at Hamilton Palace before its demolition, may suggest that the Scots' fondness for their dining rooms brought the early development of substantial tables as opposed to traditional royal trestles.

The only distinctive element in the eighteenth-century Scottish dining room was the buffet, its function possibly as much ceremonial as practical: designers of dining rooms had no need to study convenience when the processional presentation of successive courses only added to the ritual. It seems likely, however, that the buffet was used for the service of drink as well as to express an owner's rank through the display of plate. In a nostalgic chapter in his book on *Glasgow and its Clubs* of 1856, John Strang gives a clear description of this

> former invariable accompaniment of a Scottish *salle à manger*, viz. a cupboard or buffet, with shelves fancifully shaped out and their edges painted in different colours, such as green and light blue, and even tipped with gold. On these shelves were displayed any pieces of silver plate that were considered worth showing, and also the most valuable and richest coloured China punch-bowls, jugs, and cups – such in fact as are now frequently seen on the chiffonnier of a modern drawing-room. Below these shelves there was a hanging leaf which, during dinner, was upraised and served as a sideboard, and when dinner was ended, it was again let down, and shut in with doors opening from the centre and reaching nearly to the ceiling. These buffets, nevertheless, were continued in many dining-rooms long after sideboards had become common.[10]

In accordance with the architectural effect pursued by William Bruce, early buffets, when closed, vanished into the surrounding panelling (pl 132). Architects such as Smith and McGill seem to have found an appropriately architectural solution by placing them opposite the fireplace, often giving them flanking pilasters to match those framing the chimneypiece, and distinctive doors. The early Georgian buffet at Craigievar is japanned green inside, and this flash of colour against the surrounding oak panelling must have added a note of theatre to the dining room during the service of dinner. The grandest buffet of all, however, of veined white marble, is built into the marble lining of the stairwell at Dalkeith Palace, its extravagance perfectly symbolizing the Duchess of Buccleuch and Monmouth's desire to have her palace eclipse any other house in Scotland.

The impressive dimensions of the Scottish dining room, and the fact that dinner was taken during the afternoon, in daylight, made it a suitable room for the display of family portraits. At Newbattle Abbey in Midlothian the dining room was hung with an impressive collection of Van Dykes, and elements of this arrangement survived the room's subsequent function as drawing room.

Following the Union of Parliaments in 1707, state apartments seemed to lose none of their attractions for the Scots and were shoe-horned into even such tiny houses as Sir John Clerk of Penicuik's new villa at Mavisbank, designed by William Adam in 1726. By the 1730s, Adam was the dominant figure in Scottish architecture, and his flair for decoration found a new outlet through his importation of stuccoists, including Enzer and the Clayton family, to carry out his decorative programmes. One of Adam's most arresting dining rooms occupies most of the centre of the new House of Dun of about 1730 (pl 133).

132. Murrayfield House, an early Georgian villa near Edinburgh, was built about 1734. Although the dining room was enlarged to reflect later patterns of entertaining, the original buffet was carefully reset as a symbol of old-fashioned Scots hospitality and given a coat of antiquarian oak graining, played up with the family coat of arms, during the early nineteenth century.

The intricate plan of the House of Dun is also a reminder of the dual character of the Scottish house, where the state apartment was balanced by a private suite for everyday family life. It was Adam's genius to combine both requirements within a compact rectangle, allowing a family to be suitably grand and also comfortable. The only reception room provided on the family side was the parlour, and as a general living room (although there was also a library at the top of the house) it provided another, less formal, model for later dining rooms.

In many houses, both the great dining room and the parlour had buffets and it may have been Adam who introduced the fashion for classicizing their previously rectangular form into a niche with a shell motif. In grand dining rooms, stucco niches were major architectural features. Unfortunately none seems to remain intact with both its enclosing doors and gate-legged table. Many very grand dining rooms did not have buffets, however, and it may be that this was a lingering of the royal public dining ritual, where the lack of room specialization, to the extent of dining off trestle tables, was a cultivated archaism. An equally temporary buffet arrangement may have been used.

If William Adam gave the Scottish dining room a new decorative quality, there seems to have been little change in format and therefore by implication dinner service. The radical transformation of house plans in the mid eighteenth century seems to have been more to do with changes in the character of the withdrawing room. This suddenly blossomed into the recognizable modern drawing room where guests were received directly on arrival, from a room of lesser importance to which they withdrew for tea after dinner. A harbinger of this rise of the drawing room may be seen in Adam's replanning of Hopetoun, where the drawing room has so swelled in volume as to dwarf the adjacent great

133. The saloon or great dining room at the House of Dun, Angus, designed by William Adam. Joseph Enzer's exuberant stucco decorations of 1742 testify to the importance Scots attached to their dining rooms, which were the most important reception rooms in their houses until the mid eighteenth century. Enzer's decorative scheme compliments the banquets that were served here with its allusions to the chase and the riches of the sea.

dining room, although the latter is a grand space rising up into the next storey. The patron's requirements here were perhaps unusual: a large art collection required accommodation in the new great drawing room, which thus had a gallery function. But Hopetoun was a key house in setting fashionable trends.

In plans for new-built houses, or those with substantial additions such as were made by John Douglas at Archerfield in 1747, it became the norm to pair the drawing room with the dining room across a central entrance hall instead of following the old state-apartment plan. This did not diminish the importance of the dining room but raised the drawing room to a more equal partnership in terms of size. This must reflect a radical change in usage. By degrees, the drawing room was to eclipse the old supremacy of the great dining room and emerge as the principal stateroom. Because guests were now received in the new kind of drawing room, a direct route from the front door and entrance hall became essential.

The most dramatic exemplar of this change, and a possible index of its suddenness, is provided by Blair Castle. When this was repaired after the disruptions of 1745, the largest room on the 'state' floor was intended as the great dining room. It has a pair of buffet niches at each end, and the chimneypiece ordered from Thomas Carter of London was appropriately ornamented with vine leaves and grapes. At some point after 1758, however, when Steuard Mackenzie drew up a proposal for the transformation, it was fitted up as the drawing room and its walls hung with silk, leaving the resplendent marble cistern also by Carter, with its seashells, coral, and pearls, niche-less and stranded.

This new pairing of dining room and drawing room also led to a polarization. The identification of the drawing room as the pinnacle of expense with gilding, white statuary marble, looking glass, and silk had the effect of downgrading the dining room to a more robust character suited to its heavier usage for dinner service by servants. A further distinction now began to crystallize, categorizing the drawing room as feminine and the dining room as masculine (see pp 161ff). At its simplest, this stemmed from the habit of the men to linger over the bottle, ostensibly indulging in deep political discussion, while the ladies left the table to await them in their bower-like drawing room across the hall, which isolated them from the drunken rammy.

The rise of the drawing room perhaps imposed on fashionable society the need for matching drawing-room manners. Certainly there seems to have been an attempt to moderate the boorish drunkenness of the men to ensure they remained fit for female society at the end of dinner, but it was not taken up by all. John Strang, looking back from the 1850s to a period around 1800, described at length the Glasgow dinners of former days:

> There were no silver forks then in use, and forks of steel with more than two prongs were even a rarity. The dinner hour in the best families was three o'clock; and when a party was given, four was generally held to be quite *à la mode*. During the days of Fielding, only four-and-twenty years prior, the fashionable dinner hour in London was two … certainly the Glasgow four o'clock dinner hour of the period we are sketching, had followed fast in the wake of the fashion of London. It may be mentioned, also, that in the days of Queen Anne it was the common practice among the higher circles, that the dinner should be put upon the table, and the ladies placed at the dinner board, before the gentlemen were called or allowed to enter. This was also the practice almost universally followed in Glasgow up to the beginning of the final decade of the last century [the 1790s]; and was felt the more necessary when a bed-room

134. This curious painting set in the ceiling of the library at Newhall in Midlothian must date from the early nineteenth century, but it purports to show a meeting of the Worthies Club in Leith in the middle of the eighteenth century. The punch bowl, brought in by the landlady, is the centre of the convivial entertainment while the poet Allan Ramsay reads from *The Gentle Shepherd*.

was the only reception-room in the house. Most of the small company dinners in Glasgow were at this period placed on the board at once, after which there might be a remove of the upper and lower end dishes, but nothing more. On great occasions, however, there was sometimes a regular second course; but as to a third, and a dessert, these were altogether reserved for an after age. The wines generally were port and sherry … As to a bottle of French wine – such as claret – which, thirty years before, was so common throughout all Scotland, it may be said to have been, in 1793, in most houses a *rara avis in terris*. Oat cake and small beer were to be had in every family; the former was presented even at state parties, and the latter was always placed in two or more China jugs at the corners of the table, for any guest who might wish to quaff such a luxury. Drinking water at an entertainment was altogether unpractised. Cheese was invariably produced at the close of every repast, and was always accompanied with London porter, which was decanted into two silver cups, when the parties had such to display, or into a large crystal goblet or China jug; and, like the love-cups of the University, these were sent circling round the board, and were accordingly mouthed by all inclined to taste the then fashionable English beverage. Ices and finger-glasses were still in the womb of fashion; and each person generally carried in his pocket a small silver dessert-knife, which was unhesitatingly brought from its hiding-place if a golden pippin or a moorfowl-egg pear by any chance called for its aid. When dinner was over, and the dessert removed – which was invariably the case after it had stood a short time – the wine bottles made a few circles, and were immediately succeeded by the largest China bowl in the house. In this gorgeous dish, which was of course placed before the landlord, the universal beverage of cold punch was quickly manufactured … it was now the time to sit in for serious drinking – and serious, indeed, it often was … The retiring of a guest to the drawing-room was a rare occurence indeed; and hence the poor lady of the house was generally left to sip her tea in solitude, while her husband and friends were getting *royal* over their *sherbet*. The fact is, that drinking and swearing were characteristic of the dinner parties of the last century, not only in Glasgow, but everywhere else.[11]

An account by a Frenchman, Faujas de Saint-Fond, of a dinner at Inveraray in 1784 suggests that the Duke of Argyll was caught between his own fashionable habits and tradition: 'Towards the end of the dessert, the ladies withdrew to a room destined for the tea-table. I admit that they were left alone a little too long; but the Duke of Argyll informed me, that he had preserved this custom in the country …'[12] He claimed it was to avoid offending the gentlemen of Argyll, who liked to sit long over their drink as in the generation earlier; but clearly there was pressure to change. Saint-Fond also mentioned the facilities provided to cope with such customs:

> If the lively champagne should make its diuretic influence felt, the case is foreseen, and in the pretty corners of the room the necessary convenience is to be found. This is applied to with so little ceremony, that the person who has occasion to use it, does not even interrupt his talk during the operation. I suppose this is one of the reasons why the English ladies, who are exceedingly modest and reserved, always leave the company before the toasts begin.[13]

Inveraray is typical of the rearrangement of the house to the advantage of the drawing room. In the early 1770s, the room originally intended by the architect, Roger Morris, as the long gallery was partitioned to create a central entrance lobby with a new dining room and drawing room on either side. The drawing room was a whole bay larger than the dining room. In John Adam's rearrangement of his father's design for Arniston, the dining room was also smaller than the adjacent drawing room.

This new dining room at Inveraray was enlivened with elegant arabesques by two French painters, Guinard and Irrouard le Girardy (pl 130). While their dazzling Louis XVI decorations did not become typical, the idea of treating the

135. In 1773 the newly completed neoclassical stucco decorations in the dining room at Paxton House, Berwickshire, were complemented by a suite of furniture supplied by Thomas Chippendale from London. The tables, whose sections can accommodate different sizes of party, are the original ones and reflect the latest fashions. The room has recently been restored.

dining room as a field for decorative painting does seem to have been an established Scotticism. William Adam's rooms had been ornamented by the Norie family of decorators and housepainters. The panelling in the great dining room at Mavisbank had blue and white 'Landscops' by Norie, and at Milton House in the Canongate, designed by John Adam for Lord Milton in about 1755, the dining room was decorated with 'Arabesque painting and Landskips' by William Delacour, a Frenchman. These seem to have been in the style of Watteau's rococo engravings. John Adam also employed Delacour to soften the severity of the great dining room at Yester: his light distempered panels depicting classical ruins, which was further embellished by Robert Adam in 1789, make this the most beautiful room in Scotland. It clearly demonstrates the importance the Scots have attached to the dining room.

Many of Norie's landscape schemes were carried out in dining rooms and prepared the ground for such developments as Charles Steuart's views of local topography, with which he decorated the walls of the dining room at Blair Castle in 1766-78. In a letter discussing the design of Penicuik, Sir James Clerk makes clear that Ossian's Hall, with its cycle of decorative painting by Alexander Runciman of 1772, was intended as the dining room for company. At a lesser artistic level, the fictive framed pictures in the dining room at Woodside House near Beith demonstrate the decorative vitality of the west of Scotland at this time. At Woodside, only the overdoors and large central panel have remained exposed, but the architecturally placed landscape panels would have been linked by further decorative painting to create an overall scheme.

So far we have been discussing Scotland's grandest houses. This is because the dining room as a specialized room could be found only above a certain level of society and social ambition before the mid eighteenth century. Most Scottish houses had only a single public room which, if it was called the dining room, must also have functioned as a parlour-living room.

John Adam's plans for a new house at Ballochmyle of about 1760, engraved for *Vitruvius Scoticus*, did not include a drawing room, although the dining room was finished expensively with a rich stucco ceiling.[14] In his *Anecdotes and Egotisms*, Henry Mackenzie recalled that in many houses the lady's bedroom was used as a drawing room.[15] Similarly, when William Adam had planned Duff House in 1735 the family apartments on the first floor merely had a dining room, but when the house was fitted up in the late 1750s one of the bedrooms was sacrificed to provide the 'Private Drawing Room' now deemed essential.

The New Town of Edinburgh, built from 1767, gave rise to a new type of terrace house, based on London models, where the street floor was the dining-room flat with the drawing room above. Although conceived on the grandest possible scale, Robert Adam's plans for Baron Orde's Queen Street house of 1770–1 established a pattern for the builders of lesser houses. Adam's apsidal sideboard recess in the dining room was to become a standard feature of many New Town houses.

In the second half of the eighteenth century, specialized furniture was developed to suit increasingly particularized room use. Furniture makers and upholsterers were quick to invent an ever wider range of goods for consumers to aspire to. Endeavours such as Edinburgh's New Town, and the building of similar properties in Glasgow and Aberdeen, presented a commercial opportunity on a scale previously unknown in Scotland. The idea that different rooms should have a distinct and easily recognizable character was, however, rooted in convention rather than simply following function. House furnishers thus soon developed a hierarchy which only the bravest could dare flout.

The fashionable neoclassical vocabulary not only stimulated designers such as Robert Adam to create new forms in his houses, but also encouraged furniture makers to pick up the architectural ornaments and follow them through in the furniture, creating a unified effect throughout the room. The dining room was also to benefit from efforts to promote arts and manufactures, leading to the more widespread use of porcelain and pottery tablewares. Processes such as Sheffield plating, introduced in the 1750s, could imitate silver at a fraction of the expense for the middle-class market.[16]

If the concept of a unified suite of furniture began in the melting pot of the new kind of drawing room, it rapidly moved into the dining room. One of the best examples of a dining room fitted up by a single supervising cabinetmaker and upholsterer is to be found at Paxton in Berwickshire (pls 135, 136). Ninian Home's West Indian sugar plantations provided the cash for a modish metropolitan refitting in 1774. His dining room was finished with neoclassical plasterwork, imitating the antique stucco discovered in excavations of Roman houses.[17] Dining room and drawing room were both fitted up by Chippendale from London, and many of his furnishings survive. The most arresting is the elegant sideboard table with its flanking pedestals bearing vases, an evolutionary stage in the invention of the modern sideboard. Such new architecturally placed sideboards challenged the supremacy of the old Scots buffet, which began to disappear from more fashionable dining rooms.[18]

An even rarer survival at Paxton is the original dinner table (pl 135). Like the sideboard, tables were the subject of innovation by furniture designers. The telescopic table of the early nineteenth century proved the fittest and survives in quantity where earlier experiments, as exemplified by Paxton, have been discarded. The key feature of the dinner table was the polished boards which were revealed at the dessert when the servants removed the stained linen cloths. The cabinetmaker's challenge was to achieve a more or less unbroken expanse of superbly matched timber – its quality an advertisement for his firm and the centre of attention – which could also cope with a variable number of diners. A further pressure came from the late eighteenth-century tendency to entertain larger numbers. The Paxton table, with its freestanding middle section and 'D' ends, which could serve as detached side tables when the party was small, demonstrates the ingenuity of the maker's solution to these problems. Typically, Chippendale's chairs do not survive at Paxton: no item of household furniture was to be more frequently replaced. At first this was for reasons of comfort, particularly when sprung upholstery was invented, and then the reasons became mainly aesthetic.

Some of Scotland's most elegant neoclassical dining rooms are by Robert Adam. At Mellerstain during the early 1770s, Adam effectively installed a traditional state apartment, kicking off with a great dining room with attractive stucco ornaments in white on tinted grounds. Many of his later designs for Scottish patrons were for intricately planned smaller houses, where the dining room and drawing room are so similar in size and access arrangements that it is often impossible from the plan to distinguish them. Both enjoyed a variety of inventive shapes, as at Sunnyside, an Edinburgh villa of the late 1780s. Mellerstain is also a reminder that there were no set rules about style. Its castellated gothic exterior was deemed suitable for its dramatic setting in the Borders landscape, but although Adam did much to popularize the castle revival in Scotland, his interiors remained classical. The popularity of the gothic revival, however, fuelled by its compatibility in picturesque terms with the rugged Scottish landscape, was to have an important impact on some Scottish

136. A corner of the dining room at Paxton (see pl 135). The Chippendale sideboard flanked by urns lined with lead to hold water for the rinsing of glasses, and with plate warmers in their pedestals, represented the latest London fashions and marked a move away from the traditional Scottish buffet niche.

dining rooms and led to a deliberate re-invention of that room's history.

The key Scottish house in the gothic revival was Inveraray, designed by Roger Morris for the third Duke of Argyll in 1744, although in its interior the gothic windows were transformed with circular heads to suit the classical French tastes of the fifth Duke from 1772 (pl 130).[19] As the picturesque line hardened, however, it began to be accepted that the exterior style of a house should be followed through into the interior. This was soon set as a rule. As a solution to this difficulty, architects found it convenient to recast their dining rooms as baronial halls in a process that was to have a profoundly regressive impact on Scottish taste. Thus at Taymouth, where the Elliots reworked the Inveraray theme for Lord Breadalbane, the dining room emerged as a baronial hall with gothic shafts and vaulting, theatrically played up by the housepainter's new-found skills with graining, marbling, and imitation ashlar. Stained glass completed the effect.

During the early nineteenth century this mood had a significant impact on old houses. When the architect John Smith of Aberdeen was asked in 1824 to modernize Craigievar, he declined. Through the chances of inheritance the castle had escaped alteration and he suggested it was 'well worth being preserved as it is one of the finest specimens of architecture in this country of the age and style in which it is built and finely situated.'[20] Acting on his advice, the Forbes family modernized their other seat at Fintray, nearer Aberdeen, and used Craigievar as a summer holiday villa, the more attractive because of its old Scots character. By the end of the century, the family found it had been in the

137. The hall as dining room at Craigievar, Aberdeenshire. Although many old Scottish tower houses were to be ruthlessly modernized during the nineteenth century, Craigievar was preserved. The family played up its antique character by continuing to dine at the seventeenth-century table, and a suite of appropriate dining chairs was made up to match, copied from seventeenth-century originals. The tartan upholstery confirmed the deliberately Scottish character of the room.

vanguard of a reappraisal of Scotland's past in which both Sir Walter Scott, and unexpectedly, Queen Victoria herself, had played a part.

Smith's improvements at Craigievar were so restrained that they have tended to go unnoticed. It was relatively easy to convert the great hall into a dining room (pl 137) with the addition of a butler's pantry in the screens passage and a wine cellar below. The contents reflected the baronial mood, which possibly went as far as rushes on the floor. Willingness to sacrifice comfort for the sake of looks is demonstrated by the family's determination to dine at the old table which was so high that the set of antiquarian seat furniture required foot cushions to sustain the awkward elevation. Almost inevitably, the new chairs were covered in the Forbes 'ancestral' tartan to achieve an effect that is so visually persuasive it seems churlish to question that it could possibly date from later than the 1620s.

The identification of an apparently 'Scottish' species of the picturesque fuelled the baronial revival but a vocabulary of ornament proved elusive. It was relatively easy to latch onto the Jacobean ceilings in castles like Craigievar and Glamis, but regrettably, more was known of the ornamental vocabulary of Pompeii and Herculaneum than that of medieval Scotland. Without a range of sources to pave a high road of design excellence, the Scots took the baronial low road to Brigadoon. But if the visual stimulation was limited, the emotional justification was profound, for even at the end of the eighteenth century there was a widespread sense of the passing of peculiarly Scottish, and therefore precious, customs.

One feature of this emotionalism was the buffet niche, still lingering in the early nineteenth century, as described by John Strang above (p129), but beginning to be replaced by the sideboard. A fondness for the old-fashioned buffet is perhaps betrayed by the Scots continuing to place the fitted sideboard in an elaborately architectural mural recess, and in the characteristic stepped back of the Scottish variant on the London sideboard which may reflect the buffet's tiered shelves.

It was this kind of feeling that lay behind Sir Walter Scott's coinage of a specifically Scottish idiom at his beloved Abbotsford. This was done partly

138. At Abbotsford in Roxburghshire Sir Walter Scott created Romantic interiors in an earlier Scottish idiom that were to have a profound impact on later taste. In his dining room, mahogany was eschewed and the dinner tables were made from ancient oaks from Drumlanrig. Unromantically, the Turkey carpet had a matching oilcloth in front of the sideboard to protect it from spillages of food.

139. In 1906 Charles Rennie Mackintosh and his wife Margaret Macdonald bought 6 Florentine Terrace (later 78 Southpark Avenue), Glasgow, which has now been faithfully reconstructed within the Hunterian Art Gallery. They brought with them the dark-stained oak dining-room furniture designed for their previous flat, and their new dining room has a subliminal baronial air. The contrast with the pale drawing room upstairs (pl 178) is notable.

through an inspired *bricolage* of early fragments and casts of ancient carvings at Melrose or Roslin, but also through the selection of Scottish materials. Thus the boards of Scott's dinner table were not of fancy foreign mahogany but 'of Scottish oak with room for thirty people and clouded in the most beautiful style … They were made of particular parts of the growth of certain very old oaks which had grown for ages … in the old and noble park at Drumlanrig Castle'.[21]

Scott's attitude, however, was far from simple, and if his table looked backwards, the gaslight flickering above was so new-fangled and untested that it was subsequently cited as contributing to his death. But if Scott's approach was also lighthearted, as the cabbage substituted for a medieval boss above his chair at the head of the table at Abbotsford reveals, the pursuit of an elemental and unquestionably Scottish primitivism continued in earnest. It went on to spawn hundreds of grisly revived baronial dining rooms devoid of aesthetic merit. Two exceptional flashes of interest are the late nineteenth-century, and as yet anonymous, refitting of the hall at Crathes with a very early revival of Scottish tempera decoration; and the subliminally baronial dining room that the Mackintoshes created for themselves at 78 Southpark Avenue, now in the Hunterian Art Gallery (pl 139). The idea that to sit on crude furniture covered in deerskin and wield implements made from antlers in a room with walls of granite rubble is somehow more worthily Scottish than the approach of the fifth Duke of Argyll and his Duchess, who went to Paris and ordered Beauvais tapestry and quantities of gilt chairs for Inveraray, and then trained up a band of Edinburgh craftsmen to make cheaper copies of the French originals, has had a persistent but deleterious effect on Scottish taste ever since.

If Sir John Forbes at Craigievar and Scott at Abbotsford could take social risks with idiosyncratic decoration in their dining rooms, many others did not dare. Among the best accounts of an early nineteenth-century Scottish dinner is one in the *Early Reminiscences* of Mrs Janet Story. This includes a nostalgic memoir of her childhood at 37 Melville Street, at the fashionable west end of Edinburgh's New Town. After a successful career in the Indian navy, her father had sufficient money in the bank to settle in Edinburgh, educate his growing family and marry off his daughters respectably. Extravagant formal dinners were the lynchpin of this kind of upward social mobility and the family was not alone in living at the limit of its income. The warmth of Mrs Story's recollections is tinged with the knowledge that the high life came to an abrupt halt when the bank failed. Her account is worth quoting at length because it reflects the extent to which the character of the dining room was being set in a rigid etiquette based on conspicuous consumption.

> My father furnished No. 37 from the upholstering firm of Messrs. Whytock & Co. No scamped work came out of their shop, and to this day the drawers run and the hinges work as if Japanese artificers had been employed on them. The furniture was nearly all rosewood and old Spanish mahogany, especially the many leaved dining tables, my mother's particular pride. ... You could see your face in them almost like a mirror. And all this was true 'elbow grease,' for no modern French polish was ever allowed to desecrate those sacred panels. In winter, when ... no social interruption seemed probable, the tables were hauled out of their corners, the leaves inserted, and the entire household set to work to polish them up, first rubbing them hard with a small square piece of cork, and then finishing with dry rubbing, with a piece of flannel or even an ordinary duster.[22]

This work was assisted by the occasional employment of two Highland porters; they did numerous jobs for the households in the neighbourhood and were especially good at polishing the boards, which were easily damaged by hot dishes or spilled wine.

Mrs Story's father took great pride and pleasure in entertaining, with his handsome wife at the head of the table, and she had much to do:

> The dinners then were something to speak of, and were affairs that required much arrangement and forethought. The cook who was to assist on the occasion must first of all be secured, long before the guests were invited; for the ordinary kitchen performer of that day was a mortal of very ordinary attainments, and would have been quite over-weighted with the prospect of preparing a dinner for twenty-two, or even a larger number ...
>
> The cook secured, the next most important matter was the head waiter, a very superior functionary, who was answerable for the arrangement of the table service and appointments, and for the ushering in and general superintendence of the company ...
>
> Mrs. Clerihew, the female *chef*, and my mother between them always concocted a feast for the gods: no cheese-paring economy was ever practised in our house, for though my mother, like John Gilpin's wife, 'even when on pleasure bent had a frugal mind,' my father had not: he liked everything to be of the best, which usually meant the most expensive: and in those days a very elaborate and costly succession of viands was almost a matter of course, if people gave a dinner at all.
>
> Two soups, and Mrs. Clerihew was not niggardly in her stock, two large dishes of fish, and these were all placed on the dinner table, my father serving the one, my mother the other. We had two very handsome silver soup tureens ... One was always placed at the head of the table, the other at the foot ....
>
> In succession to the soup and to the fish, four massive *entrée* dishes were placed heavily on the table to be 'seen of all men'; and were then lightly removed and handed, one after the other, to the guests. One of them was

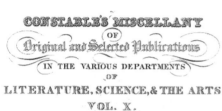

CONSTABLE'S MISCELLANY
OF
Original and Selected Publications
IN THE VARIOUS DEPARTMENTS
OF
LITERATURE, SCIENCE, & THE ARTS
VOL. X.
TABLE TALK.

Engraved on Steel by W.H.Lizars.

EDINBURGH:
PRINTED FOR CONSTABLE & Cº
1827.

140. Although Lizar's elegant dining-room scene is imaginative and was intended only to decorate a title page of 1827, it gives a vivid impression of the conspicuous consumption pursued in the 'Modern Athens' and may record accurately the service of the dessert course at the end of a dinner.

invariably a curry, which though served out of its proper order, which, in India, is at the conclusion of the meal, was of an excellence so superior as very speedily to win great renown for my mother's recipe …

The silver *entrée* dishes were removed, and a huge roast of beef or a leg of mutton was placed before the host: the opposite end of the table being graced by a gigantic turkey, roasted or boiled. While my father devoted his attention to the beef, the male guest of honour carved the turkey …

Then came the sweet course. At the foot of the table there was usually a dish of macaroni and cheese, more especially for masculine tastes; while at the other end towered a magnificent erection of spun sugar and pastry, filled with luscious preserves, a perfect death trap for indigestion, especially after all that had gone before. Two side dishes, one occasionally a simple pudding, duly appeared; while four handsome cut crystal dishes took the place of the previous *entrées*, containing a white vanilla and a pink raspberry cream, a pale wine jelly, and one tinted crimson with drops of cochineal: very pretty and tempting they all looked.[23]

As described by Mrs Story, the citizens of Edinburgh during the 1830s had created a formulaic performance. The set-piece quality of a typical Northern Athenian dinner is reflected by the extreme standardization of the dining rooms in which they were held. In 1831 or 1832, William Trotter, the leading cabinetmaker in Edinburgh, presented an estimate for fitting up Number 3 Moray Place to Sir Duncan Campbell of Barcaldine.[24] The suggested dining room furniture matches the suite that survives, by a miracle, at 31 Moray Place (now the Hope Trust), down to the 'Handsome Roman mahogany Sideboard richly carv'd 8 feet long'. This is a measure of the extent to which Edinburgh, a city of careful professional conformity dominated by the legal profession, was in thrall to social conventions.

Trotter's estimate also reveals how Edinburgh's New Town houses accommodated large parties. Although the dining room at Number 3 was to have the regulation twelve single chairs plus two armchairs, the parlour immediately behind the dining room was to contain '8 Mahogany Chairs same as in dining room'.[25] When the table was pulled out to its full extent, twenty-two diners could thus be seated in matching elegance.

By the 1820s, the dining room had fully evolved into a conventional form from which only the most socially secure might risk deviation. A photograph by Magnus Jackson of the dining room at Megginch Castle in the 1870s illustrates this norm (pl 142). It is also of interest in showing a reduced table for a small family meal, whereas most dining rooms were photographed on gala days. Partly through deliberate contrast with the drawing room, as well as for obvious practical reasons, dining rooms had a hard surface finish with plain painted, and thus durable, wall surfaces. This plainness was promoted by the Greek Revival style, which eliminated the earlier Georgian dado in favour of an unbroken expanse of wall.

During Victoria's reign, 'art' gravitated with the lion's share of the available cash to the drawing room, leaving family portraits in the dining room. The drawing room had rosewood furniture and painted imitations of expensive cabinet-woods on its joinery, silk upholstery and curtains, chimneypieces of white statuary marble, and extensive gilding. In contrast, the dining room furniture was normally of dark mahogany with joinery often painted like oak. For heavy duty a rug of coarse red and blue Turkey pattern knotted pile had perhaps a strip of oilcloth in similar style in front of the sideboard to protect the floor from careless servants. Leather or horsehair chair covers were standard, with heavy cloth curtains − red being a favourite colour. The dining room

141. In contrast with the overt Scottishness of Craigievar, Balmoral before its redecoration in the 1850s (see pl 16) had a series of interiors in very straightforward mid nineteenth-century taste. This watercolour by James Giles of 1854, with its green walls and Turkey carpet, makes it easier to imagine the original effect of rooms recorded only in black and white, such as the dining room at Megginch in the plate below.

142. An 1870s photograph of the dining room at Megginch Castle, Perthshire, full of detail documenting dining customs. The dark chimneypiece, painted walls, Turkey carpet and leather upholstery are all conventional, and diversely framed family portraits testify to the family's long lineage. Note the Landseer-inspired embroidered firescreen to the right of the fireplace and the wicker chair screens tucked in behind it.

chimneypiece was often of black marble, in the form of unornamented Greek Revival slabs, and gilding was seldom used.

There was a limit to which innovation could be encouraged if hierarchic distinctions were to be maintained in order not to confuse dinner guests. Effort was therefore concentrated on improving the planning of houses and methods of keeping dinners hot. The 'Modern Athens' was to prove second to none in all departments. Sir John Robison, Secretary of the Royal Society of Edinburgh and inventor, was one of the first to install gas for cooking in his new house at 13 Randolph Place, where he also had a sophisticated ventilation system. But the master country-house planner of the early nineteenth century was William Burn, whose approach focused on the careful siting of public and private rooms. Since the dining room required both 'family' access and efficient dinner service, Burn placed it in an isolated part of the house to be close to the kitchens and to a new, but all-important, dinner service room, often with hot plates (which survive at Camperdown House designed by Burn in 1821). Sunshine was considered a nuisance in a dining room, which thus could face north, an aspect not suited to other public rooms. This complex programme is recorded in the manual published in 1864 by a fellow Scot, Robert Kerr, entitled *The Gentleman's House, or how to plan English residences from the Parsonage to the Palace*.

With a logic anticipating a computer programme, Kerr explains how the size of the dining room had to reflect the proportions of the table itself; the necessary circulation space for service; the placing of the fireplace; and the desirability of having the sideboard immediately behind the master's chair for instant communication with the butler. Something of this scientific codification can also be seen in dining-room furniture at this time. The principal innovation remained the telescopic table, conveniently supported on four corner legs and a certain amount of unseen ironmongery to resolve the traditional conflict of the diner's legs with the earlier claw-legged sectional tables. Sprung seats and deep buttoning gave maximum comfort, and a further luxury was supplied by upholstered backs for dining chairs. Dinner wagons of various kinds (Hopetoun was to have a miniature railway running through the house) increased the chance of dinner arriving hot. An entirely new piece of furniture was the case designed to store leaves of the dinner table until they were required. This usually matched the sideboard and could be a handsome thing in its own right.

Such innovations were pursued with no less vigour in old houses, but arguably it was the increased size of the dinner table itself that pushed out the walls of the dining room in a general rearrangement of eighteenth-century houses throughout Scotland at this time. This reflected the custom of holding ever larger parties and also a fashion for elaborate table centrepieces. A popular rearrangement in older houses was to turn the outer great dining room of the state apartment into the drawing room, whose new status suited its more ornamental character, and to gut the old drawing room and state bedroom to provide a new dining room. This brought the new drawing room into immediate proximity with the entrance hall, while the new dining room was in contact with an existing service stair. This happened not only at the House of Dun but also at Haddo, designed by William Adam in about 1730 and rearranged in about 1822. A similar rethinking (but leaving the drawing room intact) can be seen on the grandest scale at Hopetoun, which was apparently ready to receive George IV during his state visit in 1822.

The air of codification which now attached to the dining room was reflected in its associated social customs. Even when James Hogg had dined at Inveraray in 1803 (pp 125–6) the gentlemen had changed into black evening dress, to his discomfort and disapproval. Another standardization related to the dinner hour, as Lord Cockburn summarized: 'within my memory, the hour has ranged from two to half-past six o'clock; and a stand has been regularly made at the end of every half-hour against each encroachment and always on the same grounds – dislike of change and jealousy of finery.'[26]

This standardization, however, was not achieved without resistance. At one extreme there were a few people who strove for fancier dining rooms. D R Hay, the Edinburgh housepainter and Scotland's pioneer interior decorator in the late 1820s, tried to induce his clients to select more elaborate effects from his repertoire to enliven their dull dining rooms, his favourite treatment for their plain walls being raised damask patterns in sanded paints.

In his newly aggrandized palace at Hamilton, the tenth Duke in the 1820s devised a sumptuous gilded state dining room with marbled walls and a marble sideboard used for the display of plate whose value, 'including a magnificent gold set, is probably about £50,000'.[27] If his gilded 'Louis Revival' dining chairs were exceptional, it is interesting to see in a photograph of about 1880 that their placement would have won Kerr's approval:

> One feature which has always a substantial and hospitable aspect in this apartment is the unbroken line of chairs at the wall. Although it is not desirable to make a Gentleman's Dining-room like the Assembly Hall of a Corporation or the Long-room of a tavern by carrying this principle to extreme, yet it is not well when dinner waggons, cheffoniers, or whatever else, are placed at intervals in such number as to give the apartment the character of a Parlour. In fact, as much as possible, every chair ought to stand at the wall facing its place at table; whereby, if no more, a species of association is kept up with the primary purpose of the room.[28]

Behind Kerr's somewhat puzzling logic there may be a deliberate attempt to preserve the eighteenth-century custom of lining furniture against the perimeter of the walls of each room when not in use. At the start of the nineteenth century it had become usual in fashionable circles to pull drawing-room furniture into the centre of the room in pursuit of a picturesque, 'lived-in' look, but a rare furniture plan of about 1850 for Springwood Park, near Kelso, shows a stiff line up of furniture in the dining room while the rather tentative pulling out of the drawing-room furniture suggests that in less fashionable Scottish houses old customs may have lingered.

143. This Victorian furnishing plan for Springwood Park, near Kelso, Rox-burghshire, shows the persistence of eighteenth-century formal customs in the dining room, where the furniture is arranged around the walls, while in the drawing room a few items have been pulled into the centre of the room in pursuit of a more informal arrangement.

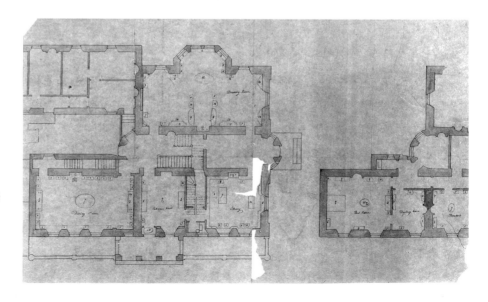

144. *The family of Woodhouselee assembled in the Dining room. September 1804.* Painted by Lord Woodhouselee's daughter Isabella, who is standing by the harpsichord, it shows this large family following various pursuits in the 'gothick' dining room at Woodhouselee, Midlothian. They are using this room, with its cosy fitted carpet, as the everyday sitting room according to Scottish custom.

145. This portrait by David Cooke Gibson shows Sir Adam and Lady Ferguson using their dining room at 27 George Square, Edinburgh, as a parlour or sitting room. It was painted between 1847 and 1851, and seems to be a very accurate rendition of the room.

The other line of resistance to prescriptive dining customs came from those who resented the disruption of cosy, old-fashioned, and often apparently Scottish habits by smart London notions of propriety. Thus when an anonymous American was invited by Lord Jeffrey to dine at Craigcrook Castle in 1827, he was delighted that

> At six o'clock we were introduced into the dining-room, and seated at the table, crowned with a series of Scotch dishes, from barley-broth down to the bannock, which is a thin cake made of oatmeal ... Two species of fish from the Forth, a desert of native fruits, half a dozen kinds of wine one of which was old Madeira from his friends in the United States, and a round of whisky, the usual *finale* of a Scotch dinner, were among the varieties of the festive board, which was spread with neatness, but with no marks of extravagance.[29]

Craigcrook, however, was the Jeffreys' country retreat; it would be fascinating to know if dinner at their town house in Moray Place was more like those given by Mrs Story's parents.

The later dinner hour had the effect of killing off the traditional Scottish supper, though Lord Cockburn's *Memorials* record the defiant attempts of his Edinburgh circle to retain it:

> Early dinners begat suppers. But suppers are so delightful that they have survived long after dinners have become late. Indeed this has immemorially been a favourite Edinburgh repast. I have often heard strangers say, that Edinburgh was the only place where the people dined twice every day. It is now fading into paltry wine and water in many houses; but in many it still triumphs in a more substantial form ... Almost all my set, which is perhaps the merriest, the most intellectual, and not the most severely abstemious, in Edinburgh, are addicted to it. I doubt if from the year 1811, when I married, I have closed above one day in the month, of my town life, at home and alone. It is always some scene of domestic conviviality, either in my own house or in a friend's. ... The refection is beginning to be thought vulgar, or at least superfluous ... But its native force makes it keep its place even in polite societies. How could it fail? ... Supper is cheaper than dinner; shorter; less ceremonious; and more poetical.[30]

Strang's book on Glasgow clubs of the early nineteenth century shows that there too, when dinner parties were less numerous, most visiting was for supper:

> those agreeable reunions, although not quite so ceremonious, partook much of the same style as a dinner of the present time ... on such occasions it was the custom for the ladies to continue at the table till a very short time before the general break-up. These, too, were generally very merry meetings, and the evening's pastime was always enhanced by a glee, a catch, or a song; or sometimes where there were young ladies, by a rondo or air on the spinnet or piano.[31]

This polarization between formal dinners and delightful suppers also perhaps preserves a contrast between the baroque dining room and the cosy family parlour which had once balanced it. This was increasingly under threat in many houses where, from the late eighteenth century, the no less elegant breakfast room was replacing the parlour, and dinner was always served in the dining room, even for a small family party like that photographed at Megginch (pl 142). Obviously, as dining rooms became more specialized and scientifically planned, it was difficult to change into the less formal mode favoured by the Cockburn set.

The survival of the parlour model may also be reflected in the common Scottish practice of using the dining room as the family's ordinary sitting room in smaller houses. The drawing room having developed to such a degree of finery that there was a danger of spoiling every surface, it was easier to leave it shut up against the arrival of guests; whereas the robust dining-room furnishings could more readily stand family wear and tear. This living-dining room concept is exemplified by the portrait of the Fergusons seated at their black marble dining-room fireplace in their townhouse in George Square, Edinburgh (pl 145). An earlier example is probably shown in a watercolour of the parlour at Woodhouselee, a gothic Edinburgh villa (pl 144).

A poignant inventory of one such living-dining room is to be found in the sequestration papers of Trotter's firm when it foundered in 1860. George Potts had been the firm's traveller and had advised on the fitting up of the grandest dining rooms in Scotland. The inventory of his estate clearly describes a more informal room in Potts's own house, Carlton Cottage, Spring Gardens, Edinburgh:[32]

Dining Room

	£	s.	d.
Grate Fender & Irons		12	
2 Jugs			2
Easy chair in Mor Cloth		12	
Small Fly table		4	6
Drawers & Bookcase	2	10	
Sofa in Mor Cloth	2	5	
Telescope Dining Tables		4	
6 Mahogany chairs	2	2	
Enclosed Mahogany sideboard with Back fitted for Books	6		
2 Light gas Lustre		14	
Carpet, Rug & Waxcloth		15	
Curtain & Pole		5	
Wood vase		5	
Books	9		
[Total]	29	6	6

Having set out to treat *The Gentleman's House ... from the Parsonage to the Palace*, Robert Kerr was obliged to deal with the living-dining room, which merited a section of its own entitled the 'Dining-and-Sitting-Room'. But his sneering asides imply the disapproval of a professional architect whose profit derived from a percentage of the total outlay. His use of the adjective 'homely' to describe this dual-purpose room suggests that it owed its popularity as much to the survival of more comfortable habits as to financial stringency.

A subsidiary function of the Victorian dining room was its use for family prayers, as for instance at Warriston House, an Edinburgh villa, where benches were brought in for the maids. A photograph of the dining room at The Cairns, a baronial villa by the architect John Burnet for J P Kidston, a coal master in Cambuslang, Lanarkshire, shows a bible resting on a linen-fold cabinet, with a suitably inspiring painting above (pl 146).

Another photograph of The Cairns shows a set table with its floral arrangement and folded napkins. The line-up of carving and serving cutlery at the master's cover is a reminder that traditional dinner service as recorded by Mrs Story prevailed in Cambuslang in about 1875 when the photograph was taken. Carving at the table prolonged the meal through ritualized performance

146. The Cairns at Cambuslang, near Glasgow, was designed by John Burnet senior, and this photograph of 1875 suggests that he also designed its dining-room furniture to match his chimney-piece. A bible sits on the matching case for the extra leaves from the dinner table, testifying to the common use of the Scottish dining room for daily family prayers.

until fashionable society liberated itself from the boredom this involved by the introduction of service *à la Russe*: meat was carved by servants at sidetables and brought to each diner at the table, greatly speeding up the process. It is not known when this arrangement spread to Scotland but it is likely, as with so many innovations, that there was a degree of resistance and a time lag. The Russian style required a larger range of plates and cutlery and was labour intensive.

A growing dislike of the hard and fast conventions that house furnishers had established for the dining room led to attempts at greater individuality, especially by designers involved in the reforming Aesthetic Movement of the 1860s and 1870s. Oak was adopted as a fashionable alternative to mahogany. Perhaps the most individual of all the proto-Aesthetic dining rooms is to be found at Holmwood, designed by Alexander 'Greek' Thomson about 1857 (pl 147). Holmwood is a small suburban villa but reflects the importance attached by Glasgow merchants to business entertaining, with its disproportionately large dining room and extensive service accommodation of larders and kitchen close at hand.

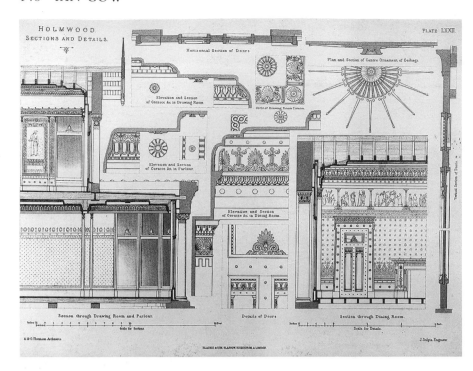

HOLMWOOD.
SECTIONS AND DETAILS.
PLATE LXXII.

Section through Drawing Room and Parlour.   Details of Doors.   Section through Dining Room.

147. Holmwood, a villa at Cathcart near Glasgow, was the masterpiece of the architect Alexander 'Greek' Thomson, who supervised every detail of its design and decoration in 1857–8. The house is now in the care of the National Trust for Scotland, and investigation has brought Thomson's original schemes to light and revealed their rich colouring.

Holmwood became a convent, and sadly its top-lit marble sideboard has been dismantled and almost nothing is known of its other furnishings at present. Aesthetic furnishings can, however, still be seen in the eighteenth-century dining room at Newhailes, a villa near Edinburgh with a superb lion-skin marble chimneypiece and inset paintings (pls 148-50). Although most of these decorations date from the second quarter of the eighteenth century, the furnishings continued to evolve. A watercolour of 1869 shows the room with the standard early nineteenth-century long dinner table and Greek Revival dining chairs (pl 148). Not long afterwards, however, the house was restored in a loosely artistic manner which played up the eighteenth-century character. The later furniture was replaced by an Aesthetic oak table and stuffed-back dining chairs (pl 149). The old marble-topped sidetable remained in use under the large pier glass opposite the chimneypiece, but an oak sideboard was introduced behind the columns at the service door. This was probably balanced behind the opposite pair of columns by a matching case for the table flaps. The fascination of Newhailes is that it represents an amateur and artistic response to the decoration of the relatively recent past, before the self-conscious development of a sense of period styles.

The first stirrings in Scotland of the Aesthetic Movement's second development into the cult of period styles and what we now recognize as 'antique' furniture occurs in a lecture delivered in 1883 to the Edinburgh Architectural Association by John Marshall, Rector of the Royal High School. Although obliged to reside in the standard Victorian speculator's villa, where the bay-windowed drawing room lay immediately over the bay-windowed dining room, Marshall rejected the allure of the upholsterer's 'twenty guinea suite' for each room in favour of an accumulation of earlier furniture which had, at least to his eye, the added value of patina.[33] His dining room (pl 151), with its Aesthetic frieze, had a mixture of pieces including the inevitable antique Chippendale chairs, which were soon to become essential in any dining room with pretensions to taste. The fact that Chippendale's chair designs were less comfortable than deeply sprung Victorian dining chairs was disregarded in pursuit of the desired look.

148. A watercolour by Walter Severn of 1869 shows the dining room at Newhailes, a villa at Musselburgh near Edinburgh, with interior decoration by Thomas Clayton of 1742. This view clearly depicts the fine marble fireplace and the standard mid nineteenth-century Greek Revival chairs.

149. A photograph of the same room, about 1928, showing that the chairs were replaced in about 1880 with a set of fully stuffed oak chairs to match the new Aesthetic dining table.

150. A Royal Commission record photograph shows that the chairs have been replaced again, this time with a suite whose eighteenth-century character is suited to the original decoration of the room, though the table has been suffered to remain.

151. John Marshall was one of the first amateur collectors of antique furniture and this sketch of 1883 of the dining room in his Edinburgh villa, Southgate, shows that in addition to a Jacobean oak cupboard (left) he has selected a late eighteenth-century Scotch sideboard with its stepped shelf on top, perhaps harking back to the Scots' fondness for their buffets, and the inevitable 'Chippendale' chairs which were to become the cynosure of good taste.

152. The taste for eighteenth-century furnishings spread rapidly at the end of the nineteenth century and was particularly taken up by architects. This view of the dining room at Kellie Castle, Fife, in about 1900 shows a harlequin set of the newly fashionable Chippendale chairs. The castle was restored by Professor James Lorimer from about 1878. After his death his sons, John, the artist, and Robert, the architect, continued to develop the interiors of this house, which was to have an important impact on Scottish taste.

Scottish architects quickly took up the eighteenth-century revival dining room. Perhaps the most magical in Scotland at this date was that created by John Lorimer and his architect brother, Robert, in their parents' rented holiday home at Kellie Castle in Fife, which had been rescued in a pioneer restoration by their father (pl 152). An attractive room with painted panelling was played up with fragments of ancient tapestry, but the Lorimers' use of a harlequin set of 'Chippendale' chairs and a rag rug was unusually relaxed. It recalls other folk revival exercises elsewhere in Europe, and particularly the interiors of contemporary artists such as Carl Larsson in Sweden. Another artist, E A Hornel, also had non-identical Chippendale chairs in his dining room at Broughton House in Kirkcudbright, whereas bourgeois convention demanded a matching set of chairs in Sir Robert Lorimer's house in the west end of Edinburgh's New Town. His dining room at 54 Melville Street was in a pretentious medieval style, akin to the taste of his friend, the rich collector Sir William Burrell, and was created round a fragment of early tapestry. Sir Rowand Anderson, Lorimer's master, made a number of revealing changes to his dining room in the modest stripped-baronial villa he had built for himself at Colinton, outside Edinburgh (pl 153). This was fitted up in what Americans would dub an Eastlake or Mission style, but as Anderson grew more interested in collecting, with a particular fondness for oriental porcelain, the house was gradually refurnished and the original contents elbowed aside by Dutch buffet commodes and lacquer cabinets. By about 1900 it had a 'Sheraton' sideboard,

153. Sir Rowand Anderson had designed his own villa Allermuir at Colinton near Edinburgh in 1879. By the time this photograph was taken some twenty years later, his Aesthetic furnishings had been overlaid by the spoils of many years of antique collecting. The shelves and cabinet display part of his collection of oriental ceramics. Although the Dutch buffet cabinet with its tiered shelves was antique, the seventeenth-century-style chairs, the sideboard, and telescopic table were all modern reproductions.

but this, like the matching mahogany telescopic table, was probably a new piece in period style. His dining chairs were of a seventeenth-century type and may have been specially made to receive a set of embossed Spanish leather covers. The historicist look was completed by his use of a table carpet. It was an eclectic ensemble.

This taste for luxury can be seen in several of the Scottish shots taken by the specialist architectural photographer, Bedford Lemere. Elaborate table centre-pieces and displays of the florist's art, like that depicted at Inglewood in Clackmannanshire, were surely not cleared away at the end of the meal, now brilliantly illuminated by electricity. There was the usual resistance to the new refinements of abundant flowers and fancy napery, and as early as 1858 Strang complained of contemporary Glasgow taste:

> There were, however, no table napkins, each with its pear-shaped roll en-closed, placed before the guests at dinner, although sometimes these modern comforts were sported at the tea-table; and such articles, if ever seen, were certainly not fringed with *lace*, which some upstarts have lately been attempting to introduce …[34]

154. This photograph of the dining room at Inglewood, Alloa, in Clackmannanshire, was taken by the distinguished architectural photographer, Bedford Lemere, in about 1900. It shows a formal dinner setting with elaborate flower arrangements in an eclectic seventeenth-century styled room designed by the fashionable Edinburgh architects Mitchell & Wilson.

With the new accent on period styles in the late nineteenth century, manufacturers responded with modern tablewares following earlier forms and there was a proliferation of practical and decorative items to add to the richness of effect. Architects designed houses with rooms in a variety of styles, showing a tendency towards early Georgian and Chippendale in the dining room. A prime example of such a dining room survives at Hill of Tarvit in Fife, designed by Sir Robert Lorimer to 'accord with furniture of a Chippendale type'.

No room was to be more often refurbished in the twentieth century than the dining room and after 1928 the early Aesthetic chairs at Newhailes were replaced with some in eighteenth-century style (pl 150). A spectacular example of this pace of change is shown by a series of photographs in the National Monuments Record of Scotland of Poltalloch, one of Burn's most expensive commissions, where the chimneypiece and the voluptuous Victorian rococo furniture were gradually replaced by more classic eighteenth-century forms.

A good impression of late nineteenth-century refinement is recorded in a series of posed photographs showing a dinner party attended by prominent Edinburgh tradesmen (pl 155). But too little is still known about dinner service

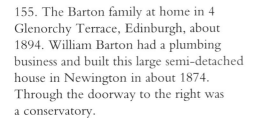

155. The Barton family at home in 4 Glenorchy Terrace, Edinburgh, about 1894. William Barton had a plumbing business and built this large semi-detached house in Newington in about 1874. Through the doorway to the right was a conservatory.

throughout Scotland to draw any conclusions about social customs at this period.

Public and ceremonial dinners expanded in the nineteenth century to the extent that they often required an elaborate temporary architecture of their own outside the home. Scotland's dining clubs, however, often met in private houses (although a few still maintain special premises), and depended, like Mrs Story's parents, on firms of specialist caterers who could supply not only the cook but waiters and tablewares. The elaboration of table settings and ever-increasing numbers created business for specialist firms who could hire anything that might be required, as Wilson's of Edinburgh still do.

It is too early to make a balanced assessment of the dining habits of our own time, but the architectural part of the equation can be readily summarized. The profound change in the second half of the twentieth century has been the disappearance of domestic service. Thanks to the efforts of architects such as William Burn, the dining room and service areas were situated in such remote zones of country houses that they were impossible to use without domestic staff. Many such houses owe their survival to a reconsideration of their planning

156. The dining room/living room at Clapperfield, Edinburgh, the home of the architect Stuart Renton, built for himself in three phases from 1959. Originally the house had a small kitchen, this room, one bedroom, and a bathroom, but it was expanded over time. The open-plan, combined living/dining room in a middle-class house is a twentieth-century phenomenon.

which has liberated numerous county families from their viewless kitchens and a life clustered round the Aga.[35] At lesser social levels, the hatch between kitchen and dining room, and, more recently, the 'hostess trolley', sought to bridge the gap, but most families have now given up the unequal struggle: the dining room is as dead as the fish knives and grape scissors that its sideboard once harboured, and is equally unmourned. Few houses now have a special room set aside for dining, and it is quite acceptable, even in Edinburgh, to eat off one's lap in front of the television.

In recent years there has perhaps been a last flicker of life, but it is a revival rather than a survival and possibly classifiable under a 'New Romantic' label. As a result, even the present writer possesses a detested dinner jacket against the call of pretension, but as the century closes, one is more likely to be asked to dine in the kitchen. What is extremely moving, however, is that after almost three hundred years of artificiality, which now survives only in the uncertain etiquette of weddings, some pockets of traditional Scottish housewifely virtues, as represented by 'high tea' and home baking, have somehow survived.

7 The Drawing Room

JULIET KINCHIN

'At a pinch it might be possible to live a tranquil, and even a useful, life without a drawing room.'

H J Jennings, 1902[1]

To judge from the mass of accumulated evidence, the drawing room in Scotland appears to have had a very uneven status and history. It was never a typical space within working–class or smaller rural homes; and it took considerably longer than the dining room to become established as a standard feature of houses of the upper and middle ranks in Scotland. By the mid nineteenth century, however, the drawing room was in the ascendant, the showpiece of the home, and its treatment had become the most hotly contested of all domestic interiors. In such a sensitive arena, where status was established by myriad references, the onus lay increasingly on women to ensure that the appropriate range of identities and values was projected through the decor, furnishing, and arrangement of the drawing room. The home in general, and the drawing room in particular, had come to be read as a statement of individual character, morality and tastes, but also had to embody the full rhetoric of domesticity. This range of cultural meanings, evolved over several generations, will be the principal focus of this essay.

The format and usage of the nineteenth-century drawing room combined aspects of a formal 'gala' interior with the roles of family sitting room and 'lady's withdrawing room'. As a room type it had first appeared as part of the new apartment system of processional 'shewed' interiors introduced to grand Scottish houses of the late seventeenth century. At this stage, however, it only played a supporting role to the glamorous lead act of the baroque dining room and state bed chamber (see p 127). The hierarchical relationship between these public rooms was clearly expressed by their relative size and position. In the 1690s layout of Hamilton Palace, for example, the drawing room appears as a buffer zone between the larger dining room and the relative intimacy of the bed chamber and closet beyond (pl 157). In a processional sequence of this kind, a drawing or 'withdrawing' room created a somewhat indeterminate space into which all or part of the company could 'withdraw' at any stage, marking a change in the ritual character or relative privacy of the adjacent rooms. Lacking specialized furniture, these early drawing rooms appeared to function only in relation to the nearby interiors and, as in the case of New Tarbat House in Easter Ross, could even double up as the best bed chamber: in the first-floor 'Drawing Room', the inventory of 1719 listed a bed with 'Moyhair' hangings, twelve chairs with fringed bottoms and green stripes, a chamber pot and close stool, and a servant's bed.[2]

It was not long, however, before the drawing room assumed a higher profile and more distinct character in the houses of the very rich, being expanded to

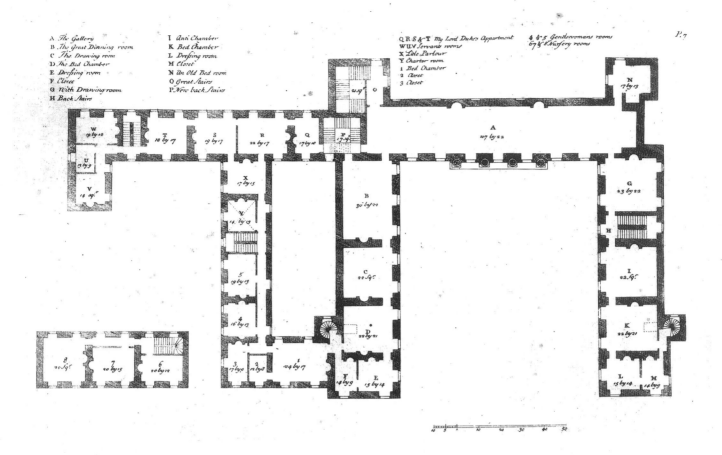

157. Plan of Hamilton Palace from *Vitruvius Scoticus*, probably drawn about 1728 from the plan as remodelled by James Smith in the 1690s. The processional sequence of public rooms was typical of the 'apartment' system introduced to grand Scottish houses of the late seventeenth century. It is clear from their relative size and position how the hierarchy of rooms works.

a barn-like 'parade' or gala space, epitomized by the Great Drawing Room at Hopetoun created in the mid eighteenth century (pl 158). Like the saloon to which it was often closely linked, such a showpiece was reserved for large-scale formal entertainment rather than day-to-day use. Movable furniture would have been set out in symmetrical order against the walls. The key signifiers of major expenditure were the white marble fire surrounds, the staggering yardage of silk damask for upholstery and wall coverings, the glass mirrors with sconces for dozens of wax candles, and lashings of gilding on the interior ornament and matching furniture. Even more expensive and glamorous than Hopetoun was the drawing room created at Inveraray in 1782 by the Duke of Argyll, who commissioned Beauvais tapestries and gilt furniture in the latest cosmopolitan fashions direct from Paris. Although these spectacular schemes were very rare, they were significant in formalizing many of the decorative conventions subsequently associated with the middle-class drawing room.

By the end of the eighteenth century a more picturesque approach was beginning to free up the disposition of furnishings in the drawing room. The formal arrangements of furniture at Archerfield in East Lothian clearly struck Lady Louisa Stuart as excessively stiff in 1799 compared to the more relaxed atmosphere at Dalkeith:

> It wants nothing but more furniture for the middle of rooms. I mean all is set out in order, no comfortable tables to write or read at; it looks like a fine London house prepared for company; quite a contrast to the delightful gallery at Dalkeith where you can settle yourself in any corner.[3]

Greater flexibility in the way the room could be used, and the introduction of more specialized furnishings allowed for varied groupings of people and

158. Glamorous furnishings and expensive decoration in the Red Drawing Room at Hopetoun House, West Lothian, photographed in the 1960s. Through the door can be seen the sequence of rooms on the principal floor.

activities. Apart from being the main reception room for both casual callers and formal entertainment, it was also becoming the space where the women of a household, and in some cases the children, would spend much of their day. J C Loudon, whose writings on gardens, architecture, and interiors were widely read throughout Britain, was Scottish by birth and upbringing. Writing in 1839, he envisaged the well-appointed drawing room as a hive of activity, describing how the ladies might amuse themselves when there was company in the house, 'some with needlework, others with a book or a drawing, others with writing or music, till they met the gentlemen at luncheon'.[4] The programme of activities might also include an excursion, making calls on other drawing rooms in the neighbourhood with the lady of the house. In the afternoon and on summer evenings the connecting doors of the living rooms could be thrown open:

> In the saloon a lady is, perhaps, playing a lively air, while the young ladies and some of the gentlemen are lounging about the room engaged in playful conversation. In the drawing-room would most likely be another group, some sitting upon a couch, while others stand round the table collecting their work, books, or drawings before they retire to dress; and all talking over the place or people they had visited in the morning.[5]

After changing for dinner, family and guests would reassemble there in more formal mode to be shuffled into order of precedence before the ritual procession in pairs through to the dining room. Later in the evening after dinner the gentlemen would rejoin the ladies in the drawing room for tea, cards, and informal conversation to round off the day. These patterns of social interaction were choreographed by a diversified range of seating and tables. Apart from the substantial, more architectural items of furniture, many of the chairs and occasional tables were now lighter and could be easily moved.

Significant adjustments to the layout and appearance of the drawing room were made not only according to the type of entertainment and time of day, but also on a seasonal basis. While a party in summer might fall into detached groups scattered all over the apartment, in winter the company tended to form into one large cluster around the fire. Heating, lighting, and maintaining such large rooms for occasional use was a formidable task. 'Case covers' of cotton or linen shrouded the precious upholstery most of the time, and candlelight was kept to a minimum. It was often easier to shut up drawing rooms out of season, particularly during a Scottish winter. Having more windows than the other public or state rooms, they quickly became dank and freezing. Cullen, the upholsterer co-ordinating the decoration of the Hopetoun drawing room in the 1760s, advised fixing the precious red damask onto the walls with fillets so it could be removed when the room was not in use as a precaution against mildew. Entering the uninhabited wilderness of a bagged-up drawing room was a depressing experience, as described here in *The Inheritance* (1824) by the Scottish novelist Susan Ferrier:

> the visitors were left to find amusement for themselves, which was no easy task where the materials were wanting … here was no fire, and the bright hand-some stove was only to be admired for itself, and the profusion of white paper

159. The Allan family in the drawing room at 28 Queen Street, Edinburgh, probably in 1810, drawn by John Harden. Harden made numerous sketches of his wife's family engaged in music-making and needlework in this room. The drawing room provided the subject matter for many nineteenth-century drawings and watercolours, another artistic activity cultivated in this type of room.

which filled it. The carpet was covered, the chairs were in their wrappers, the screens were in bags – even the chimney piece, that refuge of the weary, showed only two girandoles.[6]

With the quest for comfort intensifying, it is not surprising to find that larger houses often accommodated an additional 'Small Drawing Room' (sometimes labelled the 'Morning Room') as an escape from the chilly formality of the state apartments (pl 160). The furniture listed in a sale, or 'roup', of 1817 at Rozelle House in Ayr clearly implies the daytime use of this smaller room, with draught and fire screens for sitting cosily near the fire, a bookcase for reading matter, and a breakfast table for light meals.[7] The main drawing room, on the other hand, was equipped with greater quantities of lighting, mirrors, and seating for formal evening entertainment, along with the necessary accoutrements for tea and cards. Often such rooms would be furnished *en suite* so that the spaces could be interconnected by folding doors for large parties.[8]

Other rooms closely connected with the drawing room and falling within what might be described as the feminine sphere of influence were the music room and the boudoir. In Walter Macfarlane's Park Circus house in Glasgow, for example, one end of the 1870s drawing room was sectioned off as a music room with carved musical trophies over the door to indicate its function. By this time the pianoforte was more usually located in the drawing room than the dining room. Although originally part of the bedroom suite, 'boudoir' was a term which had assumed rather *nouveau riche* overtones. Like 'morning room' it had come to be applied to a small sitting room used by the mistress of the house, where she could talk to servants, go over the housekeeping, and perhaps

160. Morning Room at Lews Castle, Stornoway, one of the very few large houses on the Isle of Lewis, about 1900. The morning room was closely associated with the drawing room in its style of decoration, though it was likely to be less formal since it was used for private activities rather than polite entertaining.

read or write. In the 1860s, Lady Alison's boudoir at Possil House near Glasgow had rosewood furniture with crimson damask upholstery matching that of the drawing room. Fifty years later the contents of the boudoir at Craigallian (another substantial house outside Glasgow) also smacked of a drawing room in miniature, with items such as a Parian statue of 'Cupid', oriental and pink gilt vases, a writing table, gilt mirrors and a tiny model of a spinning wheel.[9]

The relationship of drawing room to 'parlour' was more ambiguous. Rather like a small drawing room, the addition of a parlour could serve as a more comfortable alternative to the formal reception areas, a kind of family common room in which informal meals might be taken. By the early nineteenth century, however, it is clear that parlours were going out of fashion at the upper end of the social scale. Returning to *The Inheritance* of 1824, we find such an interior mentioned only as a stuffy and outmoded room, reflecting the outlook of its owner, the rich old bachelor Uncle Adam:

> A small dining-table, and a few haircloth chairs stuck against the walls, comprised the whole furniture of the room. A framed table of weights and measures, an old newspaper, and a pile of dusty parchments, tied with a red tape, formed its resources and decorations.[10]

Further down the social hierarchy, on the other hand, parlours were still to be found in middle-class tenement designs throughout the nineteenth century, either in addition to the drawing and dining rooms, or as the formal 'front room' in a two-apartment flat. Such parlours seem to have contained elements of the furnishings of both drawing and dining room, in a formula neatly sketched here in the words of 'Erchie', a character created by Neil Munro in the columns of Glasgow's *Evening Times*:

> When I got married, Duffy, haircloth chairs was a' the go; the sofas had twa ends to them, and you had to hae six books wi' different coloured batters spread oot on the parlour table, wi' the top o' yer weddin'-cake under a gless globe in the middle. Wally dugs on the mantelpiece, worsted things on the chair-backs, a picture o' John Knox ower the kist o'drawers.[11]

Although speaking in about 1900, Erchie could have been describing the room depicted in Finlay's 1861 advertisement, in which a young couple relax

161. Advertisement for Finlay's, the Glasgow ironmongers, from the *Glasgow Post Office Directory*, 1861. The cosy parlour scene is similar to that described by 'Erchie' above. Note the set of haircloth chairs, the round table with a glass globe in the centre, and the clock and ornaments on the mantelshelf.

for a cosy evening with the newspapers in front of the parlour fire (pl 161). The main suite of furniture usually matched that of the dining room in style and materials (see p 140), but equally there were often ornaments and items reminiscent of the drawing room, such as a work table or a small bookcase, albeit of an inferior quality.

Clearly the vast majority of people in Scotland could not afford an elaborate and specialized sequence of rooms. The drawing room in particular tended to take up more square footage and window frontage than any other interior, and its contents were a drain on labour and resources. Quite apart from the purchase of finery, servants were required to deal with the dust trap created by having so many precious and delicate items in a room with open fires. Not surprisingly, limitations on space and disposable income brought priorities into focus, the result being that drawing and morning rooms were invariably ousted from floor plans before the dining room or parlour. While the dining room had rapidly become established as essential within middle-rank houses of the late eighteenth to early nineteenth centuries, the need for a drawing room – a further public space devoted to more obviously feminine activities – does not seem to have been as clearly felt. In that period the longstanding dominance of the dining room in Scotland was reinforced by the overtly masculine character of socializing within the home. William Creech commented on the desertion of Edinburgh drawing rooms in the late eighteenth century:

> In 1763 – It was the fashion for gentlemen to attend the drawing-rooms of the ladies in the afternoons, to drink tea, and to mix in the society and conversation of the women. In 1783 – The drawing-rooms were totally deserted; invitations to tea in the afternoon were given up; and the only opportunity men had of being in ladies' company, was when they happened to *mess* together at dinner or supper; and even then, an impatience was sometimes shewn, till the ladies retired.[12]

The custom of women withdrawing from the dining room, leaving the men to get on with prolonged bouts of drinking, appears to have been more entrenched in Scotland than England. At least this was the perception of Christian Ployen, a Faroese traveller touring Scotland in 1839, who summoned up a picture far removed from the 'beau ideal' outlined by Loudon above (p 157). Being a foreigner and not a heavy drinker, Ployen took a dim view of the after-dinner conversation which all too often degenerated into tedious, drunken rambling, and he regarded the prolonged segregation of the sexes as plain uncivilized. 'The sitting after dinner is in my belief a remnant of the barbarous customs of former ages and ought to be abandoned in all good society', he wrote; 'I understand that it is very much on the decline in England, but in Scotland, Orkney and Shetland it is still in full force, and probably in these places, it will take some generations to get rid entirely of the practice.'[13] With men tending to dominate any social 'front-of-stage' activities, there was perhaps less demand for a correspondingly 'feminine' public space.

Inevitably such cultural patterns in room usage were modified in Scotland (as elsewhere in the industrialized world) by the sharpening of the divide between home and work. The private interior space of the home was increasingly defined as the province of women and children, while men's work and leisure tended to shift to the public domain. Within the domestic arena the drawing room, presided over by an idealized wife-mother figure, assumed new importance as the focus of the nineteenth-century cult of bourgeois domesticity. Family values and the civilizing influence of the home were seen to emanate from the drawing room, as illustrated in the charming

1850s picture of the Mahoney family at home in Blackfriars Street, Glasgow. Framed in the window, the caged songbird and view of Glasgow Cathedral point to the spiritual, non-commercial values infusing the drawing room. The image also captures the self-conscious propriety invoked by such an interior. In their best dress and on their best behaviour, the family members are proudly displayed to the viewer. On the one hand, the drawing room was to provide a haven from the external world of work and the corrupting aspects of commerce. On the other, it was still the showpiece of the home, the focus of high-profile expenditure.

There was widespread agreement that the arrangement of the drawing room should be left to the lady of the house: 'none but a lady can do it', claimed Loudon.[14] This had not always been the case. At Inveraray, for example, it had been the Duke of Argyll who took charge of furnishing the drawing room in the 1780s. By 1807, however, when Thomas Hope published his folio of *Household Furniture and Interior Decoration*, he was taken to task by *The Edinburgh Review* for indulging in such 'effeminate elegancies', which in the magazine's view were better left 'to slaves and foreigners'.[15] Furnishing the home was increasingly seen as not an edifying or appropriate task for men. Meanwhile, through exercising choice as consumers women were beginning to wield huge power in affecting the style and appearance of objects.

Within the home, the drawing room was perceived as the most 'feminine' of the key rooms, providing an explicit contrast to the 'masculine' dining room. Writing in 1864, Robert Kerr specified the drawing room as the 'Lady's Apartment', stating:

162. The Mahoneys at home in Glasgow in the 1850s. This picture of a typically prosperous middle-class household emphasizes the projection of family values through the Victorian drawing room. Mr Mahoney worked as a brassfounder and gas fitter. The caged songbird and view of Glasgow Cathedral and the Necropolis point to an identification with spiritual, non-commercial values in this room.

163. Stencil work at 3 Park Terrace, home of Sir James Bain, Lord Provost of Glasgow in the 1870s. Something of the glamour, wealth, and sophistication of Glasgow's elite in the late nineteenth century can still be experienced in the Park Circus area of the city: apart from this glittering example, the drawing room decorated by two generations of the Macfarlane family is now run as the Register Office's most prestigious Marriage Suite.

The character to be always aimed at in a Drawing-room is especial cheerfulness, refinement of elegance, and what is called lightness as opposed to massiveness. Decoration and furniture ought therefore to be comparatively delicate; in short the rule in everything is this – if the expression may be used – to be entirely *ladylike*. The comparison of Dining-room and Drawing-room, therefore, is in almost every way one of contrast.[16]

This gendering of interiors provides a key to understanding the drawing room as a foil both to the workplace and to the dining room, the other principal 'public' interior.

Picturesque variety in the drawing room's seating, cabinets, and tables made a marked contrast with the restrained and formal symmetry associated with the dining room. Likewise the reflective glitter and high finish of the gilding, the silky fabrics, elaborate veneers, and mirrored or French-polished surfaces found in the drawing room were deliberately played off against the 'solid' and unadorned materials in more 'masculine' schemes such as the dining room or library. The proliferation and complexity of objects in the drawing room, and the variation of mass and outline in their grouping, expressed notions of civilizing 'refinement'. Smoothness was another attribute linked to the 'feminine' and to social polish. Lumbering, rough-edged men were thought to be civilized by 'the gracious refinement of woman's subtle spell',[17] and by the process of having to negotiate the apparently fragile and unstable 'clutter' of the drawing room.

The furnishings were becoming more numerous and stylistically varied than those associated with any other room, and they cost correspondingly more. The amount of space and detail lavished upon them, whether in trade literature or household valuations of the late nineteenth century, gives a clear indication of how far the relative hierarchy among the main room types had shifted since the eighteenth century. The following figures indicate a typical range in the number of entries per room in the catalogue of the high-profile Glasgow furnishing house Wylie & Lochhead from around 1900: drawing room 120; dining room 57; bedroom 35; hall 23.[18] This hierarchy was also translated into the use of materials of a perceptibly higher quality throughout the drawing room. The upholstery was usually of velvet or silk damask, for example, as opposed to the horsehair, leather, or plain repp associated with the dining room; grates were often of bright-cut or inlaid steel rather than brass or iron; and furniture was predominantly of rosewood or walnut, embellished with decorative inlays, carved detail, and gilding, in preference to the use of plain oak or mahogany.

Accents of deep subtle colours, variegated patterns, or glossy veneers could all enhance a luxuriant effect. The availability and range of household textiles and wallpapers had been transformed by technical innovations. Formerly the preserve of aristocratic households, the painted mural schemes, delicate plasterwork friezes, and stamped leather hangings could now be emulated by means of specialist wallpapers.[19] Apart from such materials and finishes, a sense of richness was also communicated through an emphasis on visual intricacy and a tendency to elaborate combinations of colours, textures, materials, and forms – both in the overall composition of the room and in single objects.

Although for the most part spun and woven by machine, textiles still retained associations of richness and refinement. The womb-like muffling of the drawing room in layers of curtains, carpets, fluffy rugs, frilly lampshades, cushions, and padded upholstery all gave the space a distinctive sound and feel aimed at inducing a state of physical and mental comfort. It also discreetly echoed the intimacy and sensuality of the boudoir, and the comfort of the nursery. The protective cocoon of textiles metaphorically communicated the refining and mediating role of woman and culture in softening the harshness of reality. If the outside world could not be controlled, at least the interior of the home could be.

Compared to the relatively stable formula for furnishing dining rooms, which could be virtually handed over to the shopman, the middle-class drawing room now presented a minefield of possibilities. To guide bewildered consumers through the plethora of options there was a booming literature on household taste and management. Authors already mentioned, such as Loudon and Kerr, whose books were among the most widely read throughout Britain, came from a Scottish background, and such writings provide a valuable touchstone against which to view the Scottish drawing room.

Further guidance was at hand through an increasingly sophisticated range of retail outlets. The most exclusive homes were supplied by a network of artist-decorators and dealers. It was also possible to purchase every conceivable drawing-room accessory in Scotland's new department stores, which offered an all-in advisory service aimed at a largely middle-class, female clientele. Although few women had money they could call their own, it is clear from diaries, novels, and advertisements that they tended to control expenditure on

164. A specimen drawing room in Wylie & Lochhead's Glasgow showrooms, around 1900. A series of drawing-room settings could be seen in the firm's Buchanan Street store and pictured in its trade catalogues. Here the dominant style is a version of the consistently popular 'Louis XV'. Note the abundance of textiles, particularly floral silk brocades, combined with luxuriant lacquerwork, ormolu (gilded bronze), and carved detail.

the middle-class home. Shops like Wylie & Lochhead or Gardner's in Glasgow had begun to display complete room settings from the 1870s to demonstrate how the entire kit might fit together (pl 164). Advances in printing technology and the transportation infrastructure meant that such stores could reach a huge hinterland through a system of mail order. With an efficiency it would be hard to parallel today, an order wired to Wylie & Lochhead in Glasgow from Ardtornish, a house on a remote West Highland peninsula, was despatched by steamer the following day.[20] With agents, buyers, and frequently branches worldwide, many Scottish producers of furnishings could now retail to a world market. Ironically, some of the most complete 'Scottish' drawing rooms are now to be found as far afield as Bournemouth, where Lady Russell-Cotes –

165. Design for Queen Victoria's Waiting Room at Paddington by the Edinburgh decorator, Thomas Bonnar, 1860s. This design shows clear continuity between the style of domestic drawing rooms and more public interiors, such as hotel and station waiting rooms.

166. Carved gilt chair by Wylie & Lochhead of Glasgow, upholstered with embroidered beadwork, 1860s. Like much drawing-room seating at this time, the swelling forms were enhanced by the use of sprung upholstery. The embroidery may have been worked by an amateur since the panels do not match the shape of the frame exactly. Such floral ornament is typical of the drawing room's references to Nature.

167. *Opposite: Spring Moonlight* by John Lorimer, 1896. Set in the spacious drawing room of the Lorimers' family home at Kellie Castle in Fife, this scene captures an intimate domestic scene just before the baby's bedtime.

168. Drawing room at Lauriston Castle, Edinburgh, as furnished early in the twentieth century. It was the home of Mr and Mrs Reid, whose business was built on the fitting out of many railway, as well as domestic, interiors. The Sheffield-plate candlesticks on the writing table are the same as those supplied for trains, where familiar domestic items perhaps made people feel more comfortable about high-speed travel. A good prospect was considered more important for the drawing room than other rooms: here the bay window commands a view of the Firth of Forth.

Glasgow born and bred – used an array of Scottish products; or Australia, in the homes created by Cottier, Wells, and Gow.[21] In the other direction, there was a constant flow of imports back into Scottish homes, stimulated by international trade and increased opportunities for travel.

The consumer imagination was primed in the public domain by the experience of new types of interiors deploying decorative conventions similar to those of the drawing room. The principle silk and satinwood interior in Glasgow's new Municipal Chambers of 1888–90, for example, was described by the architect as the 'Municipal Drawing Room'.[22] Hotel or station waiting rooms and the phenomenal number of Clyde-built trains and ships were fitted out with opulent interiors which constantly reinforced the stylistic and cultural associations of the drawing room, and disseminated new fashions (pl 165). Conversely, one of the best surviving drawing rooms of the Edwardian era is undoubtedly that at Lauriston Castle in Edinburgh, the former home of Mr and Mrs Reid, whose business was built upon the furnishing of many train as well as domestic interiors (pl 168). When ships were broken up or refurbished, their contents were often salvaged for domestic use, such as the re-use of SS *Carisbrook* in a Scottish drawing room illustrated in *Academy Architecture* in 1901.[23] Other influential public interiors were the hugely popular tea rooms, a peculiarly Scottish phenomenon. These schemes were noted at the end of the nineteenth century for being tastefully 'homely' in comparison with their equivalent south of the border.[24] Many of Charles Rennie Mackintosh's tea-room furniture designs were in fact reproduced for domestic use, including several chairs and light fittings to be found in his own drawing room (pl 178).

Since it was the showpiece of the home, watercolour, printed, and photographic images of the drawing room proliferated in the nineteenth century. The impact of such representations was intensified by the fact that they were designed to be looked at and enjoyed within the drawing room itself. Furnishing inventories often list photograph albums and stereoscopes or

169. Advertisement for Sir David Brewster's stereoscope, 'the optical wonder of the age', 1856. On the table are the boxes of glass slides featuring European landscapes, architecture, and scenes from the Sydenham Crystal Palace. The stand could be supplied in japanned tin, rosewood or mahogany to harmonize with the materials used in drawing-room furnishings.

magnifying glasses, which encouraged an appreciation of intricate visual detail. The experience of poring over densely detailed two-dimensional images was readily transferred to the three-dimensional actuality of the interiors in which the spectator was enveloped. The art of systematic looking was also encouraged through recording the drawing room in watercolour and pencil sketching, an activity deemed appropriate for the context of the space (pl 159). On another level, people were clearly conscious of composing and appreciating a drawing room as they would a painting or photograph. Imagining his ideal drawing room in about 1900, the architect Robert Lorimer envisaged himself looking into a room in which his wife performed Chopin or Brahms on the piano and a child played on the hearthrug, a scene similar to that painted by his brother at the family home at Kellie Castle in Fife (pl 167).

This act of looking, and an awareness of being looked at, come across equally strongly in novels of the period, another rich source for this study. Small bookcases and reading lamps in most drawing rooms equipped avid novel readers to consume literary descriptions of domestic interiors and to internalize them *in situ*. Novels were considered suitably lightweight reading matter for an interior which was supposed to entertain idle hours. The narratives of many bourgeois domestic dramas were unfolded in the context of the drawing room, a theatrical space in which so many values and identities were contested, and where romance could flourish. From her own experience, a female novelist such as Susan Ferrier had clearly acquired an eye for significant detail which was then used to provide a key to the character, motivation, and interaction of her protagonists. The subtleties of such observations would have been instantly

170. Four of the eight daughters of the Wilson family in about 1880, apparently oblivious of the spectator while they amuse themselves with embroidery and cards in the drawing room. The prominent musical instruments signify the suitably ladylike accomplishments which were showcased in this space. The Wilsons had a coal business and lived at South Bantaskine Estate, Falkirk.

familiar to the middle-class audience at which they were aimed, reinforcing their sense of shared experience and identity.

The mirrors over fireplaces and pier tables which dominated most drawing-room schemes constantly reflected women's appearance back to them. Indeed they were encouraged to see themselves as part of the drawing-room scheme and to match their figure, complexion and dress to the domestic environment:

> Is she a blonde? then let there be a modicum of pale blue within her bower … rose will detract from a fair skin, pale turquoise would be preferable, but it will not suit a fresh complexion … We prefer simple harmony here making the lady the concentration of the scheme.[25]

Women are often depicted against the backdrop of a drawing room in nineteenth-century paintings and photographs. In George Logan's design for a music room, the artist's daughters are so depersonalized as to merge with the setting, and become but one element within an aestheticized arrangement of surfaces (pl 177). Similarly, a photograph now in Shetland Museum features a resplendent Edwardian lady whose silhouette appears to echo that of the

171. An Edwardian lady in a drawing room in Shetland. Women were frequently photographed in this period against the backdrop of a drawing room and were encouraged to match their appearance with the furnishing scheme.

manicured tree on the table and the birds in flight on the wall, while also picking up on the fashionably stylized and elongated motif on the wallpaper (pl 171). Her fur stole provides another element of continuity with the typically fluffy rug upon which she stands. Using similar fabrics for dress and furnishing was specifically advocated by Mrs Haweis, a leading authority on matters of taste, as a means of enhancing feminine beauty.[26]

Perhaps Mr Jennings had such an image in mind when he compared a 'showy' drawing room with the indiscretion of a tiny rouged woman 'dressed to death', wearing a picture-hat with feathers and a 'shopful of trimmings'.[27] Drawing rooms were frequently sucked into the negative comment surrounding the topic of women and fashion. As with the clothes they wore, women were often criticized for 'dressing up' their interiors to be attractive, as though they were dissembling a calculating self interest. In this sense, women were in a double bind when it came to buying furnishings for the drawing room: on the one hand there was relentless social pressure to assert their identity and family's status through the purchase of 'artistic', preferably expensive, household goods, while on the other they were constantly accused of susceptibility to the whims of fashion, and of unnecessary or unethical consumption. The perspective of a typically lower middle-class husband in 1902 is voiced here in the scathing words of 'Erchie', whose parlour furnishings were described earlier (p 160):

> 'I can easily tell ye whit Art is', says I, 'for it cost me mony a penny … when Art broke oot, Jinnet took it bad, though she didna ken the name o' the trouble … The wally dugs, and the worsted thing, and the picture o' John Knox, were nae langer whit Jinnet ca'd the fashion, and something else had to tak' their place. That was Art: it's a lingerin' disease; she has the dregs o't yet, and whiles buys shillin' things that's nae use for onything except dustin'.[28]

The apparently random accumulation of small objects like Jinnet's 'shillin' things' was a particular butt of criticism. Some authors seemed to feel the habit reflected woman's innate intellectual inferiority, and an inability to grasp the larger-scale dynamics of interior decoration. Women were generally felt to have an affinity for decoration, and to be better at apprehending two-dimensional, small-scale detail than larger forms in space. As Kerr tactfully put it, 'The more graceful sex are generally better qualified, both as respects taste and leisure, to appreciate the decorative element in whatever form of development.'[29] This perceived propensity was reinforced by gendered role play from an early age. The little girl had to grow up to be the wife-mother, and presumably in preparation for the challenge of equipping the drawing room Lady Barker suggested that girls should be encouraged to 'collect tasteful little odds and ends of ornamental work' for their bedrooms, and 'shown the difference between what is and what is not artistically and intrinsically valuable, either for form or colour'; boys on the other hand were to spurn ornament and 'have bare boards with only a rug to stand on at the bedside and fireplace'.[30]

As the showcase for artistic discrimination and individual taste, the drawing room accommodated collecting interests focused on small, exquisite, and rare or curious items. In the words of Loudon, 'everything amusing, curious, or ornamental, is in its place in the drawing-room'.[31] Contemporary photographs show a myriad such items strewn around the table tops, in and under display cabinets, and stashed into the nooks and crannies of towering overmantels or hanging shelves (pl 172). It was felt that such objects would stimulate the imagination and refined conversation, providing an informal education through the emanation of moral sentiment, history, and cosmopolitan culture. Some

172. A corner of Mrs McPhail's drawing room in Paisley, 1890s. In the drawing room the owner's 'taste' and individuality were under constant scrutiny. While this type of homely, personalized ensemble of varied knick-knacks was encouraged as an expression of domestic values (note the miniature spinning wheel on the shelf), design critics loved to castigate the mindless accumulation of objects.

items had a clear iconic and symbolic value, while others, such as framed photographs and jewellery, reflected more sentimental and personal interests. The projection of artistic taste could be relatively cheaply paraphrased in less affluent homes with a few bits of bric-a-brac, souvenirs, and mass-produced china such as the 'wally dugs' mentioned by Erchie. 'Chinamania' reached its height in the 1880s and 1890s. Such collecting was a competitive, sometimes obsessive, and fashionable pastime for both men and women (pls 172, 173).

The emphasis on cultural and artistic values in the drawing room was frequently symbolized through decorative images of the Muses or musical trophies, and through inclusion of the relevant furniture and props. Most commonly a piano, music stand, and canterbury signified a musical household (pl 170), while needlework skills were revealed by the presence of a spinning wheel, sewing table, or embroidery frame; portfolios, easels, a small bookcase and writing desk indicated artistic and literary activities. It was because the furnishing of the drawing room was, amongst other things, about the art of self presentation and the reception of visitors, that it was such an important space for young unmarried women, who had to market themselves and their accomplishments rather like luxury goods in a shop window, in order to attract husbands: 'Here the fair occupant must be studied. Does she pursue art, music, or literature?'[32] The various table tops would be liberally scattered with small

173. 'Chinamania', the craze for collecting and displaying pottery and porcelain, reached all parts of the country. This photograph shows a drawing room in Orkney in about 1900, with a fashionable accumulation of dust-harbouring objects.

artworks, drawing- and work-boxes, writing equipment, folios of prints and drawings, and books of 'the best poets and novelists'.[33] When the Paterson family were individually photographed in the setting of their Helensburgh home in about 1905, Mrs Paterson was posed at her embroidery frame in the drawing room and her daughter at the piano; the backdrop for Mr Paterson was the bookshelves of the library and his architect's table (pl 28). Lady Stirling Maxwell went so far as to have an organ built in to the wall of her drawing room at Pollok House, Glasgow, in the 1890s. Such bulky accessories were part of the permanent domestic landscape, and could not be carted easily into the public domain.

Maintaining the bourgeois ideal of home as the antithesis of the workplace, while also instilling the work ethic in the young, meant that women were encouraged to fill their leisure with productive but non-commercial activity. Visual evidence of this ideology was essential, even if the actual skills required to use the objects were lacking. Hence Loudon advised putting something on most of the tables 'to make them *appear* of use' [my italics].[34] Not only did such activity usually take place in the drawing room, but the results were often displayed there as trophies of domestic virtue. In the drawing room at Pollok House are four large scrapbooks painstakingly compiled by Lady Maxwell from the 1820s to 1840s. Each page is bordered by proverbs and aphorisms cut from newsprint and contains a delightful medley of her own watercolours, fashion plates, news items, engravings, and prints. Clearly not everyone was so talented, however, and being stuck in a 'dressed drawing-room for the day', condemned to admire such handiwork could become tedious in the extreme:

> At length Miss Lilly produced her album for the amusement or admiration of her cousin, and turned over page after page, emblazoned with miserable cupids with blue aprons, doves that might have passed for termagents, stout calico roses, heart's-ease that was eye-sore ...[35]

Private tutors and various ladies' magazines or books gave instruction in a range of decorative skills or 'fancy work', which could occupy endless hours and be used to beautify the domestic interior – crafts such as chipcarving, pokerwork, staining, stencilling, china or glass painting and repoussé metal-work all came within their remit. By the 1890s, such accomplishments were also taught at day classes in the Glasgow School of Art to middle-class women, enabling an increasing number of them to set up studios in the city and earn an independent living.

In the context of the drawing room, the most established and widespread of such domestic arts was needlework. There were aristocratic and genteel models to follow, as demonstrated by the survival in the drawing room of numerous historic samplers, 'sewed' seat covers, and embroidered boxes or frames. For amateurs who had glutted the home with the fruits of their labour, there was an additional outlet in philanthropic bazaars. In a thinly veiled critique of preparations for a Glasgow charity sale, one Miss Rosie Flirtington was caricatured as trying to catch her man by 'throwing her whole soul into the manufacture of enormities in wool-work, patchwork and bead-work, the hideousness of which was only equalled by their appalling uselessness, and the drawing room at 10 Blythsdale Crescent was turned into something not unlike a very badly kept rag store'.[36]

On the one hand, women were encouraged to demonstrate accomplishments emphasizing aesthetic refinement and technical virtuosity rather than economy of means or functionality. On the other, the results of their handicraft

174. 'Miss Rosie Flirtington' zealously promoting her charitable handiwork. Illustration from *Quiz*, 18 March 1881.

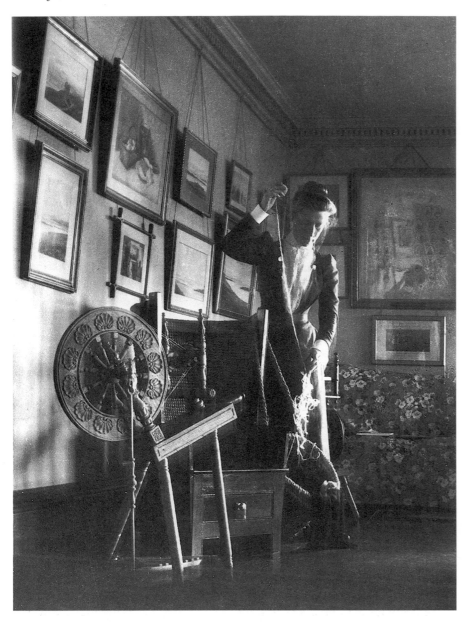

175. Lady Eliza D'Oyley Burroughs at Trumland House, Orkney, about 1900. This is a rare scene of spinning in action in a drawing room. The spinning wheel is now in the collections of Tankerness House Museum in Kirkwall. Craft traditions were clearly still very much alive in Orkney, though in more urban drawing rooms such equipment was redundant.

were often condemned as 'trivial' or 'useless' for the very same reasons. Invariably, patronage of the decorative arts by women within the home was couched in terms of philanthropy or maintaining cultural continuity rather than connoisseurship. Drawing-room concerts were another means of raising money for charity while displaying one's home-making and musical skills.[37]

Through engaging in handcrafts themselves and through buying high-quality, individually worked pieces, women were seen to be nurturing traditional skills and values in the face of industrial change. While her husband campaigned in Parliament throughout the 1820s on behalf of the Paisley weavers made redundant by mechanization, Lady Maxwell expressed her support for their plight by commissioning Paisley-pattern curtains for the drawing room in Pollok House and encouraging her aristocratic acquaintances to follow suit. Among all the artefacts associated with the drawing room, the identification of women with handcraft and Scottish tradition was perhaps most clearly signified by the ubiquitous spinning wheel, which featured in fashionable and stylistically conservative interiors alike. Although it was still a vital piece of equipment in many rural Scottish homes, by the mid nineteenth century it was clearly redundant in an urban, middle-class context, and in many cases it seems to have been little more than a decorative prop. Its attraction was largely emotive and nostalgic, as demonstrated by the inclusion of a miniature version on an overmantel shelf in Mrs McPhail's Paisley drawing room (pl 172). In the public domain the image of a woman at a spinning wheel was given iconic value by representations such as the sculpture of 'Peace' erected on the bridge over the Kelvin as part of Glasgow's International Exhibition in 1901.

Apart from particular types of objects and materials, colour provided an important conceptual cue as to the function of a space and its emotional tenor. 'The colouring of rooms should be an echo of their uses', wrote Loudon in 1839: 'The colour of a library ought to be comparatively severe; that of a dining-room grave; that of a drawing-room gay.'[38] 'Lightness' was one of the most recurrent words in descriptions of the drawing room and related interiors such as the morning room − used both in a literal sense, and to imply more abstract qualities analogous to wider cultural values. At its most prosaic the term referred to colours and materials within the interior, and the level of natural or artificial light. The drawing room usually had more windows than any other room, and ideally a southerly aspect. 'Lightness' could also describe the more delicate scale and structure of the furniture (see for instance pl 1). Some commentators extended the associations of lightness to the activities which went on in such spaces. The drawing room was after all supposed to offer light entertainment and relaxation as an antidote to the cut and thrust of the workplace. Taken to extremes, 'light' decor was occasionally perceived as a by-product of intellectual inanity or frivolity:

> An author who desires to follow out solid theories and generally severe lines of thought has been known to say that he cannot possibly do it in a room that is papered and painted in amber and white. The surroundings are too exhilarating and lead him off to lighter themes.[39]

Similarly Jennings, writing in 1902, referred to 'the lighter intellectual causeries' of the Woman's Realm, to which even 'the inferior sex' could contribute their share.[40] In the opinion of Hermann Muthesius, a German enthusiast for British domestic architecture, the 'lightness' and superficiality of the socializing which took place in the drawing room, 'precludes seriousness in the decoration and content of the room. The trend throughout is towards prettiness, casualness and lightness, a feminine characteristic'.[41] Women's brains were generally thought to be, like their physique, smaller and lighter than men's.

Construed more positively, lightness of colour and form could also provide a material analogy for the hygienic and spiritual purity of the household. In their capacity as guardians of the family's health and moral welfare, women could more easily embody such values than men, who were too closely implicated with the filthy world of work and corrupting commerce. This was reinforced by the Romantic notion of a dichotomy of temperament between the sexes which stressed a feminine propensity for spirituality. In other words, the battle against dirt had a moral and spiritual dimension. Within the home generally, and the drawing room in particular, women were expected to create an oasis of light and calm. This was no easy matter amid the squalid grime of industrial cities such as Glasgow or Dundee. Even from the exclusive heights of Park Circus in Glasgow, the relentless thudding of the Clydeside yards could not be entirely shut out. Likewise at Pollok House, cocooned in some 360 acres of parkland to the south of the city centre, the pounding of factories could apparently be heard. According to Ann Maxwell Macdonald, the trees in the park often appeared black with pollution, and she recalls how her mother got so fed up with the deposit of smut in the drawing room that she exchanged the pale chintz loose covers for ones with a brown ground. In a practical sense women were in a losing battle. The stylishly light schemes associated with the drawing room were a liability. Writing in 1876, an authority on household taste described the case of a woman who had installed a Parisian scheme, including an Aubusson carpet with a white ground, mirrored panels, and fantastical gilt mouldings. After a year it was all 'Faded flowers, blackened mouldings, layers of soot, tarnished gilding, filthy curtains, the floor sticky with a kind of black mud, the sprightly carpet the colour of yellow blotting paper after a week's use.'[42]

Light schemes constructed a vision of health and amenity which helped to bolster the home mentally against the threat of disease, particularly as contagions were thought to be transmitted by dirt and dust. In Glasgow, for example, despite efforts of the Council to clear slums, improve sanitation, and provide parks, epidemics were still rife in the nineteenth century. The authorities did not publicize the fact, but during the city's International Exhibition of 1901 there was an outbreak not only of smallpox but even of bubonic plague. Like many other middle-class Glaswegians, Charles Rennie Mackintosh and Margaret Macdonald moved from Mains Street to the more salubrious air of the West End partly to escape the smog and filth of the low-lying heart of the city. In the context of urban grime, and the threats of crime, pollution, and disease which accompanied it, one can see the exaggerated whiteness of the drawing rooms they created, and the cultivation of light schemes by many of their contemporaries, as an attempt to control their immediate environment and to exclude the threatening elements of society.[43]

The regenerative, colourful, and sensual power of Nature enhanced the concept of the drawing room as an antidote to the drab and deadening world of work. In moral terms, such a link evoked the virtuous countryside, fostering the notion of the drawing room as an 'unsullied' environment feeding the imagination and spirit. From the eighteenth century onwards, great importance was placed on the view from the drawing room, to the extent that in the 1790s the Maxwells of Pollok House forcibly removed the inhabitants of the ramshackle 'Pollock Toun' to improve the vision of undulating, rural tranquillity from inside. A projecting window box or view into a conservatory served a similar purpose. In the drawing room at Bowhill near Selkirk in the 1840s, William Burn went to great lengths to design the conceit of a window through to the garden placed immediately above the fireplace.

On a metaphorical level, references to the reproductive capacity of Nature provided an allegory for the reproduction of wealth. At the same time, organic movement or form could operate as a signifier for the pliability and weakness of the female character, and the more instinctual, sensual aspects of her make-up. Femininity was invariably connected with the pastoral, decorative, and sweet-scented side of Nature, as opposed to the whiff of blood and violence implicit in the dining-room iconography of the hunt. Indeed the drawing room's perfumed, airy scent was as important as an olfactory reference to femininity as was the wood panelling and leather impregnated with smells of food, drink, and smoke of the dining room in terms of masculinity. There was an unavoidable paradox here in the idea that women should embody 'the Natural' in what must have been the most intensely artificial room within the home.

This axis between femininity and nature was directly symbolized in the drawing room and boudoir through the inclusion of 'vegetable jewellery' – dried and cut flower arrangements, potted plants with elaborate jardinieres, and collections of natural objects such as shells or semi-precious stones (pl 5). In the 1850s and 1860s, fern cases and aquaria were particularly in vogue. Still-life or landscape pictures could be displayed on the walls or in albums compiled by the females in the household. Gardens were also evoked more indirectly through conventionalized ornament derived from nature, and drawing-room upholstery, carpets, and wallpaper were frequently floral in design (pl 160). George Logan took such imagery to extremes in his 1902 scheme for a Music Room (pl 177). Whether highly abstracted or straightforwardly representational, such imagery was so commonplace that its associations could be triggered off merely by the generally curvaceous, swelling forms of the furniture; also through the picturesque variety of objects and their apparently natural grouping which contrasted with the formal symmetry of the dining room arrangement.

As in the many other nineteenth-century Scottish interiors, historical and foreign styles were used to conjure up the appropriate sensual qualities and social nuances for a drawing room. In relation to all the themes discussed above – richness, refinement, lightness, the evocation of nature – the eighteenth-century French styles had everything going for them, offering 'a palatial richness, united to a playful elegance of effect', and patterns of an 'exquisite delicacy' and 'pretty tint'.[44] A combination of elements from 'Tous les Louis' created an impression that was organic, glitzy and cushioned, with overtones of aristocratic refinement (pls 164–6). No wonder their many admirers resisted the zeal of reformers and critics like Mr Jennings, to whom a Louis XV bureau suggested 'a frivolous court and Aphrodisian dames – an age of meretricious glitter, of excessive luxury of cupids, and quivers and amourettes',[45] and who did not realize that this was part of their appeal. There was a Scottish tradition of collecting the real thing, particularly after the French Revolution in 1789, and for collectors like the Buccleuchs or the architect Robert Lorimer and his clients, there were rich pickings of both provincial and state furniture to be had. Lorimer reworked the decorative vocabulary of the more provincial *boiserie* and

176. Inglenook of the drawing room at 12 University Gardens, Glasgow, illustrated in *The Studio* in 1900. A relatively austere, 'artistic' scheme designed by the architectural firm of Salmon & Gillespie. Even in this progressive arrangement, however, one can still make out the edge of a spinning wheel on the right-hand side, an icon of traditional craft values. The mosaic above the fireplace shows an Arthurian scene. Such poetic literary themes were often featured in the drawing room.

177. *Design for a Music Room* by George Logan, about 1900. In this interior the female figures – one reading on the couch and others making music – seem to merge with the overall decorative scheme. It has a dreamlike, fantastical quality which was seen as an important facet of drawing-room culture. The room was felt to be an environment in which the imagination and spirituality could flourish.

furniture for the drawing rooms of Monzie Castle and Hill of Tarvit. Moresque and oriental styles offered a further discreet hint of colourful luxury, mystery, and sensuality; and *chinoiserie* or the more exotic aspects of eighteenth-century styles were frequently recommended as a means of releasing the imagination: 'There is a certain irresponsibility, gaiety and naivety about Chinese ornament which makes it particularly suited for use in a Drawing Room where pure fancy may legitimately have play', wrote Gregory in 1913.[46] The use of such styles was so widespread that an impressionistic evocation was enough to provide a shorthand code for the function and character of a drawing room. The outline of a large-scale, overstuffed chair, for example, sufficed to mobilize the association 'Turkish' without even reproducing a specifically oriental fabric type or pattern. Similarly a paper fan or tall vase shape could signify 'oriental', and a curved leg 'eighteenth century'.

More progressive and fashionable 'Aesthetic' drawing rooms of the 1880s and 1890s were characterized by an eclectic blending of styles and materials, and a self-conscious integration of old and new elements (pl 176). This mish-mash was to be given coherence and made 'homelike' through the individual 'taste' of the owner; conspicuous expenditure was no substitute for the exercise of a 'cultivated' sensibility. John Marshall's 'Ideal Drawing Room', described in his lecture to the Edinburgh Architectural Association in 1883,[47] contained a Louis XVI clock, a 'Sheraton' table and escritoire, 'Chippendale' seating, a Persian carpet, oriental vases, and a 'French' grey and gold colour scheme. Although eclectic, however, the emphasis in this and comparable drawing rooms was still very much on eighteenth-century styles.

The cult of simplicity, which developed from the 1880s and continued into the twentieth century, entailed a paring down of the drawing room's ornamental features and the thinning out of its contents. In 'Artistic' drawing rooms the expression of 'lightness' became merged with the concept of refinement in a new, more reductivist, aesthetic. This tendency was given momentum in

178. The Mackintoshes' drawing room from Southpark Avenue, Glasgow, reconstructed in the Hunterian Art Gallery. Margaret Macdonald and Charles Rennie Mackintosh moved from their Mains Street flat to the West End in 1906, taking this fire surround with them. Although striking for its simplicity, the room is recognizably in the tradition of light drawing rooms.

Scotland through the distinctive schemes associated with the Glasgow school of designers at the turn of the century. The interiors devised by Charles Rennie Mackintosh with his wife Margaret Macdonald offered an alternative to the associational aesthetics of historical styles. Through concentrating on a more abstract interpretation of the visual and tactile conventions of the drawing room, they were able to move from a positivist, value-laden evocation of history or other cultures, to a more open-ended and poetic expression of style. Even their most dramatic white scheme was instantly recognizable as a drawing room, however, by virtue of its position within the house, the range of contents, and the way it was used.

The rarified atmosphere of a Glaswegian 'artistic' drawing room could be as inhibiting as the ostentatious richness of a more conventional scheme, as graphically described by Catherine Carswell:

> the rooms, though they were neither so large as the rooms in Collessie Street, nor nearly so rich as Aunt Georgina's, imposed a peculiar restraint. The way in which a few flowers stood up from a shallow glass dish; the black sofa bolsters tasselled with gold; the signed scribbles in pencil (generous as to margin) by Sargent or Burne-Jones which leaned unfixed on a moulding against the drawing-room wall; and here and there, resting on the same ledge for the convenience of handling, a framed autograph letter – these were evidences of a world in which Joanna did not yet move easily, a world where the small talk, like the material furnishings, had its own shibboleths of seeming freedom and simplicity.[48]

179. Furnishing scheme by Thomas Justice & Sons, Dundee, 1930s. The informal cosiness of the three-piece suite and cottagey window is offset by the genteel display cabinet, the artwork above the fireplace, and the traditional elegance of the candlestick, furniture with cabriole legs, and lacquered cabinet. A note of exoticism is communicated through the oriental rug and tray table, and the tasselled bolster.

Even in less self-consciously artistic households, social change was rendering the historical baggage and function of the drawing room obsolete. Like the hall and library, the drawing room was increasingly furnished as a family 'living room', and simplified, more open, planning was leading to greater continuity between adjacent interiors. Various authors on household taste in the 1920s referred to 'the passing of the drawing room', not least because ladies were 'fast becoming men', and therefore did not need a space to which to 'withdraw'.[49] The preferred terms were 'living room', 'sitting room', or 'lounge'. Usage of these labels was more linked to style and class connotations than clear differences in the purpose of the room. While the familiarly lumpen and cosy forms of the three-piece suite marked the rise of the lounge and sitting room, the drawing room was generally distinguished by references to eighteenth-century styles with their overtones of genteel and elegant living. From its sumptuous Victorian and Edwardian heyday the drawing room had been diminished to a label which then, as perhaps now, persisted only 'amongst a few who still have early Victorian tendencies'.[50] Nevertheless, putting considerations of terminology on one side, it is clear that for many this type of room has retained its power to contain the accumulated memories and identities of its inhabitants. Penned by Chaim Bermant in 1976, this closing description of a Glasgow drawing room suggests a range of associations which would not have been out of place in the late Victorian or Edwardian period:

It was choc-a-bloc with memories and ghosts. I was attached to the furniture, the carpets, the ferns in the huge brass pots; the odd bits of crockery and silver, the paperweights and bric-à-brac we brought back from holidays; the show-cases with the fine china I hadn't used since Hannah died; the walnut cocktail-cabinet with its stock of sticky liquor bottles (some of which hadn't been touched since Ellis's Barmitzvah); the large radiogram in birds-eye maple-wood; the heavy, walnut mantelpiece clock, which chimed the hour every forty minutes or so as the mood took it, and which I received on my retirement as Hon. Treasurer of the Jewish Burial Society. I couldn't see them in a different setting. I couldn't see myself in a different setting for that matter. I loved the very walls, and the real reason that I hadn't changed the wallpaper was because I felt that when I sat by myself on an evening sometimes it breathed back the impressions it had breathed in over the years ...[51]

8 The Bedroom

NAOMI TARRANT

'Nothing adds so much to the comfort of a man's life as good roomy bed-rooms, and nothing to the convenience of a family as plenty of them.'

Anon, 1864[1]

The bedroom as a separate room used merely for sleeping is a fairly recent innovation. In the past it would normally have been considered a waste of space to have rooms which did not serve several functions. Three hundred years ago only a nobleman could afford a grand parade of state rooms used on rare occasions. Today, however, single members of a household generally expect their own sleeping room and some houses even have guest bedrooms which are used for no other purpose.

Although the dedicated bedroom is recent, its main function, to provide a place for a suitable piece of furniture on which to sleep, was earlier fulfilled in several parts of the house. Inventories dating from around 1600 to 1750 show that most rooms in houses of moderate size contained at least one bed. It was only in the largest establishments that apartments could be set aside for special use without serving also as a bedroom. Adding up the number of beds in inventories can give some idea of how many people one household contained, although it is not normally clear how large the beds were, nor how many people were expected to share.

Attitudes to privacy were different in the past, and all sorts of activities which would now be regarded as private were carried out in a semi-public way. The conventions of behaviour may have demanded that some things were disregarded or not commented upon. Nineteenth-century books prescribing behaviour for servants make it clear that any conversations overheard, or private matters of the family which they came to know, should be discussed with no-one since they were no business of the servants.[2] The indiscreet servant makes a good theatrical device but in practice must have been less common than literature implies. Servants were, after all, dependent on employers for work and references. However, lighting was poor in castles and houses with small windows before the advent of the sliding sash in the late seventeenth century, and much indoor activity took place in semi-darkness. Even after the introduction of the Argand oil lamp in 1784, the level of illumination depended very much on income and willingness to pay for light.[3] It is also impossible to know how many people were long- or short-sighted and to what degree, and therefore how much they were able to observe.

The change from the public life of a medieval castle to the private homelife with which we are familiar today took place over a long period of time. It occurred at different rates in different levels of society and the reasons for it are complex. Privacy was not the only objective satisfied by separate rooms.

180. *Opposite:* Carved wooden bedstead in Gladstone's Land, Edinburgh. This tenement room is furnished as it might have been in the early seventeenth century, when such painted ceilings were fashionable in Scotland. Below the frieze, the stone walls were probably hidden by tapestries or hangings like those in pl 184.

181. The Saltonstall Family by David des Granges, about 1636–7. This depicts a gentry family in England but wealthy Scottish families probably had similar furnishings. The room has been made cosy with tapestries or painted cloths on the wall and carpet or floor cloth. As often found in inventories, the rich bed curtains have a matching armchair. In the bed, the woman is dying, lying on a bank of pillows with a lace-edged top sheet.

Perhaps a major motivating factor was a desire for status, to set the owner apart from the servants. In the seventeenth and eighteenth centuries, the grand parade of state rooms in a palace or noble house was designed to awe lesser mortals and to impress upon them the wealth and power of the owner, not just in the national or political sphere but also in the eyes of the immediate inhabitants. This was indeed a useful way of underlining the hierarchical relationships of a feudal society in which all gave allegiance to superiors.

In the public area of the hall in the sixteenth and seventeenth centuries, the king's or lord's chair was the most important article of furniture and often had a mark of distinction over it such as a canopy. In the less open area of the lord's private chamber, it was the bed which became the main focus, and it too could have a canopy. The private apartment, often called the 'Chamber of Dais' because it was behind the high table of the hall,[4] was where the lord could retire with his immediate family and guests away from the noise of the hall. Lords had to keep large retinues of followers for whom the hall served as living room by day and sleeping room at night, when they laid out straw sacks in any space they could find. The chamber also gave the women of the household a safer and more secluded place for their daytime activities. As well as the master's bed there could well be 'hurle' beds on wheels for children and servants. Other furniture might include one or more chests for the family's smaller and more

costly possessions, as well as their clothes. A table and benches might also be found here, depending on the wealth of the laird.

In grand houses this type of furniture probably remained standard for chambers throughout the period up to 1600, and continued in smaller dwellings after this date. With more settled conditions in Scotland and the Union of the Crowns in 1603, new ideas of comfort began to influence both the country and town houses of those with money and power. More small chambers were added, although they might still be used for other purposes as well as sleeping. Changed attitudes to comfort and privacy came from France, where the aristocracy's Paris homes were made more luxurious with additional furniture and textiles. The engravings of Abraham Bosse dating from the 1630s illustrate this new comfort, which spread throughout most of western Europe in the first half of the seventeenth century (pl 182). In these pictures women hold dinner parties, receive guests after the birth of a child, or view wedding presents, all in private chambers. Evidence for this kind of lifestyle in Scotland at this date is lacking, but even if the details are not the same, the ideas were certainly appealing and were brought back by Scots after visits to the Continent and London.

182. Engraving by Abraham Bosse, showing the interior of a Parisian home in the 1630s. The women are dining together in a large bedchamber while their husbands are out hunting or on business. The bedstead is of the type known as a 'French bed', which seems to have been standard in western Europe. Portraits are rather curiously hung over the tapestries on the back wall. Unfortunately, there appear to be no paintings of Scottish bedchambers from the seventeenth century.

New fashions did not immediately oust old ones and the style of bed in use in the late sixteenth century continued after 1600. Inventories make a distinction between the bedstead or frame and the 'bed', which described the mattress and hangings. The bedstead had two parts, frame and canopy, the canopy being above the bed with fabric hanging down behind the head to protect the occupants from the cold wall. Eventually a fully curtained bed evolved. This had many advantages, not least warmth at night with the curtains drawn; it also gave a certain degree of privacy, creating a room within a room. These two desirable features, warmth and privacy, remained fundamental to beds used in Scotland into the twentieth century, including the alcove beds in tenements. During the day the bed curtains would be looped up and a decorative cover, often matching the curtains, would be spread over the bed.

The sixteenth century saw the development of what is now generally known as the 'four poster' bed, though this term was never used at the time. Usually of oak, with a post at each corner to hold a wooden canopy, these developed

183. A Dutch lady at her dressing table, about 1670, by an anonymous painter of the Utrecht School. A middle-class interior with plain bed hangings, possibly in a wool fabric. The wooden bed frame is concealed by valances. A mattress is just visible as a striped cover below the sheet, and there is a full pillow and a brown blanket. During the day the white linen lace-edged toilette cover would be removed and the table could serve other purposes. On the floor is a pewter chamber pot and a close stool is visible in the closet at the back.

into elaborate and imposing items of furniture. A particular style of decorative bed has been associated with seventeenth-century Aberdeen carvers, and examples can be seen at Crathes Castle in Aberdeenshire and Gladstone's Land in the High Street, Edinburgh (pl 180). The original hangings from this type of bed do not survive but it is obvious that the rich carving must have been a dominant feature, so the curtains may have been relatively plain compared with later examples.

Although there are no illustrations of the rectangular curtained bed, known as a 'French bed', in use in Scotland, it was widespread throughout Europe in the first half of the seventeenth century and can be seen in many paintings. In this type the simple wooden frame has no ornate carving. It had a canopy of fabric and curtains on all four sides which hid the posts when they were drawn.

The bed frame or bedstead was basically four pieces of wood forming a hollow rectangle, filled with wooden slats, cords or canvas, onto which one or more mattresses were laid. The lowest was usually of straw but the upper ones could be feather, horsehair, wool, or down. To stop the contents from escaping, the outer cover was of a strong, closely woven fabric called ticking. For the head, most beds had one or more pillows and a bolster, a long sausage-shaped item stuffed with feathers which went the full width of the bed. These remained popular for double beds until about 1960, and other items of bedding similarly show little change over centuries. Linen and 'holland' (unbleached linen) sheets appear in inventories, along with bed plaids and the occasional Spanish or English blanket.[5]

Under the sumptuously decorated bedsteads were often kept trundle, truckle, or as they were usually known in Scotland, 'hurle' (and later, 'hurley') beds. These simple wooden frames on wheels were often used by servants who slept in their master's or mistress's room, but they were also useful for guests or children.

Another form of bed found in Scotland from at least the sixteenth century is the box bed. These did not need hangings as they were usually closed up by a slider of panelling or a door. During the day this resembled part of the room-panelling or a cupboard (pl 17).

In a society involved in frequent military campaigns, there was a need for some kind of camp bed. Folding beds were also useful for journeys in an age when the court and most nobles moved from castle to castle. Kings and nobles probably had quite grand temporary beds rigged up with a canopy and curtains. Camp beds of various kinds recur throughout the centuries, used by soldiers and later by travellers in an age before comfortable and bug-free hotels; and surviving today for camping holidays (though now displaced by airbeds and camping mats).

Decoration of the chamber in the early seventeenth century could include a matching set of wall hangings or painted cloths or woven tapestries, usually described in the inventories as 'Arras', after the Flemish town where tapestries were made. All these textile hangings had been common in the fourteenth, fifteenth, and sixteenth centuries, bringing warmth and colour to the rooms. They were transportable and were carried from castle to castle of the owner's estate, carefully packed up.

Tapestries were the most expensive wall covering and generally came from Flanders, although there were attempts to establish an industry in England in the late sixteenth century. A more successful workshop was set up at Mortlake in London under Charles I's patronage, but these enterprises produced only a small quantity of the numbers of tapestries used in homes in Britain. The really wealthy would commission a set from a weaver's workshop but others could buy a set or single pieces from stock patterns, or find them secondhand. Painted cloths provided a cheaper imitation. The subject matter of both could be figurative, with stories from the bible, mythology, legend, or history, told in a set of from five to seven pieces; or purely decorative, usually depicting trees, flowers, and other plants. Although tapestries continued to be made and used until the end of the eighteenth century, the production of painted cloths seems to have ceased in the early seventeenth century.

Wall hangings were often made to match the bed curtains for a unified *en suite* effect. They were usually of plain wool or a mixed wool fabric with embroidery or applied braid known as 'lace'. No full suites survive but two partial sets provide evidence of one distinctive form of decoration. These are the so-called Lochleven and Linlithgow hangings, which are 'paned', that is, vertical bands of embroidery divide the whole into smaller panels of cloth.[6] There are also motifs in the centre of each panel in rows, and a band at the bottom. The embroidery was done in a professional workshop, probably in Edinburgh, and consists of black velvet appliqué and yellow silk to give a rich effect resembling expensive Italian velvets.

Bed curtains were usually lined with a different coloured fabric, often a lightweight lining silk. At the top of the bed, a valance concealed the hanging loops of the curtains and examples of these survive, but there are no sets of bed hangings from this period. Then and later, the large expanses of fabric would usually be re-used, so such domestic textiles are now rare. Heavily embroidered valances which would have decorated the massive carved bedsteads survive from the late sixteenth century,[7] and a dated set of 1632 made by Dame Juliana Campbell of Glenorchy has small motifs on green lining silk (pl 185).[8] These are similar to the 'slips' – small motifs such as flowers worked individually – which were a popular form of embroidery because they could be done at home and did not need to be worked on the large frame required by such as the Lochleven-style hangings. Remains of a set of wall hangings covered in slips survive at Glamis Castle in Angus and Scone Palace, Perthshire, where the small embroidered motifs are scattered over a velvet ground.

184. A panel of the Lochleven wall hangings, in red wool with appliqué in black velvet and yellow silk embroidery, early seventeenth century. The ribbons at the side tied the panels together. Such surviving textiles give an idea of the sumptuous furnishing of some houses in Scotland at the time.

185. Eleven small panels in green shot silk, embroidered with the names of the owners and the date, 1632. These were for the valance of a bed. They have probably survived because of the impressive embroidery and because it would be difficult to use them for anything else.

Matching bed and wall hangings continued in use throughout the seventeenth century, as can be seen in a detailed inventory of the House of Binns, in West Lothian, taken after General Tam Dalyell's death in 1685.[9] This was a tower house of about twenty rooms, with domestic offices in two wings; the General also had a town house in the Canongate, Edinburgh. Dalyell's own chamber had suitably sober 'brown drogat hingings', but other rooms were more brightly decorated. In the 'chamber of Dyce' (or 'Desse'), which would be used by important guests, was a bed of cloth of unstated colour lined in pink taffeta. The Stone Studie had 'clow-coloured' (clove pink) hangings, while the South Chamber's suite of 'blew hingings with yellow pasments' (trimmings) had a bed to match. The bed in the kitchen, perhaps not unexpectedly, sounds dismal in grey serge.

The Binns housed at least thirty beds according to the 1685 inventory, usually two to a room. Different types are described as 'cloth', 'standing', 'hurle', and 'folding'. Cloth beds are listed in what were the best chambers, where there is usually also a folding bed. Standing beds – wooden frames on which the top corner posts extended a short way above the base – are found in the servants' rooms, although hurle and folding beds appear there too. It is not clear how wide most of the beds were, but some are described as two or three breadths, which would suggest that two or more could sleep in them. All told, about forty people might have been accommodated in the house at once.

Other furnishings in the chambers appear from the lists to have been fairly standard, though the differing values indicate that the richer quality was in the 'chamber of Dyce', the 'vault chamber', and 'green chamber', and these three rooms each contained what must have been impressive suites of '2 arm chayers. 2 backed chayers. 4 stools. A foot stool.'[10] In the General's 'brown drogat' room, the furniture included three 'ruschie laigh chayers' (probably low chairs with Russian leather backs and seats) and two presses, one of which contained important estate papers, the other his clothes. There was a looking glass, a chamber box and pan, a chamber pot, 'three brase cleicks for hinging anything on' and a 'chimnay' with fire irons and a pair of bellows. The General's pursuits are revealed by a large collection of weapons from different countries. This room reflects the business concerns of the owner as well as his personal interests and suggests a snug apartment where he could get away from the rest of what was obviously quite a large household.

At The Binns, the dining room, laigh (low) hall, and General Dalyell's room were at ground level of the main tower, with the High Hall, Chamber of Dyce, vault chamber and 'stone studie' on the first floor and six more chambers on the second. In the new type of classical, symmetrical house built in Scotland from the 1660s, based on precedents from Europe which had been seen already at the royal residences of Falkland Palace and Stirling Castle in the 1530s and 1540s, dining room, withdrawing room, and state bedroom followed in a sequence on the same floor. At the culminating point of the procession was the state bed, which in the late seventeenth century rose to new heights of grandeur. They were elaborately draped affairs with carved tops and *panaches* of ostrich plumes at the corners. The weight of the canopy might need supporting from the ceiling and often there would be an embroidered coat of arms. Something of the pomp of a state bedroom has been recreated at Holyroodhouse in Edinburgh in the King's Bedroom and another grand Scottish state bed, once at Melville House in Fife, is now in the Victoria and Albert Museum in London (pl 186).

A detailed costing of what appears to be a state bed for the Earl of Tweeddale survives in a bill dated 1674.[11] Seventy-two yards of 'rich morella mowhayr' at six shillings and ninepence a yard were required, along with linings of thirty-five ells of changeable flowered sarsnet. Decorating the outside were three different sizes of gold and silver 'lace' (braid), with four carved and gilt double knobs to finish it off. Inside were embroidered cyphers and coronets. The bedstead was a large French one with a raised roof and double sacking bottom. Rods outside supported a case cover of fine Indian dimity, protection for the expensive item which in all cost £86 1s 6d.[12]

Such richness was confined to a minority, but inventories of the early eighteenth century begin to show an increase in the number and type of goods found in bedchambers. An example of 1722 from Castle Fraser shows that Lady Fraser's room must have been rather dramatic, with a bed hung in black and white striped fabric and black wall hangings and window curtains.[13] There were two cabinets with drawers, a big glass, a press, a sleeping chair, four other chairs, and two tables. The closet contained another press, a press cupboard, privy box and pan, two chairs, table shelf, clock, a picture, more bedding and two 'skriter drawers' (an escritoire or writing desk).

Of similar date is the inventory of Charles Stewart, Steuard Clerk of Orkney, who lived in Kirkwall in 1726.[14] It lists the contents of eight rooms. The 'Studie' has a feather bed and other bedding, including a 'calligo Twilt' (quilt) and blue 'stamped' hangings, but no bedstead; possibly there was a built-in box bed. Also in the room were six cane chairs, a small dressing table, a mirror, and a hanging press full of small books. There were two box beds in the hall and a bedstead with yellow hangings in the back room, which also had two chests, a coffer, a cabinet, a sealskin trunk, and five chairs. This inventory was compiled before Stewart set off for a visit to Edinburgh, where it seems he went shopping, since on his return he added more items to the list, starting with 'ane pair fashionable brass Candlesticks'.

In contrast to the country, where householders could spread themselves out, the house in town usually consisted of few rooms. Edinburgh's citizens generally occupied one floor in one of the tall tenements and an inventory of 1716 of the possessions of Robert Drysdale, a merchant burgess and draper in Edinburgh, provides evidence of what was contained in such a house of five rooms.[15] Three 'stouped' beds appear in three different rooms, two of them described as 'hung'. The 'North room' appears to be the main apartment, with six cane chairs and two arm chairs, a looking glass, folding table, two pieces of hangings for the walls, a chamber pot and two standers. In the 'Mid room', besides the bed, were seven old green chairs, three old curtains, an old fir table, a press, a broken looking glass and a chamber pot, whilst a third room had two old 'Rushier' leather chairs, an old dressing ambrie (cupboard), a little wainscot

186. The state bed from Melville House, Fife, about 1700. Daniel Marot, a French Huguenot, is credited with making this style fashionable by his designs for beds for King William III. According to J Macky in 1723, describing Melville House in *A Journey Through Scotland*, 'The Bed of State is very noble, of Crimson Velvet, richly lin'd and adorn'd; the Chairs of the same.'

table and two old hangings. The kitchen was equally sparsely furnished but the trance (passage) was clearly used for storage, with several chests and barrels, the bedding, and a press for clothes.

Inventories of people who rented accommodation may not show bedsteads if there were built-in beds in the house. Dr James Blair's inventory of 1747 lists 'Two pair Sheets, Two pillowcases, Two pair Blankets and a bed Quilt' but no bedstead, although other furniture is mentioned.[16]

Although the term 'Bedchamber' appears as early as 1653 in the inventory of the Earl's Palace at Kirkwall in Orkney, it was not usual for rooms to be specified by their function and they were commonly named by colour or position in the house. The term 'Bed Room' came into wider use from around the middle of the eighteenth century, suggesting that this apartment was then taking on a more specialized function, and reflecting a similar increase in the number of parlours and drawing rooms mentioned. William Gairden's inventory of his dwelling in Edinburgh in 1759 lists six rooms including a garret and a writing chamber – he was a Writer to the Signet (lawyer) – but also a bed room.[17] This was furnished with an old blue curtain bed, a small writing table of marble, chairs, a basin stand of mahogany, two close boxes, carpet, chest, water pots and a crossbow. Two other apartments, the 'fore room' and 'back room', had folding beds.

When the New Town houses were built in Edinburgh in the latter part of the eighteenth century, the main bedroom was sited on the ground floor rather than upstairs. This placed the householder in a strategic position to oversee the movement of people within the house.

The second half of the eighteenth century saw an increase in the amount of furniture and other household possessions owned, and this is reflected in the inventories. While sleeping chambers had remained general-purpose rooms there was little specialized furniture apart from the bed, but now items designed for the bed chamber began to be listed. In the past, people owned fewer clothes than today, so their storage did not demand the numerous wardrobes and drawers which houses now have. Chests with drawers, being more complex to make, were more expensive than coffer chests, so clothes were usually kept in coffers, laid flat inside with sweet-smelling herbs scattered amongst them. People in small houses continued to store their clothes in kists in this way until

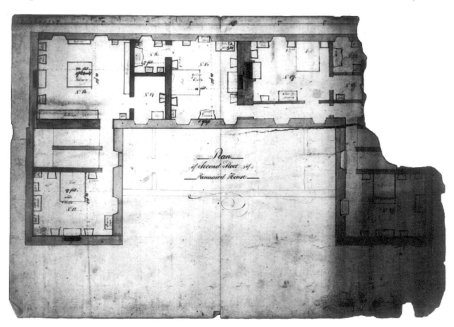

187. The second-floor plan of Kinnaird House, Stirlingshire, about 1770. The rooms numbered 12, 15, 17, and 24 show the very formal disposition of furniture in the bedrooms, some of which are named after the colour of the fabrics used, such as 'White Chintz'.

well into the twentieth century, and even among the better-off, chests of drawers and wardrobes were not universally used by the beginning of the nineteenth century. Elizabeth Grant of Rothiemurchus, for instance, describes how 'having no wardrobe, my dresses were kept in a trunk; the one I wanted seemed generally somehow at the bottom of it, and so troublesome to get at.'[18] An alternative to squashing garments into a chest was to hang them in a closet, usually by the armhole onto a peg in the eighteenth century, though later on, loops were provided inside the garments (it was not until about 1880 that the coathanger came into use). Wardrobes, linen presses, and chests of drawers were increasingly made and used in the late eighteenth century, however, and appear more frequently in cabinetmakers' records as well as in inventories.

Apart from storing clothes, the bed chamber was usually where people washed themselves. Washstands to hold a bowl were mentioned in the 1759 inventory quoted above (p 189) but the more elaborate stands with marble tops, and matching wash basin, jug, slop pail, soap dish, and tooth mug were a nineteenth-century innovation. Eighteenth-century stands usually comprised a small frame holding the basin with a shelf below for the ewer. This kind was probably used only for washing the hands during the day. Baths were taken in portable tubs brought into the bedroom and filled with hot water carried up from the kitchen. Afterwards the dirty water had to be carried down again. Providing the water for bathing, washing, and shaving in the bedroom required plenty of servants. Elizabeth Grant describes how a guest, Irish Mr Macklin, having worn out the patience of the laundry maids by the number of shirts he put on per day, 'took a bath twice a day, not in the river, but in a tub – a tub brought up from the wash-house, for in those days the chamber apparatus for ablutions was quite on the modern French scale.'[19]

Although medieval houses had often included 'garderobes', privies, or latrines, it was considered a sign of greater luxury and comfort to have a portable convenience in each bed room. These were of two kinds: the chamber pot, which could be of metal or pottery and which was for liquid waste; and the chamber pan housed in a close stool. Pans were usually of metal and the stool could be an elaborate chair-like frame with padded seat. The pot was usually stored under the bed for night-time use, but the close stool was often housed in a cupboard or closet off the chamber, affording a degree of privacy and some barrier against odours.

Chambers and bedrooms in large households were used as private space where individuals could retreat to pursue their own study, read, or write letters. Bookcases and card tables are often listed in inventories, as are writing tables, 'escritoires', and 'scrutoires', probably the type of writing desk that could be locked to protect personal papers. In the bedroom, people could dress in a comfortable manner, wearing unconstricting clothes, but once outside in the public spaces of the house they were 'on show' and expected to behave accordingly and to be properly dressed. In towns and in small houses in the country, women held gatherings in these chambers – for example, tea parties from four to eight in the evening – as this was the only space available for such entertaining. In the nineteenth century, with the increase in country house parties, the guests' bedchambers remained welcome retreats from the bustle of a full house.

Four-post beds remained in use in the eighteenth century but the trend was to lighter styles with slender wooden supports and lighter-weight fabrics than the wools and heavy silks of the earlier period. At the very end of the century in 1797, the new young laird of Rothiemurchus, an estate in the Highlands

188. A lady's writing table, much influenced by French style. It was supplied by Chippendale, Haig & Co for Paxton House, Berwickshire, in 1774. The bedroom provided privacy for writing letters, and desks and writing tables are often listed in inventories of bedchambers.

189. A mahogany chest of drawers by Chippendale at Paxton, 1774. Two items of this serpentine shape can be seen in the plan of Kinnaird House (pl 187).

190. A grand bed by Chippendale at Dumfries House, Dumfriesshire, 1759. Although more elaborate than the beds found in the houses of people in the middle ranks, the elegant carved bed posts are of a type which were used widely, not just in the mansions of the aristocracy. This room was clearly not in use when the photograph was taken by the National Monuments Record.

opposite to Aviemore, brought his bride to their Highland home in which 'the state bed and bedroom were curtained with rich green silk damask heavily fringed', and furnished with a japanned toilet-table, a mirror to match, and 'numberless boxes, trays, and baskets of japanned ware'.[20] These were obviously the choice of an earlier generation. Printed cotton, first imported from India in the seventeenth century, became fashionable in the late eighteenth century for family bedrooms with matching room curtains. Ingenious ways of making folding beds disguised as other pieces of furniture exercised the minds of the cabinetmakers. In less affluent households the box bed remained popular and the hurley bed was still mentioned in inventories.

A fascinating inventory of Benjamin Moodie from Melsetter, Orkney, in 1772 gives the names of the woods used for furniture as well as other details.[21] Mrs Moodie's room contained a folding bedstead of beech with green watered stuff hangings. Twelve yards of ticking were used in the bed, bolster, and pillows, with three and a half stone of feathers. The 'east' or 'Yellow room' had a beech bedframe with mahogany footposts fluted and carved with vases and yellow damask curtains. The dressing glass, easy chair, and six other chairs were of mahogany, but the dressing table was of fir covered in gauze, perhaps like that seen in Zoffany's famous portrait of 1764 of Queen Charlotte and her two eldest sons.[22] The floor had a yellow and black floorcloth and there were a basin, water bottle, and bed pots of stoneware. The 'Red room' had a similar

191. The 'alcove' bedroom at Paxton House, near Berwick-on-Tweed, restored to look as far as possible as it did in the late eighteenth century. Much of the furniture was supplied by Chippendale, Haig & Co in 1774. This bedstead has fluted columns similar to those described in the Melsetter inventory (see p191). The door leads to a closet used in the eighteenth century for powdering hair, to prevent the powder flying all over the room.

bedstead hung with red and white cotton check and in the 'Paper'd room' was a 'setee bedstead buff'd with a tent roof made in an extraordinary manner' with blue and white check curtains and slips for the back and seat. Other types of bed in the house included close and box beds in what were obviously the servants' rooms.

During the eighteenth century, wall hangings and tapestries fell out of favour and wallpaper became fashionable as the technology for making it improved. It was seen as a lighter, cheaper, and more hygienic alternative to fabric wall covering. In contrast, bed hangings became more elaborate on some beds shown in the cabinetmakers' and upholsterers' pattern books. The thinner silk and cotton fabrics were more suited to draping than the heavy earlier textiles. Window curtains also became more usual in the eighteenth century and are listed in Scottish inventories. In 1774, Thomas Chippendale supplied Ninian Home at Paxton, Berwickshire, with three wallpapers for bedrooms, one of '16 pieces fine Chints paper … the pattern made on purpose to match the cotton [bed furniture] 8/- £6.8.0'.[23]

More modest ways of draping beds are given in *The Workwoman's Guide* by 'A Lady' of 1840, showing that even at this period four-post beds were regarded as normal.[24] However the half tester, where the canopy only reached over half the bed with curtains at the head end, seems to have become more acceptable for the main bed rooms, perhaps reflecting the advent of more efficient firegrates as well as the beginnings of concern about ventilation and fresh air. In 1838 James Boag, Commission Agent in Edinburgh, had seven rooms, with beds in three of them.[25] What appears to be the main bedroom, next to the dining room, had a French bed with curtains, a wardrobe, two chairs, glass, bootstand, washing stand and table. At this period the term 'French' bed meant one where the long side was against the wall and a pole with draperies hung over this in a purely decorative arrangement, with no curtains to draw around. By the 1850s, beds with headboards rather than canopies were gaining in popularity and gradually came to be the standard type.

Bed linen usually consisted of a pair of sheets of plain white linen, which started to be replaced by cotton in the mid nineteenth century. Sheets, pillow,

192. Diagrams of draped beds from *The Workwoman's Guide* of 1840, showing the rich variety of treatments of bed curtains and valances. Figs 21–3 are various forms of French bed, 26 and 28 are folding beds disguised as other pieces of furniture, 31 is a simple stand bed, 27 a folding bed suitable for travel, and 30 a hammock.

PLATE 22

Fig 1 Fig 2 Fig 3 Fig 4 Fig 5 Fig 6 Fig 7 Fig 8 Fig 9 Fig 10 Fig 11 Fig 12 Fig 13 Fig 14 Fig 15 Fig 16 Fig 17 Fig 18 Fig 19 Fig 20 Fig 21 Fig 22 Fig 23 Fig 24 Fig 25 Fig 26 Fig 27 Fig 28 Fig 29 Fig 30 Fig 31

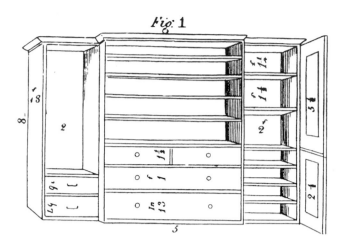

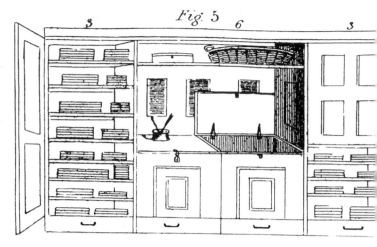

and bolster cases were made of different types of linen for different levels of the household, the finest being kept for guests, the next quality for the husband and wife, with coarser sheeting for the children. Servants would be allowed harn sheets, the coarsest kind of linen. In *The Workwoman's Guide* the number of sheets for each bed is recommended to be two pairs, or three sheets as a minimum.

Care was taken to mend torn linen, and sheets were regularly turned sides to middle when they became worn in the centre. Linen was marked with the family's initials and often a date, enabling the owner to keep track of items when they went for washing, particularly necessary if this was done by outside launderers. In the earlier period this marking was done by embroidery but later on ink was used. It meant that items could be used in rotation, ensuring even wear. *The Workwoman's Guide* also gave detailed instructions on the storage of linen, prices to be paid for laundering, and how to ensure that the right items were used on particular beds.[26] Victorian housekeeping if done as thoroughly as this book recommends was certainly a time-consuming affair.

By 1840 the list of articles to be used on a bed included the drapery, a straw mattress, wool or hair mattress, feather bed, bolster, two or three pillows, quilt or counterpane, blankets, and watch pockets to keep watches to hand at night before alarm clocks were in general use. The straw mattress was to be made as hard as a board. Horsehair or wool mattresses were for adults whilst children should have chaff, seaweed, beech leaves, or paper, but chaff and horsehair were the coolest. Bolster and pillows were stuffed with chicken, goose or turkey feathers or down, but the poor had mill-puff, a kind of cotton. A mid Victorian bed piled high with mattresses can be seen in the Gladstone family home, Fasque House at Fettercairn in Kincardineshire.

Warmth was provided by blankets. These were of several sorts and it is not always easy to distinguish them among surviving examples. In the 1685 inventory of The Binns nearly all the blankets are described as bed plaids. This probably means they were made of a coarse twill-weave woollen fabric called plaiding or pladding, not that they were in tartan. Later inventories list 'Scotch' and 'English' blankets. From the values quoted, English blankets were more expensive but it is not clear what the difference was in use. Blankets are usually described as being in pairs. This means they were a double length which was used folded over to give a double layer. Sometimes a half blanket is listed, meaning that the length has been cut in half to form a single layer. The Castle Fraser inventory of 1722 lists nine pairs of bed plaids on one bed, which is surely

193. *Left:* Drawing of a wardrobe for women's clothes from *The Workwoman's Guide*, 1840. On the left is hanging space with drawers below for furs. In the centre are sliding shelves for dresses, collars, and so on, with drawers below for heavy linen. The shelves on the right are for bonnets at the top and shoes below. All sections have doors except the centre drawers, and there is a mirror inside the left-hand door.

194. *Right:* Suggestion for a linen press from *The Workwoman's Guide*, 1840. Two bins with hinged lids in the centre are for dirty personal and household linen. Above are pinned linen lists and on the shelf is a clothes basket. In the cupboards on either side are the piles of clean linen, sorted into different categories.

excessive for use on the bed and must refer to storage of the plaids when not in use.

By 1840, Witney in Oxfordshire had become the main centre for blanket making, producing thick and light blankets with a soft raised nap. They were sold in pairs or woven together, in which case they had to be cut to put on the bed and the raw edges button-hole (or blanket) stitched. 'A Lady' (author of *The Workwoman's Guide*), recommended using one blanket on the bottom and two or three on the top. A particularly Scottish feature appears to be embroidered blankets, but it is not known at present if these were covered or were intended to be seen (pl 195).[27]

Further warmth could be achieved by adding a 'twilt', as The Binns inventory describes them. These were stuffed with wool and possibly more like a modern duvet than the later type of quilt. The term quilt came to be used to cover a variety of items which in the eighteenth century were usually more decorative pieces and therefore formed the outer cover of the bed. There are examples of elaborately embroidered satin covers which are false quilted: there is no stuffing but the background is closely sewn with a decorative design usually in yellow silk. These often had matching pillow, bolster, and small cushion covers to form a very costly daytime cover to the bed. An example embroidered with the date 1699 was owned by Margaret Hamilton, wife of the Earl of Panmure.[28]

Over all the bedding came a cover, and there was a variety of different types. Patchwork covers, which could be quilted or not, gained in popularity from the late eighteenth century onwards. *The Workwoman's Guide* ascribes patchwork quilts to cottagers, 'made by them at school, or in their leisure moments … These quilts are durable when lined, and may be good work for school-

195. *Left:* Blanket of cream twilled wool embroidered in coloured silks with various flowers, including a thistle, with IC for Isabel Carmichael and the date, 1705. Embroidered blankets seem to have been particularly Scottish items.

196. *Right:* A piece of Scotch carpet from Mellerstain House, Berwickshire, 1818. This type of carpeting was widely used in bedrooms and in the more private areas of houses. It is a double-weave cloth with the pattern reversed in colour on the other side. This was a useful feature since it could be turned over when it became worn.

children, though they certainly take up a good deal of time in making.'[29] One is mentioned in an inventory of 1795 of Andrew Henderson's household goods.[30] Henderson was a haberdasher and his house had a kitchen, store, and Fore Room, with a Parlour in which the bed was situated. The decoration of these covers depended on the skill and interest of the maker, and Scottish examples are not usually as elaborate as those made in America. Some patchwork quilts include suitable biblical texts printed on cotton which were incorporated into the design.

Some inventories mention Scotch covering. This is probably the double weave (similar to today's 'Welsh tapestry') which was used in a heavier wool for carpets in the late eighteenth and early nineteenth centuries. When made for the floor this double-woven cloth was called Scotch carpeting and was often used in bedrooms (pl 196). Castle Fraser in Aberdeenshire has some very good examples of this from the 1820s to 1840s, and at Shambellie House Museum of Costume at New Abbey there is a modern example based on an old design.[31] Some fragmentary examples of double-weave bed covers exist from the nineteenth century, including one made by Matthew Fowlds of Fenwick, Ayrshire, probably dating to about 1880.[32] Another type was the overshot coverlet which was taken by Scottish immigrants to Canada and developed into a particularly attractive form of bed cover.[33]

A regional style of cover is the Shetland 'tattit' rug. These have a shaggy wool pile on a cloth backing, and were made in two pieces, roughly sewn together, so that they could be separated for washing. Surviving rugs mostly have geometric designs but others are floral and one has a Union Jack.[34] When they were getting worn they could be used as floor coverings. These attractive bedcover rugs are recorded in house descriptions in the eighteenth century and were made until about the 1930s, but appear not to be made today.

In the nineteenth century, other forms of bed cover became popular, including machine-woven examples imitating quilting. Made in white cotton, they are usually called Marseilles quilts. These white covers were seen as hygienic, because they could be washed, and very suitable for use with the iron bedstead. They were particularly used on children's and family beds whilst the guest rooms might retain grander covers. White cotton knitted covers also became very popular towards the end of the century and in the years up to the First World War (pl 204).

The dressing room as a room separate from but allied to the bedroom was found in eighteenth-century houses of a certain level (for instance, houses in Edinburgh's New Town), but their use increased in the nineteenth century, when even small country houses had them. They were usually next door to a bedroom and might share a small lobby, with a common door onto the landing. Rooms provided for honoured guests usually had an attached sitting room, while houses built in the twentieth century might also include a bathroom, to form a suite for the most important guest room. The dressing room was essentially the husband's room, where his clothes were kept and there was usually a single bed (pl 197). This could be used occasionally, for example when his wife had a new baby, or on a regular basis if the couple did not particularly want to sleep together, a common practice in aristocratic households. Some writers advocated separate beds for couples but it was seen by most middle-class people as right for couples to share a double bed unless there was a medical reason against it.

Apart from a single bed, the dressing room would have wardrobes and chests for clothes and a washstand with matching china. Sometimes a chest would act

197. Dressing room at Cullen House, Banffshire, photographed in 1960. It was usual for the dressing room, since it was customarily a man's room, to have a single bed and fairly plain furnishings.

198 & 199. Details from a page of a Wylie & Lochhead, Glasgow, catalogue, illustrating furniture suitable for a gentleman's dressing room, 1900–10: a shaving stand, and a chest of drawers which includes a trouser press in a sliding drawer.

as a dressing table but if there was space, a dressing table with mirror was provided and an array of toilet equipment laid out on top. A shaving stand with a mirror at a higher level than found on dressing tables became quite popular, especially for the man who had to shave himself (pl 198). The dressing room next to the 'Tiger Room' at Brahan Castle in 1862 had a bed, chest of drawers, looking glass, basin stand, two tables, chair, bath, screen, foot bath and carpet.[35] In an inventory of 1925 for a farmhouse near Berwick, the dressing room had a combination bedstead with wire mattress, chest of drawers, washstand and ware, mirror, clothes rail, three cane chairs, carpet, and invalid's chair.[36]

Both the bedroom and the dressing room often had a pair of steps which were needed to get into high beds. Bedside tables might be small cupboards holding the chamber pot. On top would be placed the candle stand, as most bedrooms continued to have no other lighting than this until well into this century. There was often a bedside rug so that the carpet did not get too worn in the area where there was most use, and this was sometimes shaped to fit all round the bed. Separate freestanding looking glasses were another popular item, and a towel rail was needed in the bedroom if there was no bathroom. There were various small chairs, some more for decoration than for use. At night, clothes were often draped over chairs to air and in the Victorian period and later, women's underwear might be covered by a piece of fabric so that husbands did not see their wives' corsets.

Pictures were used in all rooms in the nineteenth century but the bedrooms usually had more intimate paintings or engravings than the public rooms. Dressing rooms might have sporting subjects or portraits of politicians, while ladies' bedrooms could have flower paintings or sentimental engravings, embroidered pictures or children's samplers. Elizabeth Grant mentions that in 1813 'A court beauty by Sir Peter Lely was sent up to a bedroom, she was not dressed enough to be downstairs'; and 'A few old landscapes, not so well preserved, were hung about in the bedrooms.'[37] Later on, family photographs were commonly displayed here.

Advice on how best to furnish bedrooms was offered to Victorian house-holders by numerous publications. J C Loudon's *An Encyclopaedia of Cottage, Farm and Villa Architecture and Furniture*, first published in 1833, is one such book, while Lady Barker wrote on *The Bedroom and Boudoir* in 1878. By the late nineteenth century the idea was to make the bedroom as light and airy as possible to counteract the unwholesome exhalations of the body during the night. Greater concern about the spread of diseases, such as tuberculosis, played a part, as did the feeling that too warm a bedroom was debilitating. Fires were for invalids or when someone was ill, not for every day, even for the wealthy unless they were really decadent. The emphasis was on fresh air to counteract the frowstiness of a bedroom in the morning and bedclothes and furnishings had to be washable and hygienic. The introduction of iron and brass bedsteads reflected this new interest – the draped bed was considered to harbour dust and bugs. In the mid nineteenth century the spring base made up of coiled wire springs started to become popular. These springs were used in seat furniture too and were strongly recommended by Loudon in his book of 1833.[38] Later, wire mesh bases were introduced, described by Lady Barker in 1878 as resembling a coat of mail.[39] She considered them cleaner and more comfortable than the older slatted or roped bases.

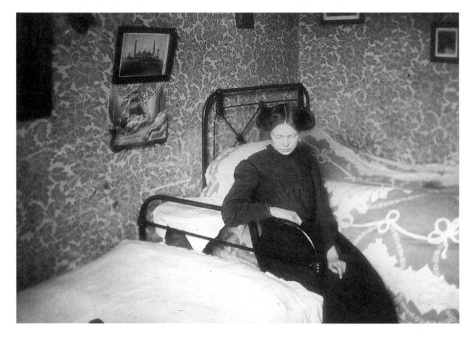

200. In contrast to bedrooms in large country houses, those of the less affluent could be very crowded. This photograph of about 1910 from the Environmental Health Department of Edinburgh District Council highlights the concern felt at overcrowded conditions which could help to spread infectious diseases such as tuberculosis.

Furniture for the bedroom was increasingly available in suites from the mid nineteenth century, comprising wooden headboards for beds, a wardrobe, washstand, chest of drawers, dressing table, full-length mirror, bedside tables, and chairs. Manufacturers and retailers promoted matching sets in different price ranges to increase their trade (pl 202). Depending on the size of the room and the wealth of the purchaser, more or fewer pieces could be bought. The bedroom suite became an essential part of a young married couple's house furnishings in the first half of the twentieth century, when a middle-class marriage was expected to start with the complete kit.[40]

In the early twentieth century the eiderdown gained in popularity. This was a highly stuffed feather quilt covering only the top of the bed. The outer covering was often of rayon or silk satin in a limited range of colours or else a floral pattern, with a less slippery fabric on the underside. The eiderdown was

intended to be kept on the bed at night, but during the day it could sit on top of the bed cover. Ensuring that it did not slip off during the night meant that it was sometimes anchored under the top blanket. By the late nineteenth century in Scotland a sheet was often used to keep both quilt and blankets on the bed over the sleeper.

201. Bedroom at Corehouse, Lanarkshire, photographed in 1951–6 but showing the survival of a typical Scottish country-house bedroom of the late nineteenth and early twentieth centuries. On the small bed is a plump eiderdown. The washstand appears to have been still in use, with its ewers and basins, slop bucket and chamber pot, and to the side, a towel rail. A touch of modernity is the electric light on the bedside table.

202. 'A Massive and Commodious Suite' offered by Wylie & Lochhead, Glasgow, early twentieth century. This is a little old-fashioned compared to some other pieces in the catalogue, but would fit in well in the large late nineteenth-century tenements of Glasgow.

No. 687. Bedroom Suite, in Mahogany, Carved, comprising :
5 ft. Three Door Wardrobe, Fitted Drawers and Hanging Space inside,
3 ft. 6 in. Half Cheval Toilet Table,
3 ft. 6 in. Washstand, with Marble Top and Back,   Complete, £36 10/
2 Chairs, with Upholstered Seats,
A Massive and Commodious Suite.

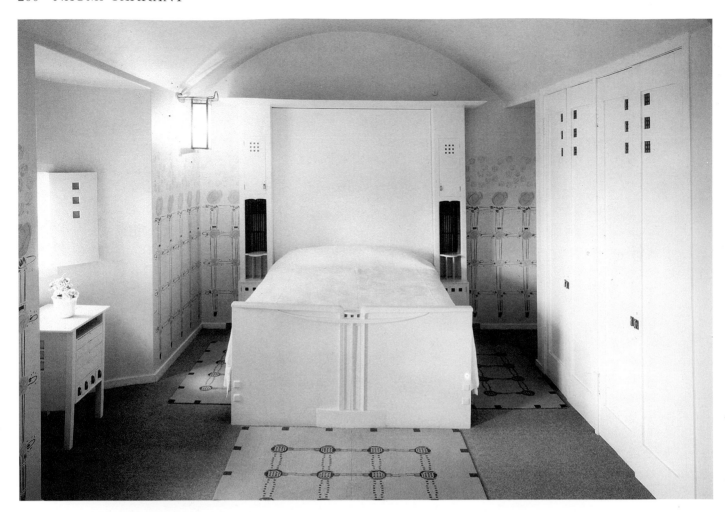

Further comfort in beds was brought about in the early twentieth century by the adoption of interior sprung mattresses and bed bases. Beds started to lose their bed heads and footboards in the mid twentieth century. They fitted in better to the lower ceilinged rooms of modern houses as they took up less room. The bed bases could also be used against a wall with fitted cupboards and bedside tables incorporated into a full wall unit, again taking up less space and allowing more furniture to be fitted in. In architectural literature of the turn of the century it was often recommended that furniture should be built in to a house to save cleaning but it was not until the 1960s that manufacturers began to promote fitted bedroom furniture to a wide market.

Another addition to comfort was the wider use of central heating in Scottish homes, though this is by no means universal today. Few children, however, now face the rigours of an icy bedroom, as David Daiches remembered from 1920s Edinburgh and many readers will recognize from their own experience:

Every winter morning began with that tremendous summoning of the will to enable me to leave the beatific warmth of my bed for the cold linoleum floor of the chill bedroom; time never made it any easier; it was always an act of tremendous resolution, worked up with enormous effort. Yet it never occurred to me that the situation was anything to complain of, and the notion that bedrooms might be heated (except in cases of illness) would have struck me as bizarre in the extreme if I had ever heard of it, which I hadn't.[41]

Along with changes in furnishing and ambience, there has been a revolution in bed linen in the last thirty years. In the past, white was considered the only

203. Hill House, Helensburgh, a house designed in 1902 by Charles Rennie Mackintosh for Walter Blackie. The bed has fixed side cupboards and headboard, and there are fitted cupboards to the side, in accordance with thinking in architectural circles of the time about the labour-saving advantages of built-in furniture. This is a fully co-ordinated room with even the wall decoration and carpet designed by the architect.

204. *Waking* by Sir John Everett Millais, 1865. Metal bedsteads were considered more hygienic than wood because they could easily be cleaned. Similarly, the knitted cotton bed cover could be washed thoroughly. The bedspread survives in the collections of Perth Museum and Art Gallery, which also owns the painting.

colour for sheets because it could be boiled. Linen is still thought the best fabric for sheets, being cool and soft, but it is now extremely expensive as well as difficult to launder correctly. The introduction of mixed cotton and polyester sheeting – polycotton – has allowed new ideas for bedding to be introduced. Cotton takes well dyes which do not fade quickly with frequent washing, and polyester helps to make virtually crease-free material. Together these two fibres can therefore be used to make decorative and easy to launder sheeting.

Housework for women in the first half of the century was very time-consuming and heavy. Reading the recommended ways of cleaning the house in the manuals of the day, one forms the impression of work increasing to fill the time available to the middle-class woman, who often did not have a large family to look after by the 1930s. But the rise in female employment, particularly for married women after 1945, meant that the old routine of housework – washing on Monday for example – was no longer possible. So there was an interest in new forms of bedding which appeared to enable the bed to be made quickly. This probably helped to make the continental quilt or duvet, often known in Scotland as a 'downie', so popular. The use of bright covers for these quilts, frequently with matching curtains, has been an essential decorative feature of bedroom design in the last twenty years. However, sheets and blankets are making a comeback in some quarters.

The large families of the nineteenth century meant that children often shared beds and even in wealthy households they would normally share bedrooms. Moral reformers pushed for the segregation of the sexes and it therefore came to be considered necessary to have a minimum of three bedrooms in a house, one for the parents and one each for boys and girls. The smaller family size of the twentieth century led to children often having their own bedrooms, particularly where there was only one of each sex. This is the standard which most families would consider necessary today, as it allows children to indulge in their own leisure activities and to decorate their rooms as they wish (pl 205). Children's bedrooms usually accommodate furniture suitable for all their activities, while the parents' room is used more frequently only as a sleeping room, though bedrooms often now house a personal computer and have become the location for much home-based work.

Today, bedrooms in most new houses are so small that built-in furniture is necessary to make the best use of the space available and sofa beds and futons seem to be increasingly popular. It is difficult to see how much smaller the bedroom can get. Perhaps the future will see a return to living in one room where all activities take place during the day and the beds are unfolded for the night. This would be to return full circle to the way all Scots lived in the distant past and how the majority lived until recent times.

205. Young girl in her bedroom, 1988. Springburn Museum in Glasgow organized a project in which young people were lent cameras to record their rooms. The results show a number of common themes: pets in the room, TV or audio systems, bright duvet covers, and personalization of the space.

9 The Bathroom and Water Closet

MILES OGLETHORPE

'the advantages of bathrooms with proper water supply over portable baths, both in point of convenience and economy of labour, can scarcely be over-rated.'

S F Murphy (ed), 1883[1]

Although the bathroom and water closet (WC) are now indispensable components of modern living in all but the most primitive of Scottish homes, the provision of such facilities is rarely discussed in architectural literature, appearing with regularity only in modern building regulations, and during the last few decades in growing numbers of DIY books. Indeed, a trawl through published material reveals that from Roman times until the early nineteenth century very little was either written or done about sanitary facilities.

Part of the problem appears to have been that, in British society at least, the subject of personal hygiene was taboo, and where mentioned at all, is even today riddled with awkward euphemisms. Such has been the discomfort associated with this sensitive subject that even the technical terminology has become warped, with 'lavatory', which used to mean 'wash basin', now being used in common parlance to describe the water closet (which has itself been superseded by 'toilet' or 'loo').

Fortunately, this state of embarrassment has not always prevailed, the late nineteenth century being a golden era for publications and propaganda on domestic and institutional plumbing facilities, fired, no doubt, by Prince Albert's unhappy encounter with typhoid. A number of seminal texts provide detailed and enthusiastic instruction on how to fit the home with sanitary fixtures, and how to ensure that adequate connections, with precautionary traps, are made to the local sewers.[2] One particularly interesting chapter by an architect, John Cash, appended to a book entitled *The Modern Home*, also enthuses about drains, commenting that 'A little knowledge of drains may be dangerous, but that little, properly used, is better than none'.[3] Cash was proud to count himself a 'sanitarian', initiated into the 'mystery of Sanitary Science'.

It is, however, regrettable that the author has so far failed to discover any evidence that the provision of bathrooms and WCs in Scotland was significantly different from that in the United Kingdom as a whole. Scotland has, nevertheless, a proud history of municipal water and sewerage infrastructure, and a particularly important sanitary-ware industry. In these respects at least, there is a distinctly Scottish story to be told.

In Scotland, as elsewhere in the United Kingdom, the provision of domestic plumbing facilities is a relatively modern phenomenon, dating from the early nineteenth century. Before this time, it has been said that the 'Midden Ages' prevailed, characterized by, in today's terms, unimaginable rural and urban squalor, filth and disease.[4] Before the bathroom and WC, excretory relief was usually achieved with the aid of a commode, chamber pot, or privy; or directly through an appropriate orifice in a building.[5] For those who could afford to pay, private bathhouses were available in Edinburgh, and presumably elsewhere, as Lady Grisell Baillie's accounts indicate: in 1695 she paid £4.16.0 (Scots) 'For baithing in Rees baithing hows' and £9 'To the Bainio in the Canigate'.[6] In the home, however, portable water carrying devices and furniture, such as ewers, basins, and tin baths were used for personal ablutions. Indeed, until the beginning of the First World War in 1914, washing in most working-class households was done at the kitchen sink, with weekly baths taken in a tin tub (pl 78).[7] The ideal of separate rooms dedicated to personal hygiene could not have been achieved without a piped water supply, and some means of heating the water. This in turn brought the need to dispose safely and efficiently of the resulting waste and thus necessitated increasingly sophisticated sewerage systems.

Before the development of mains water supply in Scottish towns and villages, water was drawn from local wells, streams, and rivers, a situation which was sustainable where population density remained relatively light. Inevitably, the rapid urbanization encouraged by the industrial revolution generated major problems, not the least of which was that water supply and human waste tended to become indistinguishable.

The first water supply schemes in Scottish cities appear to have been in Edinburgh (1674), Stirling (1774), Greenock (1796), Glasgow (1806), and Paisley (1834).[8] These were, however, generally limited to the wealthier classes, and conditions for most people in the towns and cities continued to deteriorate. Nowhere was the problem better documented than in Edinburgh, where the French phrase 'Garde à l'eau!', or 'Gardyloo', was associated with the co-ordinated throwing of excrement into the streets.[9]

Such insanitary arrangements shocked visitors to the capital. Joseph Taylor in 1705 described his experiences with distaste:

> Every street shows the nastiness of the inhabitants: the excrements lie in heaps … In a morning the scent was so offensive that we were forc't to hold our noses as we past the streets and take care where we trod for fear of disobliging our shoes, and to walk in the middle at night for fear of an accident on our heads. The lodgings are as nasty as the streets … every room is well-scented with a close-stool, and the master, mistress and servants lye all on a flour, like so many swine in a hogsty … We have the best lodgings … and yet we went thro' the master's bed-chamber, and the kitchen and dark entry to our room, which look't into a place they call the close, full of nastinesse. 'Tis a common thing for a man or woman to go into these closes at all times of the day to ease nature.[10]

Thirty five years later, Edward Burt found himself trembling at the sound of an opening window 'while behind and before me, at some little Distance, fell the terrible Shower'; and having safely reached his lodgings, was 'almost poisoned with the stench.'[11]

The total inadequacy of private water supplies led to the incorporation into municipal control of most cities' supplies in the mid nineteenth century. Dundee was the first to end private ownership in 1840, with Glasgow following in 1855, the ensuing Loch Katrine scheme justly receiving international attention as it approached completion in the 1860s.[12] Other cities to follow suit included Greenock in 1867, Edinburgh and Dundee in 1869, and Inverness six years later.

206. An extensive network of pipes is indicated on this map published in 1890 in Colston's *The Edinburgh and District Water Supply, a Historical Sketch.*

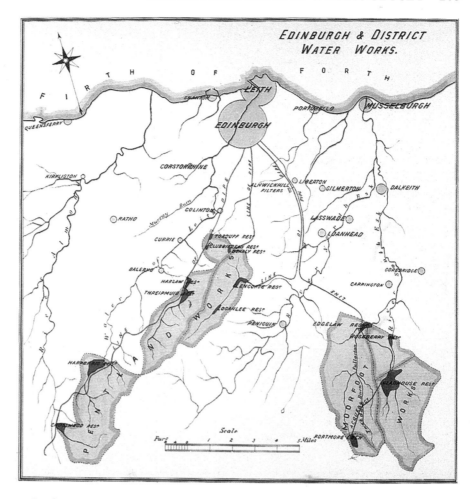

Such improvements were made possible partly by the advent of new materials for the manufacture of pipes and mains. In 1674, Edinburgh's first piped water supply was provided in three-inch diameter lead pipes, which carried water from Comiston to the now defunct reservoir at Castle Hill. The pipe was increased to four and a half inches diameter in 1722, and augmented by supply from Swanston in wooden pipes in 1760. However, it was the advent of cast iron which after 1787 transformed Edinburgh's water supplies (pl 206).[13]

During the early nineteenth century, Scotland became one of the world's most important centres for the manufacture of pig iron, and developed a reputation for high-quality iron castings. The forerunner of the modern Scottish iron industry was Carron (near Falkirk), but several companies grew to specialize in the manufacture of cast-iron water mains and associated products. A leading producer was Thomas Edington of Glasgow, whose Phoenix Foundry supplied mains pipes for towns and cities throughout the country.[14] Another famous Glasgow company, Walter Macfarlane & Co, whose Saracen Foundry produced a wide range of architectural cast-iron products, manufactured an assortment of sanitary appliances, including cast-iron baths, water closets, wash-hand basins, and urinals (pl 207). Scotland also became famous for its engineering industries, and it is no coincidence that companies such as Glenfield Kennedy of Kilmarnock came to specialize so effectively in products associated with water supply, such as pipes, valves, and other hydraulic engineering fixtures (particularly those relating to reservoirs). In addition, Scottish expertise appears to have pioneered the development of 'pressure pipes', capable of containing high-pressure supplies both of water and gas.[15]

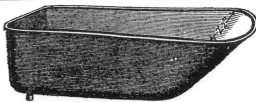

Unfortunately, water supply is only half the equation, as was apparent from the 'Gardyloo' problem: there was little point in having piped clean water if there was nowhere for the dirty water and waste to go. With the rapid urbanization of the nineteenth century came huge problems of communal filth and disease, resulting in epidemics of cholera, typhoid, and related diseases.[16]

Taking Glasgow as an example, we find that the need for more sewers was recognized comparatively early, the first significant developments occurring in 1790. Sequences of serious epidemics, affecting both rich and poor, provided the impetus for major works from the mid nineteenth century onwards, and by the 1890s, sewage treatment had developed to cope with the huge quantities of effluent generated.[17]

Before the provision of sewers, most tenement houses had been equipped with privies or trough closets. Sometimes a whole stair housing dozens of families shared a single privy, usually located in the back green, adjacent to ash bins. The excrement was mixed with ash and the resulting night soil was taken away in dung carts during the night. Before the city grew too big, it was usual for night soil to be sold as fertilizer on behalf the landlord, generating extra income, or perhaps as part-payment of rent.[18] A similar situation prevailed for urine, the chemical properties of which were of value to the textile industries in particular.

Inevitably, the rapidly growing metropolis became awash with 'human fertilizer' (adding to the already substantial problems created by horses), and action was urgently required to deal with the problem. A report on the housing of Glasgow as late as 1891 noted that:

> The provision made for the disposal of the excrement of the inhabitants of these tenements demands immediate attention. Several places are noted where there is no provision whatsoever, but in our opinion, the privy (a public facility in the back yard) is in no case a sufficient provision for flatted tenements. It is never used, and cannot in the nature of the case be used by females, and seldom by children. The result is that every sink is practically a water closet, and the stairs and courts and roofs of the outhouses are littered with deposits of filth cast from windows.[19]

In the last decades of the nineteenth century, therefore, the development of sewerage infrastructure was rapid, encouraged in particular by Snow's discovery in 1849 that cholera was a water-borne disease.[20] There was also substantial

207. This advertisement from *The Builder*, 7 July 1860, depicts the utilitarian cast-iron baths of the day. The text seems to suggest that the 'plain' version above would have to be filled and emptied by hand.

investment in public baths from the 1880s, providing bathing and swimming facilities; public laundries further promoted standards of personal hygiene.

At the domestic level, the Industrial Revolution not only provided the materials from which a dwelling's water supply could be built, but also a wide variety of products without which the modern bathroom would be incomplete. The more obvious examples include cheap, effective factory-produced soap, absorbent textiles for towels and flannels, and latterly, 'toilet tissue'.

The history of toilet or 'bathroom' tissue is elusive. Materials commonly used in the past for such purposes have included sponges, cloths, and leaves; and newspapers provided an obvious source from at least the early eighteenth century. Specially made sheets were on sale in the United States in the 1850s, such as 'Gayety's Medicated Paper' from New Jersey. Scott Brothers were making several brands of bathroom tissue in Pennsylvania by 1880, having patented a paper-perforating machine in 1871, suited to the production of rolls of tissue. In the United Kingdom, hard and often medicated bathroom tissue was widely available by 1900, but it was many years before softer varieties became popular. The first of these was made in 1932.[21]

One of the most important requirements of the bathroom was an adequate supply of piped hot water, which was made possible by the installation of high-pressure plumbing, storage tanks, and domestic boilers. On a more mundane note, the presence of comparatively large quantities of water (and resulting condensation) in a room required the use of sturdy, water-resistant materials, favouring the adoption of waterproof flooring such as floorcloth and linoleum (much of which was produced in Fife, especially in Kirkcaldy). In addition to wooden boarding, other favoured materials included ceramic bricks and tiles, which again protected porous walls and floors that were vulnerable to rot.

The need for such materials emphasizes the fact that, unlike other rooms in the home, the bathroom (and associated WC) are almost entirely functional, bearing few of the social responsibilities expected of rooms elsewhere in the home. There was, nevertheless, some potential for indulgence, as is clear from the range of sanitary fixtures and appliances and decorative tiles which became available, particularly in the twentieth century.[22] It is also hard to believe that the more lavish bathrooms were never shown off to friends, especially such fine examples as that shown in plates 212 and 225, which is almost a scale version of Andrew Carnegie's palatial bathroom at Skibo of 1900–3.

Introducing a bathroom into a dwelling was a relatively simple matter for a new building, where the room and associated plumbing could be included at the design stage. It was rather more complicated in existing structures, where it meant either building extensions, or converting other rooms. In tenements an extension was often added up the back of the building, the early examples containing only WCs for the shared use of the houses on each landing (pl 74). In dwellings where existing rooms were sacrificed to make way for bathrooms, obvious candidates for conversion included dressing rooms and bed closets. A particularly attractive example from the mid twentieth century can be seen at Craigievar Castle in Aberdeenshire, where a lemon yellow bath fits neatly inside a dark-panelled bed space.[23] In recent years, especially in smaller dwellings with only cupboards available for conversion, shower rooms have been preferred to bathrooms, though as late as the 1940s a writer on modern homes could say that 'Shower baths are not normally installed in private houses.'[24]

It is significant that bathrooms tended to be located near to bedrooms, and in larger, more luxurious dwellings, some bedrooms had their own wash basin,

208. Shower bath at Hill House, Helensburgh, built for the publisher Walter Blackie in 1903–4. The grid-like windows are typical of Charles Rennie Mackintosh's design, but the panelling is simply a smarter version of the wooden boarding often found in bathrooms. The shower itself must have been the height of modernity, though its extensive pipework would be difficult to clean.

209. The bathing facilities at Lauriston Castle, Edinburgh, were particularly good because of Mrs Reid's family's plumbing business. The bath is of painted zinc, which was more comfortable than cast iron because it retained heat well. The WC disguised as a chair in French style in the background was an expensive 'Optimus Sanitary System'.

210. A coffin-shaped bath on display at Fasque House, Fettercairn, Kincardine-shire. It bears the label of W & P Steele, a 'Furnishing Ironmongers' at 61 George St, Edinburgh, and dates from about 1835.

or an *en suite* bathroom. Lauriston Castle in Edinburgh has some fine examples because of the connections of the owners at the turn of the century: Mrs Reid, née Margaret Johnstone Barton, was from a family of sanitary engineers (pl 209). In dwellings with upper floors, it is normal for bathrooms to be on the same floor as the main bedroom. Plumbing requirements also often dictate that bathrooms are located near to (although rarely now with direct access from) kitchens, the other room in the house where water is used as part of a daily routine.

The bathroom is now perceived as containing a bath or shower (or both), a wash basin, and usually a water closet, although the latter may be housed separately in a smaller adjacent room. More salubrious bathrooms may contain a bidet, or an extra wash basin. Today, the modern bathroom frequently does not have a window, and is required by law to have ventilation ducts and fans. There are, in addition, large numbers of fittings and accessories that can be added to a bathroom, ranging from basic items such as mirrors, cupboards, and towel rails, through to less specialized personal intrusions, such as chairs and bookshelves. The centre of any bathroom, nevertheless, remains the sanitary ware itself.

Usually the largest single item in the room is the bath. Writing in 1929, the ceramics expert, Alfred B Searle, observed that earlier types of bath were often made from sheet metal, generally zinc or copper, and were generally coffin shaped, narrowing at the foot (pl 210). These were superseded by vitrified-enamel cast-iron or fireclay baths, which initially retained their coffin shape, but eventually evolved to the parallel sides now customary (pl 211). Searle noted that specialized corner and recess baths had also been developed, and

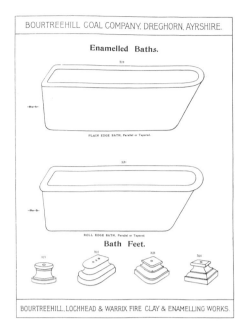

211. Enamelled clay baths from a 1902 catalogue, showing the feet on which the baths were raised so that cleaning could be carried out underneath.

212. *Right:* A Shanks & Co shower bath combination installed at Belmont, Eskbank Road, Dalkeith, in 1900. The row of taps enables the bather to experience a range of different water sensations.

213. *Below:* A 'Savaspace' bath in a house in Helensburgh, about 1900–10. It seems that the bather might have had a problem with privacy.

Lawrence Wright also illustrated a variety of other types and shapes, including 'Sitz' and 'Hip' models.[25]

Searle's preference was for fireclay baths because of their resilience and the tendency of iron baths to rust if chipped. However, the space-saving baths which were sometimes installed in smaller dwellings and in servants' quarters in larger houses were designed to tip up on hinges, allowing them to be stowed away in cupboards, and most of these were made of sheet metal to reduce the weight (pl 213).

Although very much part of the modern bathing experience, showers have appeared in the earliest bathroom arrangements in a variety of guises. These range from the familiar detached compartment to a simple fitting above a bath. Most elaborate of all were showers integrated into the bath itself, as illustrated by the example above from Dalkeith .

The second most prominent fixture in a bathroom is usually the 'lavatory', now generally known as the wash-hand basin, which can be described as a form of washing bowl, sometimes on a pedestal, sometimes wall-mounted (pl 214) or in a cabinet, to which is attached a permanent supply of hot and cold water and a waste pipe connecting to the drains. Searle noted that the earliest lavatory basins were like those sold with ewers for bedroom use, but with an outlet at the bottom to which a waste pipe could be fixed (pl 215). Wash basins ranged from plain simple designs to extravagant models forming part

of extensive and often highly decorative suites, embellished with moulding or printed designs.

Perhaps the most important of the sanitary fixtures is the 'water closet' or WC, which Searle described in 1929 as a form of basin, many different patterns being available, which should be so shaped as to be self cleaning with only two gallons of water.[26] Early models were, however, not necessarily so efficient, usually being built from cast-iron, lead, and wood components. The introduction of WCs was made possible by the availability of sewers and cesspools into which they could discharge. This was itself dependent upon the development of non-porous (usually internally-glazed) pipes to carry the waste without leakages. Although many early WCs were installed outside in outhouses, replacing privies, in time the WC was incorporated within the home, and subsequently within bathrooms. This was not only because of the enhanced hygiene, comfort, and convenience of such arrangements, but also because of problems caused by severe winter weather and frozen pipes.

Lawrence Wright's book of 1960, *Clean and Decent*, and Roy Palmer's *The Water Closet, A New History*, provide the best chronologies of the WC. Sir John Harrington is alleged to have invented the water closet for Queen Elizabeth I of England but the main technical improvements did not occur until after 1850, particularly with the introduction of heavy ceramic materials.

The earliest mainstream WCs may be classified as 'Valve Closets' (pls 216, 217), the first patented example being the Cummings model in 1775. The system involved a pan with an opening at the bottom sealed with a leather valve. The action of flushing, by a complex arrangement of handle, lever, and counterweight, admitted water to the bowl whilst temporarily releasing the valve. Such devices were usually encased by wooden surrounds, sometimes requiring the attentions of a skilled cabinetmaker. The major disadvantage of these closets was the valve itself, which usually leaked, allowing nasty odours and gases from the soil pipe to escape into the dwelling. However, later sanitary engineers, such as William Ross of Glasgow, produced improved designs, and valve closets were still being installed many years after more sophisticated alternatives were available.[27]

214. *Left:* Wash-hand basin with glass and soap holders in the East Bathroom at new Knock Castle, Ayrshire, from around 1900. The tiles would be in a rich dark colour with a shiny glaze.

215. Early versions of 'lavatories' were made to resemble washstands. The bowl may have been plumbed in or possibly tipped up. From *The Plumber and Sanitary Houses* by S S Hellyer of about 1886.

216. *Right:* A valve closet surviving in a house in Dunbar, East Lothian, with its wooden panelling, lid, and handle mechanism. This kind of boarding was frequently fitted in bathrooms and WCs.

217. Diagram of the complex workings of the valve closet, from *The Plumber and Sanitary Houses* by S S Hellyer, about 1886.

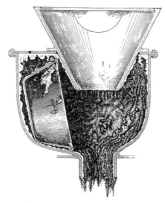

218 & 219. Examples of new and used pan closets, intended to deter any prospective purchaser. From Hellyer, about 1886.

Next on the evolutionary scale is the 'Pan Closet', which Palmer describes as 'highly objectionable'.[28] It comprised an upper earthenware basin with a shallow copper pan containing three to four inches of water as a seal at its base: the pan could be tipped away to discharge its contents into a lower cast-iron receptacle connected to the drainage system (pls 218, 219). Hellyer (about 1886) comments that:

It has always been a puzzle to me to understand how such a water-closet as a pan closet should become so great a favourite with architects, plumbers and the public. The only 'bliss' that the public can have about so foul a thing is 'ignorance' of its nature, but what excuse for architects and plumbers I know not, except that it was the custom of their father to specify and to fix pan closets, and this became a law unto them.[29]

Many nevertheless were tolerated well into the twentieth century, although the author has perhaps been fortunate not to encounter any surviving Scottish examples so far.

With the advance of the heavy ceramics industries came the ancestor of the modern WC, in the form of the 'Hopper'. 'Hoppers' were simple basins, either in long or short format, with primitive flushing systems which again incurred the disgust of Hellyer, who observed that:

the Hopper ought never to be used, even in the very poorest water closet. The faeces on using such a closet fall upon the side of the basin and foul it, and as the basin is generally dry, hardly any amount of water brought to bear upon it will flush it off. There is left a 'fixture', like the basin itself, which the *out-going* tenant is generous enough to leave behind him for the *in-coming* tenant to see, and have the benefit of without anything to pay.[30]

A principle advantage of 'Hoppers' was that they were simple to make and comparatively cheap. They were consequently often installed in servants' quarters, while the householders reserved the more sophisticated (although no less inefficient, if Hellyer is to be believed) 'pan' and 'valve' closets for themselves.

Great advances in the evolution of water closets came with the advent of 'Pedestal Closets', which could be made from clay, and could therefore be manufactured in bulk at relatively low cost. Water closets of this type were being installed in houses in Scotland in increasing numbers in the 1880s. Examples of 'sideways-flushing' Doulton models, installed in 1887, can be found still in use at Viewfield House, Portree, Isle of Skye (now a hotel). Similar specimens no doubt survive elsewhere in Scotland.

The few books that exist on the history of sanitary ware tend to distinguish between three types of pedestal closet. These are the 'Wash-Out' (or 'Flush-Out'), the 'Wash-Down', and the 'Siphonic'. Well-known early examples included the Twyford's 'Deluge' and Ducket's 'Clencher', but as is illustrated in J & M Craig's catalogue of 1914, there were many Scottish examples with equally evocative names, including the 'Plinius' wash-out, 'Centric' and 'Excentric' (both 'wash-down' models), and the 'Torentia' (a siphonic design).

THE "PLINIUS"	THE "EXCENTRIC"	THE "TORENTIA"
WASH-OUT CLOSET.	WASH-DOWN CLOSET.	SINGLE JET SYPHONIC CLOSET.
In Finest Earthenware, with or without Seat Lugs, Outlet at Back.	*In Finest Earthenware, with or without Seat Lugs, Outlet at back.*	*In Finest Earthenware*

Of the three pedestal WCs, the first, the 'wash-out', broke with tradition by abandoning the concept of a valve to close the bottom of the pan, favouring instead a small amount of water sitting in the 'U' or 'S' bend, acting as a seal after each flush. 'Wash-outs' became popular in the last decades of the nineteenth century, and by 1900 were being produced in great numbers by Scottish manufacturers. Despite the significance of this innovation, it is difficult to determine who first developed WCs of this type.

The 'wash-down' closet grew to become the most common type of WC in use in the United Kingdom. Its principal attraction was that its flush was exerted directly on the water in the basin, forcing the waste away more effectively, and enhancing the self-cleaning properties of the closet. Perhaps more impressive still is the siphonic closet, in which the water and contents of the basin are carried away by means of siphonic action. The earliest known example is thought to be that designed by John Randall Mann in 1870,[31] and it was again being manufactured in Scotland by 1900. Extra features of 'siphonic' closets,

220. A selection of J & M Craig's strikingly named water closets from the 1914 catalogue. Minor variations were clearly seen as of significance when selling such goods.

221. *Opposite:* A Shanks & Co bathroom from a catalogue of the 1930s. Note the clean lines and gleaming surfaces and the fashionable shade of green. Matt glazes for ceramic tiles were now more popular than the very highly reflective surfaces of the turn of the century.

Shanks

PLATE F8161
Bathroom Suite in No. 5 Green

Comprising :—

F7577 "Carnock" Bath, combined taps to plunge and shower, inlet nozzle to bath, standing waste and overflow, curtain rail and curtain.

F7478 "Coral" Bidet, in Vitreous China, "Eureka" mixing fitting to rim and ascending spray, pop-up waste.

F7427 "Carlford" Pedestal Lavatory, in Vitreous China, taps and pop-up waste.

F8096 Towel Rail with inlet and outlet connections.

F7970 "Argos" Siphonic Closet and 3 gallon (14 litres) "Parva" cistern, in Vitreous China, "New Rotunda" valveless siphon fittings, "Decosan" finished seat and lid.

F8106 Wall Cabinet for building into wall.

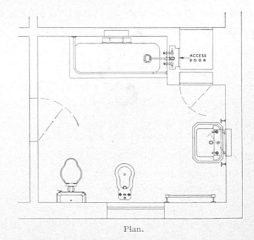

Plan.

CRAIG'S PATENT SYPHONIC CLOSET
THE "MAELSTROM."

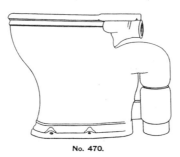

No. 470.

Syphonic Closets have the important advantage over the ordinary wash-down form that they discharge the water in a mass, thus serving the very useful purpose of cleansing and flushing out the drain pipes—an advantage which is patent to everyone.

Most of the Syphonic Closets hitherto put on the market have been either too intricate in construction or too expensive to be largely used, but in introducing the "Maelstrom" we can safely say that it is the acme of simplicity, besides being little more expensive than an ordinary wash-down.

The following are a few of the advantages which can be claimed for this closet:—

(A) It is as easily fitted up as an ordinary wash-down.
(B) It has no valves to get out of order.
(C) It is reliable and certain in its action.
(D) It can be used with any Syphonic cistern having an after service of half-a-gallon.

Made in one piece of Earthenware or Fire-clay, and can be had either plain, printed, or decorated.

We can supply Cisterns and Seats specially made to suit this Closet—prices on application.

222. J & M Craig's 'Maelstrom', described in the 1900 catalogue as 'the acme of simplicity'.

such as J & M Craig's 'The Maelstrom', included a flushing rim around the edge of the basin, a major discharge of at least a gallon of water into the basin (commencing the siphonic action), and a third, slow, after-flush flow. Such advanced self-cleaning WCs were able to fulfil Searle's stipulation that the basin should be cleaned with a maximum of two gallons of water.

One of the factors that originally restricted the advance of the WC was the amount of water used by most models. Valve closets in the early days were regarded as especially wasteful, particularly given the scarcity of water in the cities and the limited capacities of most piped water supplies. Indeed, rules and regulations were strictly applied, often preventing the installation of some models of WC. One of the most important areas of development was therefore that of the cistern: water-saving devices, such as the valveless cistern for which the London plumber Thomas Crapper is famous, greatly assisted the advance of the modern WC.

A further aspect of pedestal WC design was the loud noise created by the flush, usually due to the height of the wall-mounted cistern above the bowl. Although a resonant flush was sometimes a source of pride in the early days

Bidets perfectionnés Shanks

Dimensions extérieures — Longueur avec batterie, 0m781 ; Largeur, 0m394 ; Hauteur, 0m413 ; Entrées d'eau, 13 m/m. ; Sortie, 28 m/m.

No. 675, Bidet en porcelaine blanche avec alimentation d'eau chaude et froide à la gorge creuse et à la douche ascendante. Batterie nickelée et vidage combiné avec trop plein, complet.

No. 675

Dimensions extérieures :—Longueur, 0m661 ; Largeur, 0m464 ; Hauteur, 0m413 ; Entrées d'eau, 13 m/m. ; Sortie, 26 m/m.

No. 3074, Bidet en porcelaine blanche avec alimentation d'eau chaude et froide à la gorge creuse età la douche ascendante. Robinetterie nickelée et vidage combiné avec trop plein, complet.

No. 3074

Dimensions extérieures :— Longueur, 0m673 ; Largeur, 0m375 ; Hauteur, 0m394 ; Entrées d'eau, 13 m/m. ; Sortie, 26 m/m.

No. 3075, Bidet en porcelaine blanche avec alimentation d'eau chaude et froide à la gorge creuse et à la douche ascendante. Robinetterie nickelée et vidage combiné avec trop plein, complet.

223. Shanks & Co probably had more success selling bidets in France than in Scotland, where most surviving bathrooms from the early twentieth century appear to have done without them. This illustration is from their French catalogue of 1912.

(ensuring the neighbours knew of your latest stride towards civilized living), it was generally frowned upon as an embarrassment. Silent flushes were therefore an ambition, and the problem was solved by placing the cistern close to the back of the basin, admitting water to the pan through a much larger pipe, and increasing the quantity of water used at each flush from two to three gallons. The disadvantages of this design were that it took up more floor space, and in some cases, broke the two-gallon rule, incurring the wrath of the local water authority.[32]

By 1900, trade literature confirms that much of the demand for bathroom fixtures was for ceramic appliances. In simple terms, the industry had its roots in the heavy ceramics industries (especially those making firebricks for furnaces) for which Scotland was justly renowned.[33] Fireclay mining and manufacture was closely linked to the central coalfields, the most significant areas for earthenware sanitary ware occurring in the west in Ayrshire (notably Kilmarnock), and Renfrewshire (centred on Paisley and Barrhead). Many small companies nevertheless prospered elsewhere, with numerous examples appearing in Glasgow and other cities. Among the more interesting of these were Steele's of Edinburgh (Niddrie Fireclay Works) and Buick's of Alloa (Hilton Fireclay Works).[34]

As is already apparent, the larger companies included Shanks of Barrhead, whose products ranged from the basic to the exotic, and who were mass-producing bidets by 1900 (pl 223), and J & M Craig in Ayrshire. In addition to the 'Maelstrom' and other models, Craig's were well known for their decorated appliances, such as the 'Chrysanthemum' range (see pls 225, 226). Other Ayrshire companies included Howie and the Bourtreehill Coal Company, the latter's 1902 catalogue containing a broad range of products (pl 211). Among the most important of these were the white-glazed bricks widely used for the walls of bathrooms, but also suited to prisons, hospitals, and other institutions. Their principal advantage was the ease with which their glazed, non-porous surfaces could be cleaned.

224. The bathroom adjoining the principal bedroom at the new Knock Castle in Ayrshire was equipped around 1900. The bidet is very similar to those depicted in Shanks & Co's catalogue.

225. *Opposite:* Shanks and Craig both produced a printed chrysanthemum-patterned suite in 1900. This is the Shanks version in the bathroom at 47 Eskbank Road, Dalkeith (see also pl 212).

Urinal No. 300, Medium.

Fountain Hand Basin, No. 492.

226. 'Hibiscus' patterned sanitary ware from J & M Craig's catalogue of 1900. In *Nairn in Darkness and Light*, David Thomson describes an intriguing urinal in his uncle's study, which he mistook for a wash basin, as well as the 'proper basin with taps and flowers on it and in one corner a WC which was also covered with flowery patterns'.

As the twentieth century progressed, so the market for Scottish sanitary ware increased. The biggest demand came from huge public-sector house-building programmes which, because of comparatively high standards and building regulations, required well-appointed indoor bathroom and WC facilities in every new dwelling.[35] Scottish bathroom furniture was also exported throughout the British Empire and beyond. A further aspect of the industry was its close relationship with and dependence upon the shipbuilding industry. Clyde-built ships, especially liners and ferries, created substantial orders for sanitary fixtures. This market niche ensured that a significant number of the world's seaborne bathrooms were Scottish. Demand was further bolstered by rules and regulations enforcing the provision of washroom facilities in factories, offices, and other institutions, especially schools. A notable market cornered by Scottish producers consisted of the London Board Schools, for whom the Bourtreehill Coal Company made a range of fixtures at the turn of the century, including the near-indestructible 'Infantile' closet.

It has been suggested that the vast increase in the number of working-class homes with fitted bathrooms inspired a demand among those with more money to spend on their homes for suites in colours other than the utilitarian white.[36] Certainly there was an explosion of colour in the 1930s, when bright pink and turquoise suites were made, and the Royal Reception Rooms at the 1938 Empire Exhibition in Glasgow were equipped with a bathroom suite in primrose yellow.[37] It is clear from the manufacturers' catalogues that they were able to supply all the necessaries for a co-ordinated bathroom scheme, including soap and paper holders, and the chromium-plated taps which replaced the earlier brass fittings. According to one writer in 1903, the conscientious housewife would keep brass taps polished to look like gold, though this might need doing twice a day.[38] It is no wonder they were superseded in the 1920s and 1930s when both hygiene and labour saving became major concerns. The increasing use of washable ceramic or glass wall tiles in bathrooms is also evidence of these preoccupations.

Since the 1950s, demand for Scottish-made sanitary ware has declined for a variety of reasons, including the rapid reduction in house and ship building. The contracting market allowed Shanks, the most famous name in the industry, to dominate by taking over all its surviving competitors, until Shanks itself was eventually merged with the English firm, Armitage, later becoming part of the Blue Circle Group. The parent company closed down Scottish operations by shutting the Barrhead factories in the early 1990s, but the Scottish industry was kept alive by the workforce at Shanks, who formed Barrhead Sanitary Ware, setting up a new factory in Hillington, Glasgow.

The demise of Shanks was a sad blow for Scottish manufacturing capacity in general, representing the end of an era. As this extract from the company's 1930 'M' catalogue shows, the company had been at the forefront of modern bathroom design (pl 221).

One index of advancing civilisation is the importance that is now being attached to the installation of Bathrooms. Great Britain for many years led the way in sanitary appliances and realised before any other modern nation the value of the Bathroom. In recent years other nations have followed, and now, all over the world, there is great demand for comfortable, well-equipped and artistic Bathrooms. We have been pioneers in this business and in the present Catalogue many examples will be found of the latest appliances.[39]

Shanks's Barrhead factories were also unsurpassed in technical terms, pioneering fully vitrified, or vitreous china, a much lighter, stronger, and potentially cleaner ceramic material from which most sanitary ware is now made. Vitreous ware rapidly replaced heavier fireclay and earthenware products, one of its many advantages being that its glaze was less prone to craze. Another area of innovation at Barrhead was the development of battery moulding techniques, which revolutionized production on the ceramics side at the Victorian Pottery.

A further technological change to affect the bathroom has been the gradual introduction of plastics since the 1960s. These are now a crucial component of the modern bathroom, the most common plastic appliances being acrylic baths, wash hand basins, cisterns, WC seats, and a variety of fixtures such as taps, valves, and pipes. New, more resilient plastics, combined with sophisticated injection-moulding and vacuum-forming, have therefore challenged the established bathroom products, and have also permitted the production of wider ranges of colours and shapes.[40] The vivid hues of the earliest coloured suites toned down a little in the 1960s and 1970s, when 'avocado', 'aubergine', and similarly muted shades became more popular. Ironically, the type of white, heavy and ornate bathroom fitting at which the Scottish manufacturers excelled in the first half of this century has now become fashionable again, but is no longer made in Scotland. Imports come in from Germany, Italy, and Turkey to satisfy the new demand.

It is sad to have to report that, as is the case with literature, architects and draughtsmen have been reluctant to include bathrooms and WCs in their portrayals of homes of all varieties. In many cases, even where they are identified on plans, few details of the layout of appliances and fixtures are provided. Certainly, the relish with which Hellyer illustrated his plumbing and drainage arrangements does not seem to have been replicated in Scotland.

There are, nevertheless, notable examples of buildings (and drawings of buildings) in which the arrival of the bathroom in Scottish life is confirmed. Typical are Watson's Sauchiehall Street and Keppie's Hope Street tenements (pl 227).[41] A more luxurious example is Robert Lorimer's Ardkinglas in Argyllshire (pl 228). Although other architects of the late nineteenth century took pride in their knowledge of drains (most notably Norman Shaw and Philip Webb), Lorimer seems to have been exceptional in the architectural profession in having designed a WC, the 'Remirol' (his own name spelt backwards), in collaboration with the British Medical Association.[42] As indicated on plate 229, it appears to have been inspired by the 'custom of the East' and was sold widely throughout the United Kingdom.

From these, and other examples of Scottish housing, no clear pattern emerges. Some houses, large and small, have their WCs separate from their bathrooms, and some do not. Others have separate WCs as well as a WC in the bathroom. Some provide bathrooms and WCs for servants' quarters, and some appear not to. Others have a downstairs WC, and some have a cloakroom, usually described as 'lavatory' on architects' plans of the late nineteenth century. These were usually important features of larger, more formal dwellings, and frequently contain both a wash basin and WC. They were generally sited off the hall or lobby, or in smaller villas by the back door, and were convenient for tradesmen calling on business as well as for male guests using the dining room, billiard room, or smoking room.[43] One of their functions was to allow visitors access to sanitary facilities without having to penetrate the more private areas of the house, including the bathroom itself. In some instances, social habits dictate that even today men are expected to use the cloakroom, while women, especially trusted friends, are honoured by being invited to use the bathroom.

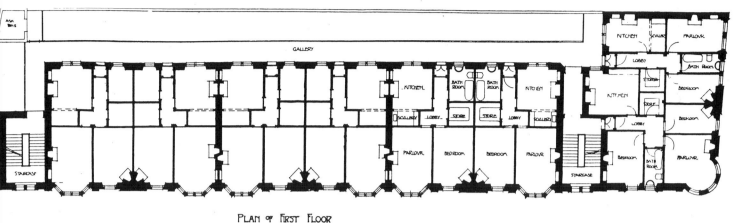

PLAN OF FIRST FLOOR

4 BLYTHSWOOD SQUARE
GLASGOW OCT 1906

227. *Above:* Plan of flats of three or four apartments, designed to be inexpensive, indicating the layout of the bathrooms. From *Flats, Urban Houses and Cottage Homes* by Walter Shaw Sparrow, about 1906. The exterior view of these tenements is shown in pl 7.

228. *Right:* Plan of Ardkinglas in Argyllshire by Robert Lorimer, 1908, showing three bathrooms on the principal floor.

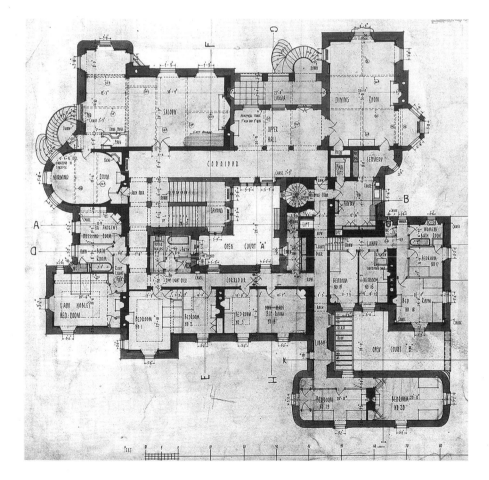

The relatively poor showing of the bathroom and WC in Scottish architectural history is disappointing, making it yet more difficult to ascertain if there are distinctly Scottish patterns of progress. The low profile of plumbing facilities may be attributed, as suggested earlier, to the socially difficult nature of the subject of personal hygiene, and to the fact that the bathroom and WC now form such a central, automatic part of daily life that, as with electricity and gas supplies and fixtures, they are simply taken for granted.

One reason for the poor appreciation of the history of bathrooms is the lack of surviving photographic archive material. This may be explained by the fact

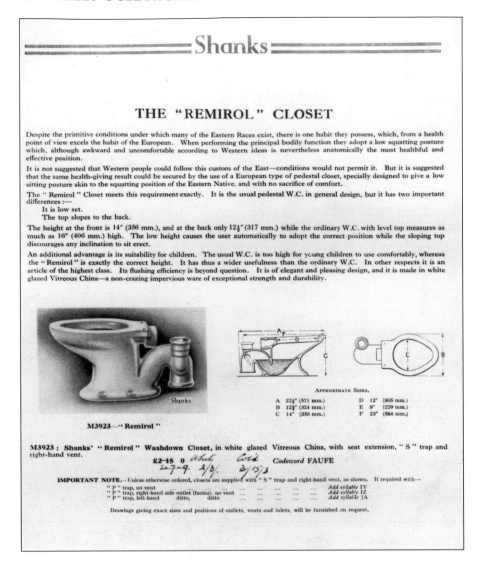

Shanks

THE "REMIROL" CLOSET

Despite the primitive conditions under which many of the Eastern Races exist, there is one habit they possess, which, from a health point of view excels the habit of the European. When performing the principal bodily function they adopt a low squatting posture which, although awkward and uncomfortable according to Western ideas is nevertheless anatomically the most healthful and effective position.

It is not suggested that Western people could follow this custom of the East—conditions would not permit it. But it is suggested that the same health-giving result could be secured by the use of a European type of pedestal closet, specially designed to give a low sitting posture akin to the squatting position of the Eastern Native, and with no sacrifice of comfort.

The "Remirol" Closet meets this requirement exactly. It is the usual pedestal W.C. in general design, but it has two important differences :—

    It is low set.
    The top slopes to the back.

The height at the front is 14" (356 mm.), and at the back only 12½" (317 mm.) while the ordinary W.C. with level top measures as much as 16" (406 mm.) high. The low height causes the user automatically to adopt the correct position while the sloping top discourages any inclination to sit erect.

An additional advantage is its suitability for children. The usual W.C. is too high for young children to use comfortably, whereas the "Remirol" is exactly the correct height. It has thus a wider usefulness than the ordinary W.C. In other respects it is an article of the highest class. Its flushing efficiency is beyond question. It is of elegant and pleasing design, and it is made in white glazed Vitreous China—a non-crazing impervious ware of exceptional strength and durability.

Shanks

M3923—"Remirol"

APPROXIMATE SIZES.

A 22½" (571 mm.)   D 12" (305 mm.)
B 12¾" (324 mm.)   E 9" (229 mm.)
C 14" (356 mm.)   F 23" (584 mm.)

M3923 : Shanks' "Remirol" Washdown Closet, in white glazed Vitreous China, with seat extension, "S" trap and right-hand vent.

£2-15 0   Codeword FAUFE

IMPORTANT NOTE.—Unless otherwise ordered, closets are supplied with "S" trap and right-hand vent, as shown.   If required with—
    "P" trap, no vent ... ...   Add syllable IY
    "P" trap, right-hand side outlet (facing), no vent ...   Add syllable IZ
    "P" trap, left-hand   ditto,   ditto ... ...   Add syllable JA

Drawings giving exact sizes and positions of outlets, vents and inlets, will be furnished on request.

229. Robert Lorimer's 'Remirol', designed in association with the British Medical Association and produced by Shanks. From a catalogue of 1930.

that bathrooms are often small and comparatively cramped, and producing satisfactory photographs is difficult because of the problem of reflection from shiny surfaces. Furthermore, taking detailed photographs of the appliances themselves is even today regarded as eccentric behaviour!

Further discouragement may derive from the fact that few old bathroom fixtures survive intact. As standards of personal hygiene have improved, there has been a desire to replace old, tarnished sanitary ware with modern, clean, and efficient alternatives. For study of the Scottish home this is unfortunate, because Scotland has played an important role in the sanitary revolution through the large-scale design and manufacture of sanitary ware and accessories. Equally significant have been the pioneering, municipally inspired water supply and sewerage schemes of Scottish cities, which transformed the quality of life for most Scots. Only recently, with the lingering threats of water privatization north of the Border, has the true extent of progress in this area of life begun to be more widely recognized.

In 1902, H J Jennings observed that in Britain

there is a room which no self-respecting householder can do without, and that is the bath room. One can only marvel at the astounding fact that, prior to twenty or thirty years back, the majority of small and medium-sized houses, and perhaps fifty per cent. of the larger ones, were built without bathrooms.[44]

230. A stylish 1930s bathroom, the walls covered with 'Vitrolite' panels, from the house of an architect, Leslie Grahame Thomson, at West Linton, East Lothian.

Even in 1914, although Glasgow had managed to replace many of its privies with WCs, over half were still shared with other dwellings.[45] The extent of progress since then is well illustrated by the fact that by the early 1990s 97 per cent of Scottish households were linked to public water authority supplies.[46] Of these, the vast majority will now have their own bathrooms.

Notes

References to publications of general interest cited in more than one chapter are given here in abbreviated form: full details can be found in the bibliography.

Other abbreviations are as follows:

NGS: National Galleries of Scotland
NLS: National Library of Scotland
NMS: National Museums of Scotland
NRA(S): National Register of Archives (Scotland) at the SRO
PSAS: Proceedings of the Society of Antiquaries of Scotland
PSOHA: People's Story Oral History Archive, Edinburgh City Museums & Art Galleries
RCAHMS: Royal Commission on the Ancient & Historical Monuments of Scotland
SEA: Scottish Ethnological Archive, NMS
SRO: Scottish Record Office

1 Studying the Scottish Home

1. S Ferrier, *The Inheritance*, London 1824, new edn Bampton 1984, 43.
2. The exceptions include J Ayres, *The Shell Book of the Home in Britain*, London 1981, and M Barley, *The House and Home*, London 1963.
3. Two useful works based mainly on written sources are M Lochhead, *The Scots Household in the Eighteenth Century*, Edinburgh 1948; and M Plant, *The Domestic Life of Scotland in the Eighteenth Century*, Edinburgh 1952.
4. For example, L Astaire, R Martine, & F von der Schulenburg, *Living in Scotland*, London 1987; and C Maclean & C Simon Sykes, *Scottish Country*, London 1992.
5. See R J Naismith, *Buildings of the Scottish Countryside*, London 1985.
6. Robinson 1984, 54–60.
7. Rodger (ed), 8.
8. Ames, 208.
9. NGS, on loan from the Earl of Mar and Kellie. The painting is dated 1783 and depicts Alloa House, Clackmannanshire.
10. See A T Simpson & S Stevenson (eds), *Town Houses and Structures in Medieval Scotland: A Seminar*, Glasgow 1980.
11. See, for instance, RCAHMS, *North-East Perth: An Archaeological Landscape*, Edinburgh 1990, 95–171; and RCAHMS, *South-East Perth: An Archaeological Landscape*, Edinburgh 1994, 113–23, 143–5.
12. G D Hay & G P Stell, *Monuments of Industry*, Edinburgh 1986, 70.

13. I Gray, *A Guide to Dean of Guild Court Records*, Glasgow 1994.
14. See L Weatherill, *Consumer Behaviour and Material Culture in Britain 1660–1760*, London 1988.
15. London 1848, new edn London 1967, 21.
16. *A Tour in Scotland, and Voyage to the Hebrides; MDCCLXXII*, i, Chester 1774, 229.
17. J & M Findlater, *Crossriggs*, London 1908, new edn London 1986, 140.
18. Ibid, 368.
19. C Carswell, *Open the Door!*, London 1920, new edn London 1986, 187.
20. Ibid, 246.
21. In the collections of Aberdeen Art Gallery.
22. The cabinet in the NMS collections is attributed to Brodie by repute but cannot conclusively be associated with him.
23. The painting is dated to 1847–51 because the Fergusons occupied this house in George Square from 1847 to 1852 and the painting was exhibited in 1852.
24. The house is now occupied by the University of Edinburgh and nothing survives of the decoration.
25. Gow, 11.
26. See T–M Morton, *Royal Residences of the Victorian Era: Watercolours of Interior Views from the Royal Library, Windsor Castle*, London 1991.
27. Photograph collections exist all over Scotland. Among the most comprehensive is the Scottish Ethnological Archive of the NMS, and the Curator keeps details of the holdings of others.
28. The Scottish Film Council in Glasgow has a particularly good example of an educational film for domestic science teachers entitled *A Day in the Home*, made in 1951.
29. The SRO keeps a register of oral history archives and staff are keen to hear from anyone with tape recordings which might be of interest to researchers. The Register gives a brief description of the contents and location of tapes.
30. See Flinn (ed), 189–90.
31. Ibid, 285–9 & 341–8.
32. For work in the home in the 20th century, see M Bulos & W Chaker, 'Sustaining a sense of home and personal identity', in Benjamin (ed), 227–41.
33. See Cowan for a stimulating explanation of this change.
34. L H Sullivan, 'The tall office building artistically considered', *Lippincott's Magazine*, March 1896.
35. J M Barrie, *The Plays of J M Barrie*, London 1928, 311–12. I am grateful to Andrew Martin for this.

36. SRO CC 8/8/86. Value of goods in the 'North roume', £54 4s 0d, in the 'mid roume' £22 16s 0d.
37. SRO GD 18/1758b, Clerk of Penicuik papers. For Clerk's response, see SRO GD 18/5014.
38. From *Housing in 19th Century Glasgow: Documents 1800–1914*, Strathclyde Regional Archives, education resource pack, 6.
39. Ibid, 13, from the *Glasgow Herald*, 14 May 1860.
40. Bamford, 29–31.
41. Published in Oldham 1877.
42. R & A Garrett, *Suggestions for House Decoration*, London 1876; W J Loftie, *A Plea for Art in the House*, London 1876.
43. R Rodger, 'Crisis and confrontation in Scottish housing 1880–1914', in Rodger (ed), 48, Appendix 2c.
44. Ibid: 27.5% of houses in Scotland had 3 or more rooms in 1861 and 35.2% of the population lived in them. The figures in 1911 were 46.7% and 52.1%.
45. A Gibb, 'Policy and politics in Scottish housing since 1945', in Rodger (ed), 158, table 6.1. The figure was 68.5%.
46. Marshall, 24–5; Franklin, 73–4.
47. See D Marshall, 'Notes of the connection of the Earls of Morton and Dick of Braid and Craighouse, with the Earldom of Orkney and Lordship of Zetland, with rental, inventory, &c., 1653, from original documents in the Charter Room of Kinross House', *PSAS* xi, 1889, 300.
48. SRO CC 8/8/128/2, an inventory of 1789, lists a dining room, two bedrooms, passage, kitchen, two garrets and cellar, and includes in the East Bed Room eight chairs, a 'Mahogany tea trea', a 'Mahogany Card Table', a 'Backgammon table', etc. These suggest that it was used for entertaining, though maybe it was for family recreation only.
49. SRO GD 18/5014.
50. Ferrier (see n1), 148–9; Grant, i, 237–8.
51. See for instance, L Weaver, *The "Country Life" Book of Cottages*, London 1913, 26–9.
52. This is anecdotal and may not always apply.
53. Loudon, new edn London 1857, 631.
54. Aslet, 111–17, Franklin 112.

2 Living in one or two rooms in the country

1. *Cobbett's Tour in Scotland*, London 1833, new edn, D Green (ed), Aberdeen 1984, 26.
2. W E Whyte, *Scotland's Housing and Planning Problems*, London 1942, 4.
3. Much evidence for shielings survives, for instance, in upland Perthshire. See J Kerr, *Life in the Atholl Glens*, Perth 1993, 95, for one such extensive set of remains at Aldvialich in Glen Fender. See also A Bil, *The Shieling, 1600–1840: The Case of the Central Scottish Highlands*, Edinburgh 1990.
4. T Pennant, *A Tour in Scotland, and Voyage to the Hebrides; MDCCLXXII*, i, Chester 1774, 216.
5. D Jones, 'Preaching tents', *Regional Furniture* viii, 1994, 42–52.
6. R Leitch, 'Salmon lodges on the Tay and Earn', *Vernacular Building* xvii, 1993, 34–47.
7. SRO AF56/1422, A Carmichael, *Fishing Lodges on the Tay and Earn*, Parliamentary Papers, 11 May 1889.
8. Ibid.
9. Ployen, 38–40.
10. Robb, 21.
11. A living van survives on the Fasque estate in Kincardineshire and there are examples in the collections of NMS and Glasgow Museums.
12. See A Fenton, *Scottish Country Life*, Edinburgh 1976, 189–92; and A Fenton, *The Shape of the Past 1: Essays in Scottish Ethnology*, Edinburgh 1985, 83–95.
13. A Fenton, *The Island Blackhouse: A Guide to the Blackhouse at 42 Arnol, Lewis*, Edinburgh 1978.
14. For Scottish and Irish dressers see R R Noble, 'Highland dressers and the process of innovation', *Regional Furniture* vi, 1992, 36–46; and Kinmonth, 99–125.
15. See H Cheape, 'Crogans and Barvas ware: handmade pottery in the Hebrides', *Scottish Studies* xxxi, 1993, 109–28.
16. D Jones, 'A sixteenth-century oak cupboard at the University of St Andrews', *Regional Furniture* iv, 1990, 73.
17. Kinmonth, 80–2; in County Cork in Ireland it is known as a 'Carbery' settle, and versions in the Basque country are called 'cicelu', or 'zuzulu'.
18. In Shetland the term 'benk' was applied to stone, turf, and wood settles in farmhouses; wider versions were known as 'pall'.
19. See D Jones, 'Darvel chairs', *Regional Furniture* ix, 1995, 64–70.
20. R R Noble, 'The chairs of Sutherland and Caithness: a northern tradition in Highland chair-making?', *Regional Furniture* i, 1987, 33–40. The Irish chairs are discussed by Kinmonth, 41–2; there are examples in the Ulster Folk and Transport Museum, County Down.
21. Ross et al, *Scottish Home Industries*, Dingwall *c*1895, 170–2, 174–5.

22. Information from Anne Brundle, Tankerness House Museum, Kirkwall.
23. The Shetland Croft House Museum at Dunrossness has some particularly good examples.
24. R Ayton, *A Voyage Round Great Britain in the Summer of 1813*, ii, London 1815, 180.
25. J C Loudon, *An Encyclopaedia of Agriculture*, London 1825, 2nd edn London 1831, 1183 & 1197.
26. D Jones, 'Everyman's furniture in Lowland Scotland', in J M Fladmark (ed), *Heritage*, London 1993, 325–34.
27. H Cheape, 'Baltic bowls and Riga cups', *Museum Reporter* xxiii, (NMS) Edinburgh 1992, 6–7.
28. There are several examples in the NMS collections, given by Miss I D J Sandison.
29. D Jones, 'Box beds in Eastern Scotland', *Regional Furniture* v, 1991, 79–85.
30. Robb, 13.
31. Ibid, 22.
32. Edinburgh District Council, City Archives. Records of the United Incorporation of Mary's Chapel, Edinburgh: Minute Book.
33. Robb, 11.
34. D Jones, 'Scotch chests', *Regional Furniture* ii, 1988, 38–47.
35. L Cooney & A Maxwell, *No More Bings in Benarty*, Benarty 1992, 48.
36. Ibid, 46.
37. Ibid, 45–8.
38. 1991 census figures (Crown copyright) show that about 8% of Scottish households were of one to two rooms. These are probably predominantly in special housing built for old people.
39. London 1930. The Weatherhouse is a dwelling formed probably in the 1880s from two 'but and ben' houses, joined by an irregular hexagonal addition. Mrs Craigmyle, its creator, furnishes it with old things such as a spinning wheel, a wooden dresser and plate racks, a cruisie lamp, and a Persian rug: new edn Edinburgh 1988, 4–6.

3 Living in one or two rooms in the city

1. Royal Commission 1917, 348, para 2241.
2. The 1991 census (Crown copyright) gives the total population of Scotland as 4,921,151. The number living in dwellings of one to two rooms was 210,965. See *1991 Census: Report for Scotland Part 1 Volume 1*, Edinburgh 1993, 269, table 22. For census figures for 1861–1911 see Rodger (ed), 48.
3. Much of the oral history quoted here is drawn from sessions with The People's Story Reminiscence Group, which was formed in 1986 to prepare for a new museum in Edinburgh. After The People's Story museum opened in 1989, the group met occasionally and a special session was organized to deal with the subject of living in small spaces.
4. For statistics see Smout in Thompson (ed), 253–4; R Rodger, 'Crisis and confrontation in Scottish housing 1880–1914', in Rodger (ed), 28, 47–8; A Gibb, 'Policy and politics in Scottish housing since 1945', in Rodger (ed), 158.
5. M Wood, 'Edinburgh poll tax returns', *Book of the Old Edinburgh Club* xxv, 1945, 90–126.
6. J Gilhooley, *A Directory of Edinburgh in 1752*, Edinburgh 1988.
7. E Topham, *Letters from Edinburgh; Written in the Years 1774 and 1775*, London 1776, 27.
8. D Defoe, 'Account & description of Scotland', in *A Tour Thro' the Whole Island of Great Britain*, iii, London 1727, 32.
9. SRO CC 8/8/100.
10. SRO CC 8/8/120.
11. A Wood, *Report on the Condition of the Poorer Classes of Edinburgh and of their Dwellings, Neighbourhoods and Families*, Edinburgh 1868, 53–4.
12. PSOHA, Pat Rogan, T275.
13. PSOHA, Robert McTaggart, T276.
14. J Butt, 'Working class housing in Glasgow 1851–1914', in S Chapman (ed), *The History of Working Class Housing – A Symposium*, Newton Abbot 1971, 68.
15. Royal Commission 1917, 113–14.
16. *Report of the Royal Commission on the Housing of the Working Classes, Scotland*, London 1885, 23, Q18,738, evidence of J K Crawford.
17. *Report on the Fourteenth Decennial Census of Scotland*, ii, Edinburgh 1933, p xii.
18. See Gibb (see n4) in Rodger (ed), 160, for a useful table of housing strategies in Scotland 1945–86.
19. *Housing in 19th Century Glasgow: Documents 1800–1914*, Strathclyde Regional Archives, education resource pack, 61; the speech is printed in A K Chambers (ed), *Memorial Volume of the Writings of John Burn Russell*, Glasgow 1905. Russell was describing the reaction to John Bright's Rectorial Address of 1884.
20. Ibid. Russell's speech was to the Park Parish Literary Institute.
21. PSOHA, Robert McTaggart, T276.
22. See R Rodger, 'The Victorian building industry and the housing of the Scottish working class' in M Doughty (ed), *Building the Industrial City*, Leicester 1986, 159.
23. PSOHA, Robert McTaggart, T276.
24. Springburn Museum Trust Archive, Andrew C Lillie, born 1911.
25. G Rountree, *A Govan Childhood, The Nineteen Thirties*, Edinburgh 1993, 3–14.
26. Pentland Centre & Calton Centre Reminiscence Groups, *Friday Night Was Brasso Night*, Edinburgh 1987, 10.
27. Examples can be seen at Summerlee Heritage Park, Coatbridge and the People's Palace, Glasgow.
28. Faley, 27.
29. R Wilkinson, *Memories of Maryhill*, Edinburgh 1993, 17.
30. Smout 1969, 414.
31. Duncan, 2.
32. Royal Commission 1885 (see n16), 36, Q19,087, evidence of James Colville, Manager of the Edinburgh Co-operative Building Company.
33. PSOHA, Newhaven Community History Group, Isa Wilson, T302.
34. I am grateful to Margaret Swain for this information.
35. Mentioned, for example, by J M Reid, *Homeward Journey*, Edinburgh 1934, new edn Edinburgh 1988, 49–50.
36. Royal Commission 1917, 57, para 449, Q18,745, evidence of Adam Horsburgh Campbell.
37. PSOHA, Joan Williamson, T232.
38. Wilkinson (see n29), 20.
39. J T Barclay & E E Perry, *Behind Princes Street, A Contrast. Report on a Survey of Housing Conditions of 443 Families Situated in St Andrew's Ward, Edinburgh*, Edinburgh 1931, 25.
40. PSOHA, Greta Conner, T283.
41. PSOHA, John Sinclair, T287.
42. PSOHA, Pat Rogan, T275.
43. Dundee Art Galleries & Museums and the late Joseph Paterson.
44. PSOHA, Betty Hepburn, T232.
45. PSOHA, Joan Williamson, T232.
46. Royal Commission 1917, 77, para 571–2. The report gives a further breakdown of the sanitary facilities in other Scottish towns.
47. H P Tait, *A Doctor and Two Policemen: The History of Edinburgh Public Health Department 1862–1974*, Edinburgh 1974, 188.
48. R Glasser, *Growing Up in the Gorbals*, London 1986, 8.
49. Royal Commission 1917, 77, para 571–2.
50. Tait (see n47), 188.
51. Ibid.
52. PSOHA, Stella Stewart, T150.
53. PSOHA, Newhaven Community History Group session, Cathy Lighterness, T302.
54. Queensferry Community History Group, *Doon the Ferry*, South Queensferry 1991, 39.
55. Wilkinson (see n29), 110.
56. Royal Commission 1917, 78–9, para 575.
57. PSOHA, Georgina Keenan, T287.
58. Ibid.
59. Dundee Oral History Project, Dundee Art Galleries & Museums, 0131/13/1.
60. PSOHA, Joan Croall, T240.
61. PSOHA, Betty Hepburn, T232.
62. St Leonard's History Group, Dundee, 29.09.94, courtesy of Graham Smith, Dundee.
63. Royal Commission 1885 (see n16), 43, Q19,306, evidence of Rev Joseph Hannan.
64. Royal Commission 1917, 105, para 731, Q20,337, evidence of Dr Chalmers.
65. Royal Commission 1917, 105, para 731, Q20,919, evidence of Mr Motion.
66. Glasser (see n48), 132.
67. Ibid, 133.
68. PSOHA, Elsie Tierney, T240.
69. PSOHA, Betty Hepburn, T240.
70. Pentland Centre and Calton Centre Reminiscence Groups (see n26), 11.
71. Leith Lives Oral History Archive, Richard Goodall, TD4.
72. Glasser (see n48), 77–8.
73. Queensferry Community History Group (see n54), 40.
74. M Weir, *Shoes Were for Sunday*, London 1970, 69.
75. PSOHA, Sybil Lindsay, T240.
76. Duncan, 17–18.
77. Dundee Social Union, *Report on Housing and Industrial Conditions and Medical Inspection of School Children*, Dundee 1905, 7–8.
78. PSOHA, Joan Williamson, T240.
79. PSOHA, Elsie Tierney, T240.
80. Dundee Art Galleries & Museums and the late Joseph Paterson.
81. PSOHA, Betty Hepburn, T240.
82. PSOHA, Pat Rogan, T275.
83. Leith Lives Oral History Archive, Mrs Gardiner, A2.
84. PSOHA, Joan Croall, T283.
85. PSOHA, Joan Williamson, T232.
86. PSOHA, Betty Hepburn, T232.

4 The Kitchen

1. *How to Plan Your House*, London 1937, 118.
2. For instance, Anon (R S Burn?), *The Grammar of House Planning: Hints on Arranging and Modifying Plans of Cottages, Street-houses, Farm-*

houses, Villas, Mansions, and Out-buildings, Edinburgh 1864, 55, figs 1–2, 4–7.

3. The Calor Gas company was started in 1936 and from the beginning promoted its product for cooking in rural areas. Information from Robin Irons, Sales Manager, Calor Gas, Scotland.

4. See Dunbar, 34, 41.

5. Statistics analysed in Flinn (ed), 194–9, tables 3.8.4 & 3.8.6.

6. Scott-Moncrieff (ed), 61, 63–4, 73, 76, 86.

7. D Marshall, 'Notes of the connection of the Earls of Morton and Dick of Braid and Craighouse, with the Earldom of Orkney and Lordship of Zetland, with rental, inventory, &c., 1653, from original documents in the Charter Room of Kinross House', *PSAS* xi, 1889, 275–313; 302, 305.

8. Ibid, 300–1.

9. Dunbar, 41–2.

10. The Stirling Castle kitchens have been restored and are open to the public with displays on cooking in the 16th and 17th centuries.

11. J Dalyell & J Beveridge, 'Inventory of the plenishing of the House of The Binns at the date of the death of General Thomas Dalyell, 21st August 1685', *PSAS* lviii, 1924, 344–70; 362–6.

12. Ibid, 365; the explanations of terms are as given by the authors.

13. Grant, i, 46.

14. See C Earwood, *Domestic Wooden Artefacts in Britain and Ireland from Neolithic to Viking Times*, Exeter 1993.

15. R Scott-Moncrieff, 'Note on the "Household Plenishings belonging to the deceist Andro Hog, Writer to the Signet, publicklie rouped and sold upon the 19th, 20th, 21st, 22nd, 23rd and 24th Days of Octr., 1691 Yeares."', *PSAS* liii, 1919, 52–63; 61.

16. Dalyell & Beveridge (see n11), 365.

17. Described in Geddes, 8.

18. Scott-Moncrieff (see n15), 60.

19. H Marwick, 'Two Orkney 18th century inventories', *Proceedings of the Orkney Antiquarian Society* xii, 1934, 45–7; 49.

20. R K Marshall, *The Days of Duchess Anne: Life in the Household of the Duchess of Hamilton 1656–1716*, London 1973, 100; Scott-Moncrieff, p lviii.

21. Scott-Moncrieff, p li.

22. Grant, i, 233–4.

23. Scott-Moncrieff, 278, 280.

24. Scott-Moncrieff (see n15), 63.

25. See Grant, i, 337.

26. The number of inventories checked is not adequate to make firm conclusions about this.

27. See Scott-Moncrieff, 243, for reference in Lady Grisell Baillie's accounts to 'plaster for Kitchen' in 1712 and also stone for pavement in kitchen and trance.

28. Grant, i, 27.

29. Ibid, i, 32.

30. Ibid, i, 98.

31. Ibid, i, 209.

32. SRO CS 96/3427, inventory of Robert Sommervell, Glasgow 1804, includes bird cage; CS 96/894 of William Naismith, Glasgow 1807, includes fowling piece; CS 96/1051 of Charles Taylor, Edinburgh 1804, lists a sword.

33. The sample of inventories used is too small to make conclusive statements about a change to ranges with ovens in the 1830s or 1840s and this requires more work, but there was also between 1841 and 1851 an increase of 44.8% in the number of bakers in Scotland, see *Census of Scotland – 1861. Population Tables and Report*, Edinburgh 1862, lv. This suggests a change in the kind of foods people were eating.

34. SRO CS 96/2043/1, inventory of Andrew Henderson, Leith 1795.

35. Information from Falkirk Museums Service. Gas was available in the house from 1841 but it is not known if it was used for cooking before the first mention of cooking with gas in 1850.

36. R Kerr, *A Small Country House*, London 1873, 55.

37. See Franklin, 92–3.

38. For Monzie, see Savage, pl 222; for Ardkinglas, see C Maclean & C Simon Sykes, *Scottish Country*, London 1992, 220–1; for Manderston, see L Astaire, R Martine, & F von der Schulenburg, *Living in Scotland*, London 1987, 106–7.

39. Dairy illustrated in Astaire et al (see n38), 109.

40. S Ferrier, *The Inheritance*, London 1824, new edn Bampton 1984, 42. This is perhaps a symptom of the obsession with 'progress' felt by many in society at this time.

41. Information from Juliet Kinchin on evidence from around 1900 found in a flat in Glasgow, where the same pattern was used in kitchen and bathroom.

42. J Milne, 'Description of Sir John Robison's House, Randolph Crescent, Edinburgh', published as a supplement to the 1840 edn of J C Loudon, *An Encyclopaedia of Cottage, Farm, and Villa Architecture*. Information supplied by Ian Gow.

43. Falkirk Museum, AO11.01, 1892; AO11.20, 1906.

44. NMS SEA, MS1973/3.

45. See Strathkelvin District Libraries & Museums, *Housing in Strathkelvin*, information pack ii, Glasgow 1989, F1h.

46. See Forty, 216.

47. A Oswald, 'Gribloch, Kippen, Stirlingshire – II', *Country Life* cix, 1951, 186.

48. Ibid, 185.

49. I am grateful to Caroline Mac-Gregor for information about Gribloch.

50. See Forty, 207–21.

51. See for instance, Cowan; Forty; and A Oakley, *Housewife*, London 1974.

52. *Abstract of Regional Statistics*, London 1971, 101, table 80.

53. *Regional Trends*, London 1994, 117, table 8.1.3.

54. Research by Professor Joy Parr, Simon Fraser University, British Colombia.

5 The Hall and Lobby

1. *Nairn in Darkness and Light*, London 1987, new edn London 1988, 33–4.

2. Anon, *The Rudiments of Architecture*, Edinburgh 1773 & 1778. New edn with introduction by D M Walker, Whittingham 1992.

3. R Oresko (ed), *The Works in Architecture of Robert and James Adam*, London 1975, 172. The 'Plan of the Principal Story of the New Building for the University of Edinburgh' shows lobbies at the entrances to the 'Class for the practice of Physick', the 'Royal Society', the 'Anatomical Theatre', and to the Professors' rooms.

4. Ibid, 48.

5. SRO GD 45/18/864, Dalhousie Papers: inventory of household furniture at Panmure, Angus. Plans of Panmure are illustrated by Macaulay, 8.

6. See A MacKechnie, 'James Smith's Smaller Country Houses' in Frew & Jones (eds), 9–16.

7. NRA(S) 3246/107 vols 49 & 51, Dundas of Arniston papers.

8. *The Edinburgh Book of Prices for Manufacturing Cabinet-Work*, Edinburgh 1805. See D Jones, 'Scottish cabinet makers' price books, 1805–1825', *Regional Furniture* iii, 1989, 27–39. Price books were guides for makers on how much to charge for their work.

9. NRA(S) 631/720, Marquess of Bute papers.

10. NRA(S) 888/607, Hopetoun papers: inventory of furniture at Hopetoun, November 1768, revised November 1780. Information supplied by Sebastian Pryke.

11. NRA(S) 3246, vols 90 & 91, Dundas of Arniston papers: inventory of household furniture at Arniston, 1850. Information supplied by Patricia Wigston.

12. Munro-Ferguson Collection.

13. Paxton House Muniments, Book 313: inventory and valuation of furniture at Paxton, 17 June 1828.

14. See J Gifford, C McWilliam, & D Walker, *The Buildings of Scotland, Edinburgh*, 1993, 352–3.

15. SRO GD 170/537, Campbell of Barcaldine papers: this was published in Bamford, Appendix I, 130–3, but was dated as c1825. The estimate was not prepared until after 1831, when Sir Duncan Campbell's baronetcy was conferred.

16. See D Ledoux-Lebard, *Le Mobilier Français du XIXe Siècle: Dictionnaire des Ebénistes et des Menuisiers*, Paris 1989, 346, 365.

17. SRO GD 226 4/10 Trinity House, Leith: Minute Books.

18. *The Edinburgh Chair-maker's Book of Prices for Workmanship*, Edinburgh 1825, 27, pl VI.

19. Kirkcaldy Museum & Art Gallery, Rothes MSS, 40/65/1.

20. Illustrated by Bamford, pl 8.

21. SRO GD 58/16/3.

22. S Ferrier, *The Inheritance*, London 1824, new edn Bampton 1984, 512.

23. See Franklin, 87.

24. See Lindsay & Cosh for a comprehensive account of the architectural evolution of Inveraray.

25. Wainwright, 200.

26. Pl VII.

27. Edinburgh 1817.

28. *The Cabinet Maker's Assistant*, Glasgow 1853, reprinted as J Gloag (ed), *The Victorian Cabinet Maker's Assistant: 418 Original Designs with Description and Details of Construction*, New York 1970.

29. See Gow, 138.

30. NMS SEA MS 1973/3.

31. Falkirk Museums A23.06: Falkirk Iron Company catalogue, 1910.

32. For an interesting analysis of the rise and fall of the combined hall stand, see Ames.

33. See J Kinchin, '"A revolution in paper-hanging": Scottish wallpapers 1850–1910', *Scottish Art Review* xvii, 1991, 16–21, pl 3.

34. 'Trance' was once used for passageways in houses of all sizes. It occurs in the 1695 inventory of Panmure House (n5) describing a passage in the domestic offices, and is still used in North Angus and Lanarkshire for an entrance passage or lobby in a small cottage. The trance is also called the 'hallan' in some parts of the country, with apparently the same meaning.

35. Information supplied by John Frew.

36. For the development and history of tenements see Robinson, 1984 & 1986.

6 The Dining Room

1. *The Dining-Room*, London 1878, title page.
2. Grant, i, 335.
3. Quoted in Lindsay & Cosh, 304.
4. See O Krog (ed), *A King's Feast: Goldsmiths' Art and Royal Banqueting Habits in the 18th Century*, London 1991.
5. Grant, i, 233.
6. Ibid, 30.
7. A F Steuart, 'The plenishing of Holyrood House in 1714', *PSAS* lxii, 1928, 181–96; 190. Obviously much of the kit described by Steuart related to the ceremonial life of the Scots' Parliament and after the Union in 1707 there was no pressing need to replace the evidently shabby items.
8. M Swain, *Tapestries and Textiles at the Palace of Holyroodhouse*, Edinburgh 1988, 68.
9. Caution is necessary because *Country Life* photographers often moved things around to make a clearer picture. See 'Melville House, Fife', *Country Life*, 30 Dec 1911, 1006–12.
10. J Strang, *Glasgow & its Clubs*, Glasgow 1857, 161.
11. Ibid, 162–4.
12. B Faujas de Saint-Fond, *A Journey Through England and Scotland to the Hebrides in 1784*, Glasgow 1907, i, 253.
13. Ibid, 253–4.
14. *Vitruvius Scoticus*, pl 63.
15. H W Thompson (ed), *The Anecdotes and Egotisms of Henry Mackenzie 1745–1831*, London 1927, 63.
16. The National Trust for Scotland has built up a good collection of Sheffield plate at the Georgian House in Edinburgh.
17. The plasterers are unknown but it seems likely that they had contact with the work of Sir William Chambers, architect of the new government offices at Somerset House in London.
18. For example, Dumfries House, also a Chippendale commission, had no buffet.
19. Robert Mylne was the architect of the fifth Duke.
20. See W A Brogden, 'John Smith & Craigievar', in Gow & Rowan (eds), 228–35; 231–2.
21. Wainwright, 169.
22. J L Story, *Early Reminiscences*, Glasgow 1911, 21.
23. Ibid, 23–7.
24. I Gow, 'William Trotter's estimate for furnishing No 3 Moray Place, Edinburgh, for Sir Duncan Campbell of Barcaldine, *c*1825', in Bamford, 130–3. The dating of this is problematic: see chapter 5, n15.
25. Ibid.
26. H Cockburn, *Memorials*, Edinburgh 1910, 31.
27. *The New Statistical Account of Scotland*, vi, Lanark 1845, 271–4.
28. Kerr, 105.
29. J H Brown, *Scenes in Scotland*, Glasgow 1833, 23.
30. Cockburn (see n26), 36–7.
31. Strang (see n10), 164.
32. SRO CS 318/7/263.
33. Marshall, 36.
34. Strang (see n10), 161–2.
35. Replanning as carried out, for instance, by Kit Martin, an architect who specializes in altering country houses for present-day use.

7 The Drawing Room

1. H J Jennings, *Our Homes and How to Beautify Them*, London 1902, 2nd edn London 1902, 236.
2. See Monica Clough, *Two Houses*, Aberdeen 1990, 85. The drawing room of Colonel Ross's house at Rosstraven adjoined both the main bedrooms, and in 1799 still contained two 'Sopha bedsteds' as well as the obligatory set of '10 painted chairs', a pier glass, '4 guilt girandoles' and covered centre table (inventory in author's collection).
3. Letter to her sister, Lady Portarlington, quoted in J Cornforth, *English Interiors 1790–1848: The Quest for Comfort*, London 1978, 13.
4. Loudon, new edn 1839, 799.
5. Ibid.
6. S Ferrier, *The Inheritance*, London 1824, new edn Bampton 1984, 88.
7. University of Glasgow Archives, Hamilton of Rozelle papers, DC 17, May 1817.
8. Such entertainments or 'routs' in early nineteenth-century Edinburgh are described in Elizabeth Grant's *Memoirs*, (eg ii, 67, 90, 102). According to Ian Gow, 'some houses in Moray Place had up to three drawing rooms in addition to an ante–room, forming a circuit around the stairwell', *The Scottish Interior*, 49. Preparations could be extensive, involving the removal of doors and the importation of pianos and flower arrangements.
9. Strathclyde Regional Archives T–BK 2, Possil House Inventory, 1867; author's collection, Mansion House of Craigallian inventory, 1914.
10. Ferrier (see n6), 148.
11. N Munro ('Hugh Foulis'), *Erchie and Jimmy Swan*, Glasgow 1904, new edn Edinburgh 1993, 102–3.
12. W Creech, *Letters Addressed to Sir John Sinclair, Bart.*, Edinburgh 1793, 33. I am most grateful to Jolyon Hudson for drawing this reference to my attention. See also Robert Clerk's remarks on p 31.
13. Ployen, 16–17.
14. Loudon, new edn 1839, 799.
15. *Edinburgh Review*, 1807, Article XIV, 478–9.
16. Kerr, 107.
17. Jennings (see n1), 171.
18. *Wylie & Lochhead Ltd. Manufacturers of Artistic Furniture, Upholsterers and Decorators. Illustrations of Furniture and Interior Decorations*, Glasgow 1903, passim. Author's collection.
19. See for example W G Sutherland, *Modern Wall Decoration*, Manchester 1893, or A S Jennings, *Wallpapers and Wall Coverings*, London 1903.
20. Private collection: Letter/Order book, Ardtornish House.
21. The Russell-Cotes's home, which contains a range of Tynecastle tapestry papers and Macfarlane ironwork, is now the headquarters of the Bournemouth Museums & Art Galleries Service. In addition to his businesses in Scotland, London, and New York, Daniel Cottier established branches in Sydney and Melbourne, where he was joined for a time by his compatriots Andrew Wells and David Gow, both of whom returned to work for Glasgow firms in the 1890s. For examples of their work in Australia see S Forge, *Victorian Splendour in Australian Interior Decoration 1837–1901*, Sydney 1981.
22. W Young, *Glasgow Municipal Chambers*, Glasgow 1891.
23. *Academy Architecture*, 1901.2, 64–8.
24. For a full account of such interiors see P Kinchin, *Tea and Taste: the Glasgow Tea Rooms 1875–1975*, Wendlebury 1991.
25. O Davis, *Instructions for the Adornment of Dwelling Houses: Interior Decoration*, London 1880, 25.
26. *The Art of Beauty*, London 1878, 205.
27. Jennings (see n1), 174.
28. Munro (see n11), 102.
29. Kerr, 86.
30. Barker, 13.
31. Loudon, new edn 1839, 797.
32. Davis (see n25), 25.
33. Loudon, new edn 1839, 797.
34. Ibid.
35. Ferrier (see n6), 219.
36. *Quiz*, 18 March 1881, 5.
37. For an amusing account of such a concert given in aid of Mrs Gobo's new pet society for 'the Prevention of Neglect of Genius' see the novel *Ethel*, by J J B, author of "Wee Macgreegor", Edinburgh & Glasgow, 1903, 25–33.
38. Loudon, new edn 1839, 1015.
39. *Evening News*, Glasgow, 7 March 1901, 7.
40. Jennings (see n1), 173.
41. H Muthesius, *The English House*, Berlin 1904, new edn in English, London 1979, 211.
42. W J Loftie, *A Plea for Art in the House*, London 1876, 40.
43. In *Purity and Danger: An Analysis of the Concepts of Purity and Taboo*, London 1966, Mary Douglas provides a classic definition of dirt as 'matter out of place' and analyses the growing obsession with hygiene and white goods in the western world as a response to all sorts of boundaries being threatened, whether to do with class, morality, or gender. For a fuller discussion of this theme see J Kinchin, 'The Gendered Interior – essays in nineteenth-century taste', in P Kirkham (ed), *The Gendered Object*, Manchester, 1996.
44. J Moyr Smith, *Ornamental Interiors, Ancient and Modern*, London 1887, 89–90. Smith was a Glasgow-trained architect-designer.
45. Jennings (see n1), 23.
46. E Gregory, *The Art and Craft of Home Making*, London 1913, 37.
47. Marshall, 16.
48. C Carswell, *Open the Door!*, London 1920, new edn London 1986, 164.
49. See E Gregory, *The Art and Craft of Home Making*, London 2nd edn 1925, introduction; and H Bryant, *House and Cottage Construction*, London 1923, 71.
50. Ibid.
51. C Bermant, *The Second Mrs Whitberg*, London 1976, 46.

8 The Bedroom

1. Anon (R S Burn?), *The Grammar of House Planning: Hints on Arranging and Modifying Plans of Cottages, Street-houses, Farm-houses, Villas, Mansions, and Out-buildings*, Edinburgh 1864, 36.
2. For example, Anon, *The Duties of a Lady's Maid*, London 1825, 57.
3. See Leeds City Art Galleries & Rutherford, 6.
4. The high table was on a platform or dais. The room is also cited in inventories as 'Chamber of dess'.
5. See for example, D Marshall, 'Notes of the connection of the Earls of Morton and Dick of Braid and Craighouse, with the Earldom of Orkney and Lordship of Zetland, with rental, inventory &c., 1653, from original documents in the Charter Room of Kinross House', *PSAS* xi, 1889, 300.
6. One panel of each set is in the NMS collections, A1921.68 & A1931.54. See M Swain, 'The Lochleven and Linlithgow hangings', *PSAS* cxxiv, 1994, 455–66.

7. For example, a set in the Burrell Collection, Glasgow, made by Kathleen Ruthven, wife of Colin Campbell of Glenorchy, dating from 1550–85. Illustrated in M Swain, *Scottish Embroidery, Medieval to Modern*, London 1989, figs 6–8.

8. NMS accession number RHB25.1–11.

9. J Dalyell & J Beveridge, 'Inventory of the plenishing of the House of The Binns at the date of the death of General Thomas Dalyell, 21st August 1685', *PSAS* lviii, 1924, 344–70.

10. Ibid, 358–60.

11. NLS Tweeddale MS 7106/108.

12. This must have been in pounds sterling, not Scots.

13. H G Slade, 'Castle Fraser: a seat of the antient family of Fraser', Appendix B, *PSAS* cix, 1978, 278–86.

14. H Marwick, 'A record miscellany III', *Proceedings of the Orkney Antiquarian Society*, vi, 1928, 27–32; 30–1.

15. SRO CC 8/8/86.

16. SRO GD 72/606 Hay of Park.

17. SRO CC 8/8/118/1.

18. Grant, i, 329.

19. Ibid, 110–11.

20. Ibid, 28.

21. SRO CC 17/7/2.

22. In the collection of Her Majesty The Queen.

23. See Wells-Cole, 45–6.

24. London 1840, 2nd edn, 22.

25. SRO CS 96/4691.

26. A Lady, London 1840, 2nd edn, 187–8, 190.

27. The NMS example, A1942.41 (pl 195), is unusual in being embroidered all over. Other blankets are more modestly decorated with only a border design.

28. M H Swain, *Historical Needlework: A Study of Influences in Scotland and Northern England*, London 1970, pl 16.

29. A Lady, London 1840, 2nd edn, 200.

30. SRO CS 96/2043/1.

31. See Gilbert, Lomax, & Wells-Cole, 89–91.

32. NMS Collection, A1994.5.

33. See H B Burnham & D K Burnham, '*Keep Me Warm One Night': Early Handweaving in Eastern Canada*, Toronto 1972.

34. Shetland Museum has a fine collection of these rugs.

35. SRO CS 96/3793.

36. Private collection.

37. Grant, i, 296.

38. Loudon, 665.

39. Barker, 40.

40. See C Edwards, 'Furnishing a home at the turn of the century: the use of furnishing estimates from 1875 to 1910', *Journal of Design History* iv.4, 1991, 233–9.

41. D Daiches, *Two Worlds. An Edinburgh Jewish Childhood*, London 1957, 26.

9 The Bathroom and Water Closet

All trade catalogues cited here are in the collection of the RCAHMS.

1. S F Murphy (ed), *Our Homes and How to Make Them Healthy*, London 1883, 90.

2. See S S Hellyer, *The Plumber and Sanitary Houses. A Practical Treatise on the Principles of Internal Plumbing Work, or the Best Means of Excluding Noxious Gases from our Houses*, London 1877, 3rd edn 1884. This covers traps at great length. A weekly journal, *The Builder*, carried many articles and advertisements concerning sanitary facilities from the mid 19th century.

3. See W Shaw Sparrow (ed), *The Modern Home, A Book of British Domestic Architecture for Moderate Incomes*, London undated, c1904, 161.

4. Gauldie, 101–12, describes such conditions in great detail.

5. The 'Garderobe' is described by G L Pride, *Glossary of Scottish Building*, Glasgow 1974, 42–4, as a 'wardrobe; by extension – a private room, bed chamber and by euphemism – privy formed in wall of castle'.

6. Scott-Moncrieff, pp lxvii, 3. There are no details of how many baths this sum paid for.

7. M J Daunton, *House and Home in the Victorian City: Working-Class Housing 1850–1914*, London 1983, 247.

8. For the development of water supplies in Scottish cities see F H Groom (ed), *Ordnance Gazetteer of Scotland*, London undated, 1890s.

9. See Gauldie, 75; Gibb, 144; for 'Gardyloo' see Wright, 76.

10. J A Taylor, *A Journey to Edenborough*, Edinburgh 1903, 134–5, quoted by Smout 1969, 367.

11. E Burt, *Letters from a Gentleman in the North of Scotland to his Friend in London*, London 1754, i, 22–3.

12. Information on the development of Scottish water supply and sewerage infrastructure was kindly provided through the Scottish and Northern Ireland Plumbing Employers' Federation by Mr Jim Robertson, formerly of Central Regional Council. For Loch Katrine, see J R Hume, *Industrial Archaeology of Glasgow*, Glasgow 1974, 133–4.

13. J Colston, *The Edinburgh and District Water Supply, a Historical Sketch*, Edinburgh 1890.

14. Hume (see n12), 63.

15. The technology involves vertical, as opposed to horizontal, casting, and was developed by D Y Stewart at its Links Foundry in Montrose in 1846; see G Gloag & D Bridgewater, *A History of Cast Iron in Architecture*, London 1948, 80.

16. Gibb, 132–3.

17. Gauldie, 74, describes conditions in Glasgow in the 1840s as possibly the worst in Britain. Hume (see n12), 136–7, describes the development of sewers in Glasgow. Similarly, information from Jim Robertson (see n12) reveals that the first slow sand filter was developed in Paisley by John Gibb in 1804, the second being established by Robert Thom in Greenock in 1827.

18. Gauldie, 75.

19. Gibb, 142, quoting the Presbytery of Glasgow *Report of Commission on Housing of the Poor in Relation to their Social Condition*, 1891, 12.

20. Gauldie, 78.

21. Information kindly provided by Mr P L Crow of Scott Ltd. Soft paper was developed by a family of German Jews, who set up a business at St Andrew's Mill in Walthamstow (and named their produce 'Andrex', after their mill). See also I Maxted, 'Sic transit gloria cloacorum', *The Ephemerist*, Dec 1990, 364–5.

22. Examples of typical accessories include those illustrated in 'Bathroom Accessories', Section 14 from 'H' Catalogue, Shanks & Co Ltd, Tubal Works, Barrhead, Scotland, August 1922.

23. Illustrated in A Stein, 'Fancy That!', *Heritage Scotland*, xi.4, 1994, 31.

24. F R Yerbury (ed), *Modern Homes Illustrated*, London undated, c1947, 142.

25. A B Searle, *An Encyclopedia of the Ceramics Industries*, i, London 1929, 62; Wright, 168, 170.

26. Searle (see n25), 226.

27. See R Palmer, *The Water Closet: A New History*, Newton Abbot 1973, 38, for William Ross. Valve closets were still being advertised in *The Builder* in the 1860s, one of the more sophisticated being Hayward Tyler & Co's 'Howard Patent Regulating Valve', which claimed to supply water to closets without the complicated arrangement of cranks and wires. Doulton & Watt were also advertising enamelled stoneware closet pans on adjacent pages.

28. Palmer (see n27), 33.

29. Hellyer (see n2), 188.

30. Ibid, 193.

31. Palmer (see n27), 42–3.

32. J Cash in Shaw Sparrow (ed) c1904 (see n3), 173.

33. See G Douglas & M Oglethorpe, *Brick, Tile and Fireclay Industries in Scotland*, Edinburgh 1993, 19; and K W Sanderson, *The Scottish Refractory Industry 1830–1980*, Edinburgh 1990, which gives a particularly detailed account of specialized Scottish fireclays.

34. Dundee Industrial Heritage's Verdant Works in Henderson's Wynd, Dundee, has retained a fine example of a Buick No7 Wash Down closet, and Alloa Museum holds a collection of material relating to the company.

35. Department of Health of Scotland, *Scottish Housing Handbook III, House Design*, Edinburgh 1950, 4.

36. See Forty, 166–8; and M Swenarton, 'Having a bath', in *Leisure in the Twentieth Century*, 2nd conference on 20th century design history, London 1977, 92–9.

37. Pink and turquoise seen by the Editor in a house in Edinburgh expensively refurbished in 1934. Yellow suite mentioned by P Kinchin & J Kinchin, *Glasgow's Great Exhibitions: 1888, 1901, 1911, 1938, 1988*, Wendlebury 1988, 136.

38. W Leverton, *Small Homes and How to Furnish Them*, London 1903, 94.

39. Shanks & Co Ltd, 1930, 14.

40. Information on the use of plastics in the manufacture of sanitary ware was kindly provided by Armitage Shanks, whose factory in Otley, West Yorkshire, is one of the major producers in the UK.

41. W Shaw Sparrow (ed), *Flats, Urban Houses and Cottage Homes*, London undated, c1906, 67, 69–70.

42. Savage, 1980, 127; and Shanks & Co Ltd, 1930.

43. An example in a grand house is at Gosford House, East Lothian, which has a WC with mahogany fittings just off the entrance hall, probably added during alterations in the 1880s. Belmont House in Dalkeith, a villa, has a sizeable cloakroom and separate WC by the back door, fitted out in 1900.

44. H J Jennings, *Our Homes and How to Beautify Them*, London 1902, 2nd edn London 1902, 236.

45. Daunton (see n7), 261.

46. Information provided by Mr Jim Robertson (see n12).

Select Bibliography

Ames, K L. 'Meaning in artifacts: hall furnishings in Victorian America', in T J Schlereth (ed), *Material Culture Studies in America*, Nashville, Tennessee 1982, 206–21.

Aslet, C. *The Last Country Houses*, New Haven & London 1982.

Bamford, F. 'A dictionary of Edinburgh wrights and furniture makers 1660–1840', *Furniture History* xix, 1983.

Barker, M A (Lady). *The Bedroom and Boudoir*, London 1878, new edn New York & London 1978.

Benjamin, D N (ed). *The Home: Words, Interpretations, Meanings, and Environments*, Aldershot 1995.

Brown, I G. *Elegance & Entertainment in the New Town of Edinburgh: The Harden Drawings*, Edinburgh 1995.

Burnett, J. *A Social History of Housing 1815–1970*, Newton Abbot 1978.

Calder, J. *The Victorian Home*, London 1977.

Cowan, R S. *More Work for Mother: The Ironies of Household Technology from the Open Hearth to the Microwave*, New York 1983, new edn London 1989.

Dunbar, J G. *The Historic Architecture of Scotland*, London 1966.

Duncan, D. *Tenements and Sentiments: Aberdeen My City*, Aberdeen undated, c1987.

Faley, J. *Up Oor Close: Memories of Domestic Life in Glasgow Tenements, 1910–1945*, Wendlebury 1990.

Flinn, M (ed). *Scottish Population History from the Seventeenth Century to the 1930s*, Cambridge 1977.

Forty, A. *Objects of Desire: Design and Society since 1750*, London 1986.

Franklin, J. *The Gentleman's Country House and its Plan 1835–1914*, London 1981.

Frew, J & Jones, D (eds). *Aspects of Scottish Classicism: The House & its Formal Setting 1690–1750*, St Andrews 1989.

Gauldie, E. *Cruel Habitations: A History of Working-Class Housing 1780–1918*, London 1974.

Geddes, O M. *The Laird's Kitchen: Three Hundred Years of Food in Scotland*, Edinburgh 1994.

Gibb, A. *Glasgow, the Making of a City*, London 1983.

Gilbert, C, Lomax, J, & Wells-Cole, A. *Country House Floors 1660–1850*, Leeds 1987.

Gilbert, C & Wells-Cole, A. *The Fashionable Fire Place 1660–1840*, Leeds 1985.

Glendinning, M & Muthesius, S. *Tower Block: Modern Public Housing in England, Scotland, Wales, and Northern Ireland*, New Haven & London 1994.

Gow, I. *The Scottish Interior*, Edinburgh 1992.

Gow, I & Rowan, A. *Scottish Country Houses, 1600–1914*, Edinburgh 1995.

Grant, E. *Memoirs of a Highland Lady*, London 1898, new edn, A Tod (ed), Edinburgh 1988.

Horsey, M. *Tenements & Towers: Glasgow Working-Class Housing 1890–1990*, Edinburgh 1990.

Jones, D. *Looking at Scottish Furniture: A Documented Anthology 1570–1900*, St Andrews 1987.

Kerr, R. *The Gentleman's House, or How to Plan English Residences from the Parsonage to the Palace*, London 1864.

Kinmonth, C. *Irish Country Furniture 1700–1950*, London & New Haven 1993.

Kirkcaldy Museum & Art Gallery, *"The Queer–Like Smell": The Kirkcaldy Linoleum Industry*, Kirkcaldy undated, c1990.

Leeds City Art Galleries & Rutherford, J. *Country House Lighting 1660–1890*, Leeds 1992.

Lindsay, I G & Cosh, M. *Inveraray and the Dukes of Argyll*, Edinburgh 1973.

Loftie, M J. *The Dining-Room*, London 1878, new edn New York & London 1978.

Loudon, J C. *An Encyclopaedia of Cottage, Farm, and Villa Architecture*, London 1833.

Macaulay, J. *The Classical Country House in Scotland 1660–1800*, London 1987.

Marshall, J. *Amateur House Decoration*, Edinburgh 1883.

Niven, D. *The Development of Housing in Scotland*, London 1979.

Orrinsmith, L. *The Drawing-Room: its Decorations and Furniture*, London 1877, new edn New York & London 1978.

Ployen, C. *Reminiscences of a Voyage to Shetland, Orkney & Scotland in the Summer of 1839*, translated by C Spence, Lerwick 1894.

Robb, J. *The Cottage, The Bothy and The Kitchen. Being an Inquiry into the Condition of Agricultural Labourers in Scotland*, Edinburgh & London 1861.

Robinson, P. 'Tenements: a pre–industrial tradition', *Review of Scottish Culture* i, 1984, 52–64.

Robinson, P. 'Tenements: the industrial legacy', *Review of Scottish Culture* ii, 1986, 71–83.

Rodger, R (ed). *Scottish Housing in the Twentieth Century*, Leicester 1989.

Royal Commission on Housing in Scotland, *Report of the Royal Commission on the Housing of the Industrial Population of Scotland, Rural and Urban*, Edinburgh 1917.

Rybczynski, W. *Home: A Short History of an Idea*, London 1988.

Savage, P. *Lorimer and the Edinburgh Craft Designers*, Edinburgh 1980.

Scott-Moncrieff, R (ed). *The Household Book of Lady Grisell Baillie 1692–1733*, Edinburgh 1911.

Smout, T C. *A History of the Scottish People, 1560–1830*, London 1969.

Smout, T C. *A Century of the Scottish People 1830–1950*, London 1986.

Smout, T C. 'Scotland 1850–1950', in F M L Thompson (ed), *The Cambridge Social History of Britain 1750–1950*, i, Cambridge 1990, 209–80.

Thornton, P. *Authentic Decor: The Domestic Interior 1620–1920*, London 1984.

Wainwright, C. *The Romantic Interior*, New Haven & London 1989.

Wells-Cole, A. *Historic Paper Hangings: From Temple Newsam and Other English Houses*, Leeds 1983.

Wordsall, F. *The Tenement, A Way of Life: A Social, Historical and Architectural Study of Housing in Glasgow*, Edinburgh 1979.

Wright, L. *Clean and Decent: The Fascinating History of the Bathroom and the Water Closet*, London 1960.

Index